Strangers, Spirits, and Land Reforms

Afrika-Studiecentrum Series

In collaboration with the South Africa-Vrije Universiteit Strategic Alliances (SAVUSA)

VOLUME 3

Strangers, Spirits, and Land Reforms

Conflicts about Land in Dande,
Northern Zimbabwe

by

Marja J. Spierenburg

BRILL
LEIDEN · BOSTON
2004

This book is printed on acid-free paper.

Library of Congress Cataloging-in-Publication Data

Spierenburg, Marja.
  Strangers, spirits, and land reforms : conflicts about land in Dande, northern Zimbabwe /
by M.J. Spierenburg.
    p. cm. — (Afrika-Studiecentrum series, ISSN 1570-9310 ; v. 3)
  Thesis (Ph. D.)—University of Amsterdam, 2004.
  Includes bibliographical references and index.
  ISBN 90-04-13957-5 (alk. paper)
    1. Land reform—Zimbabwe—Dande. 2. Rural development—Zimbabwe—Dande.
  I. Title. II. Series.

HD1333.Z552D367 2004
333.3'16891—dc22

                                                                    2004045896

ISSN   1570–9310
ISBN   90 04 13957 5

PRINTED IN THE NETHERLANDS

Contents

Preface

It is with great pleasure and a dash of pride that we present this first book in a sub-series of the *Afrika-Studiecentrum Series*, published by Brill Academic Publishers. The sub-series is the result of a co-operation between the *African Studies Centre* (ASC) in Leiden and *South Africa-Vrije Universiteit-Strategic Alliances* (SAVUSA) in Amsterdam, the Netherlands. Both institutions share a long history of academic co-operation with and research on the African continent, the ASC in the whole of sub-Saharan Africa and the *Vrije Universiteit* more in particular in southern Africa.

The ASC's *Afrika-Studiecentrum Series* came into existence in 2003 and aims to offer the best of African studies in the Netherlands. Its disciplinary scope is the same as the ASC's research profile, namely social sciences and humanities in the broadest sense. SAVUSA is a co-operative network between the *Vrije Universiteit* and a number of South African universities, with the intention of stimulating, facilitating and generating academic publications in a wide range of disciplines within the humanities field. The connecting element within this network is its focus on socially relevant subjects in the various contexts of southern Africa, each one looking at it from its own particular disciplinary background.

In the light of current developments in southern Africa, it seems appropriate that the first book in the sub-series, by Marja Spierenburg, is about a conflict over land in Dande, in the Zambezi Valley in Zimbabwe. The various developments concerning the land question in Zimbabwe have cast their shadows well beyond the national borders, influencing, amongst others, South Africa. We hope that this first book in the sub-series sets an inspiring tone for further critical debates on various socially relevant issues in southern Africa.

Dick Foeken (ASC)
Harry Wels (SAVUSA)

4 June 2004

List of Maps, Figures and Tables

Maps

Figures

Tables

Acknowledgements

Many writers complain that writing is a very solitary process, and often I have shared this sentiment. Yet, looking at the list of people I owe thanks to, I realise that this complaint is not entirely justified.

This book is based upon my PhD thesis, which I could never have finished without the unrelenting support of my supervisors Prof. Bonno Thoden van Velzen and Prof. Peter Geschiere. Bonno was the first to encourage me to embark upon this project, soon followed by Prof. Mathieu Schoffeleers. Mathieu, the *eminence grise* of Dutch Anthropology, who retired before I went to the field, but has remained a member of my committee. I would also like to thank the other members for their thorough review of my work: Professor Wim van Binsbergen, Professor Sjaak van der Geest, Professor Jojada Verrips, Professor Robert Ross and Rijk van Dijk.

In 1988 I went to Zimbabwe for a first period of fieldwork. This was my first experience with the Centre for Applied Social Sciences (CASS) at the University of Zimbabwe. Its Director at the time, Professor Marshall Murphree, has helped me a great deal in preparing my study and providing me with contacts in Dande.

In 1992 I managed to return to Zimbabwe for a two-year stint of fieldwork, made possible by the Netherlands Foundation for the Advancement of Tropical Research (WOTRO), which provided me with financial support. I was very happy to return to CASS where I was accepted as an Affiliated Researcher, thanks to the efforts of Professor Marshall Murphree and the Centre's administrator Wanda Kawadza, without whom I would never have been able to obtain a research permit from the National Scientific Council. I truly enjoyed the in-house seminars and informal discussions with fellow researchers who were working at CASS at that time: James Murombedzi, Vupenyu Dzingirai, Calvin Nhira, Nontokozo Nabane, Elias Madzudzo, Ben Cousins, Jeremy Jackson and Gordon Matzke. The joint fieldtrip I undertook with Simon Metcalfe was an unforgettable experience. I am especially indebted to Prof. Bill Derman, with whom I made several joint fieldtrips. As an external advisor on my PhD committee he provided me with most insightful comments on my thesis. Prof. Michael Bourdillon carefully reviewed some of my work. I would also like to thank Dr. David Cumming, Tim Lynam and Ivan Bond who at that time were working at the World Wide Fund for Nature's Multispecies Animal Production Systems Project. I equally benefited from discussions with Rob

Munro and Stephen Thomas at Zimtrust. Blair Rutherford, who is now back in Canada, and his assistant, Rinse, showed me the home of the new medium of Nehanda, an exciting experience for all of us. With Ingrid Sinclair and Simon Bright I made that memorable trip in 1990 to Kanyurira, to prepare a documentary on CAMPFIRE. I really hope that one day we will able to make that film on the *Mhondoro* that we have been planning for so long.

I am deeply grateful to the people in Mahuwe, Mburuma, Rutendo and Chitsungo, who endured my endless questions. I especially thank the people in Mburuma, where I lived for almost two years. In difficult times they allowed me into their lives, and shared their joys and sufferings with me. Despite the harsh conditions under which people were living, I was often invited to spend agreeable evenings in cooking huts, being treated to great stories and sadza. I thank the headman of Mburuma and the VIDCO chairman for allowing me to set up my homestead close to the big baobab tree, and my neighbours, the Chaparadza family, for keeping an eye on me. I owe a special thanks to the *Mhondoro* mediums who allowed me to consult the spirits possessing them. The experiences in Dande have left a deep imprint on me forever. Ndatenda chaizvo!

I am especially indebted to the late Lazarus Zhuwao and Phanuel Rupiya who were willing to become my research assistants. Their wives, Stella and Monica, provided hospitality and friendship on numerous occasions. I enjoyed the company of Phanuel's daughters, Precious and Patience, who may not know how much it meant to me when they once told their frightened cousin that I was not a '*murungu*', a white person, but a '*munhu*', a human being, just like them. Lazarus and Phanuel became more than assistants, they became friends, and Lazarus' death in 1996 came as a great shock to me. Both men have taught me a lot and have been infinite sources of information on almost every aspect of life in the valley. Through endless discussions they helped me make sense of all the data we gathered and things we encountered. It should be stressed, however, that they cannot be held responsible for my critical analysis concerning the Mid-Zambezi Project and the irrigation schemes.

In the Netherlands I was affiliated to the Amsterdam School for Social Science Research at the University of Amsterdam. I thank Hans Sonneveld, José Komen, Annelies Dijkstra en Miriam May for their assistance during my affiliation. I have benefited greatly from the meetings of the 'anthropology club' organised by Bonno Thoden van Velzen, Ineke van Wetering, Jojada Verrips and Anton Blok. I wish to thank the organisers and participants for their careful reading of and commenting on my work in progress: Mathijs van der Port, Rob van Ginkel, Birgit Meyer, Clementine van Eck, Talja Blokland, Maruska Svacek, Giselinde Kuipers, Erik Bähre, and my good friends Remco Ensel, Ferdinand de Jong, and Peter Odermatt. I also wish to thank James Scott, who visited the School for a week in 1995, and carefully read and commented on some of my work.

I would like to thank the participants of the 'Africa seminars' organised by Peter Geschiere and Robert Ross at the Leiden University: Anke van der Kwaak, Karen Biesbrouck, Jan Jansen, Karin Nijhuis, Adri van den Berg, Berend Timmer, Dmitri van den Bersselaar, Gerhard Seibert and, last but definitely not least, my good friend Jan-Bart Gewald.

I was privileged to be part of the 'Working Group on African Religion' organised by Mathieu Schoffeleers. The members of this group; Henny Blokland, Rijk van Dijk, Annette Drews, Cor Jonker, Ria Reis and, of course, Mathieu, carefully reviewed my contribution to the book we published together on Ngoma. I also thank the anonymous reviewers of our manuscript. I thank Rijk and especially Ria and Henny for their support when things were a little difficult. May we attend many more of Ria's famous 'peanut-soup nights'.

Parts of this book I presented at seminars and conferences, where I received very useful comments. The Advanced Research Seminar organised by Norman Long was a very pleasant seminar to attend, and there I met Jan-Kees van Dongen, who has encouraged me to continue to write. I also have very fond memories of the Colloquia on 'Religion in Africa', organised by Prof. Richard Werbner, for which I was invited several times, and where I benefited from comments from: Richard Werbner, Alcinda Honwana, Philip DeBoeck, Maia Green, Prof. Terence Ranger, Jocelyn Alexander and JoAnn McGregor. Richard Werbner provided me with Prof. Kingsley Garbett's e-mail address, to whom I hesitantly sent my paper. He replied instantly with most useful comments. Terence Ranger invited me to the annual Britain Zimbabwe Society Zimbabwe Research Day. Heike Schmidt and Jan-Georg Deutsch invited me to attend the 1997 conference on 'Afrika und das Andere' at the Humboldt Universität, where I presented a preliminary version of Chapter Seven, and received insightful comments from Ute Luig. Heike Schmidt and Albert Wirz reviewed the paper for their book. Bernhard Venema and Hans van den Breemer invited me to present a paper at their 1997 conference on 'Co-management of natural resources in Africa'. There, I received most useful comments from Marleen Dekkers, Ton Dietz and Mayke Kaag on a paper that was published in the book edited by Bernhard and Hans.

Jesse Ribot from the World Resource Institute in Washington invited me for a panel at the Annual Conference of the African Studies Association in 1998, and the 2002 meeting of the International Association for the Study of Common Property. I became an 'honorary member' of the WRI research group on the 'Re-emergence of traditional leadership in natural resource management', whose members provided comments on a paper that is now part of Chapter Two: James Murombedzi, Vupenyu Dzingirai, Lungisile Ntebeza, Frank Muhereza and Bréhima Kassibo. Achille Mbembe and Mamadou Diouf invited me to present a paper at the 1998 General Conference of CODESRIA. Amanda Hammar, who also presented a paper there, carefully read and commented on parts of what is now Chapter Two. Rijk van Dijk invited me to present a paper in the 2000 African Studies Centre (Leiden) seminar series on 'Mobility in

Africa'. I like to thank Todd Sanders for his comments, as well as Rijk, Mirjam de Bruijn and Dick Foecken for carefully reviewing my contribution to their volume. It is now part of Chapter Eight. Anke van der Kwaak, Karen Biesbrouck and Rachel Spronk diligently reviewed my contribution to a book that was presented to Peter Geschiere on the occasion of his retirement from the University of Leiden. That contribution is also part of Chapter Eight. Frans Kamsteeg, Harry Wels and Prof. Paul Bate invited me to present a paper at the 2002 EGOS conference. Their comments were taken into account while I rewrote the paper, which is now Chapter Five. Finally, I would like to thank Bill Kinsey for his comments on parts of what is now Chapter Seven.

I thank Harry Wels for inviting me to apply for a job as lecturer at the Vrije Universiteit, and for trying to keep me out of the wind while finishing this book. The discussions with him and my colleague Jens Andersson have been very stimulating. I owe a big thank you to Saskia Stehouwer, who has carefully reviewed and edited the manuscript of this book.

These acknowledgements of course would not be complete without thanks to my friends and family. While finalising this book I have not been a very sociable person, and especially those of my friends who do not live in Amsterdam have suffered from a severe lack of attention on my part: my sincere apologies. I thank my parents and sister, who have always supported me, and have had to miss me for long periods of time.

Introduction: Of narratives and land reforms

This book is about the introduction of land reforms in the northern part of Zimbabwe and the ways in which local populations reacted to them. These reforms were not about transferring land from white farmers to black farmers. On the contrary, they were meant to reduce the necessity of such land transfers. The underlying assumption of the land reforms introduced in Dande was that if the small-scale farmers in that part of the Zambezi Valley could be induced to use their lands in a more efficient manner, there would be room to accommodate about 3000 families awaiting resettlement on former European-owned land. However, as I will show in this book, things did not happen as foreseen; the land reforms were not the solution they were thought to be.

Zimbabwe has not been short of news coverage lately. The invasions of Commercial Farms spearheaded by war veterans have featured in newspapers and television news broadcasts. The 'land issue' now has become a familiar topic for a wider audience in Europe and the United States. Most attention is paid to the white farmers, who were driven from their homes by, sometimes violent, mobs of land invaders, and to a lesser extent, their labourers who are victims of the invasions as well. President Mugabe - who in 2002 was re-elected for another six-year term in office in elections that were widely denounced as unfair - has accused Great Britain, Zimbabwe's former colonial master, of having hindered past attempts by his government to solve the problem of a highly skewed distribution of land between white and black farmers. At the Lancaster House Conference, where Zimbabwe's Independence was brokered, all parties signed an Agreement stating that during the first decade of Independence no land could be alienated from white farmers; land for resettlement purposes could only be bought on a willing-seller-willing-buyer basis. President Mugabe accused Great Britain of protecting the interests of white farmers by supporting this clause in the Agreement and of not providing enough funds to the post-Independence government to buy land for its land hungry peasants. White farmers were accused of mobilising and intimidating voters into voting 'no' in the 2000 referendum on a proposed new Constitution, which, apart from granting more powers to the president, would also have allowed the government to alienate land from white farmers without paying compensation. Numerous land invasions took place soon after the referendum, in the run-up to the 2000 general elections. Despite violent intimidation the opposition party, the Movement for Democratic Change (MDC), won a considerable number of seats in Parliament from the ruling ZANU(PF) party. The invasions continued after the 2002 presidential elections. But why did the land issue flare up again twenty years after Zimbabwe had gained Independence? What happened in those first twenty years of Independence? These are questions that have a wider significance than just the Zimbabwean case, and many political commentators are speculating about the ramifications of the Zimbabwean land invasions for other countries in the region.

After Independence in 1980 the new government promised the return of the stolen lands to the African farmers and developed plans for an ambitious resettlement programme. The first post-Independence development plan presented, envisaged the resettlement of 162, 000 families onto former European Land before 1986. By 1991 about 48,000 families had been resettled (Palmer 1990; Blanckenburg 1994: 30); by 1998 the number had risen to about 70,000 families (Moyo 2000: 5)[1]. Though quite an achievement, this was far less than the target set. During the first years after Independence, the government had been able to acquire a substantial amount of land from farmers who had abandoned their farms during the war or who wanted to leave the country just after the war, uncertain of the new government's intentions. However, after a number of relatively stable years, far less land became available for sale (Palmer 1990: 169-70). The first decade after Independence confiscation was no option because of the above-mentioned Lancaster House Agreement, and despite its supposed Marxist orientation, the new government was keen to assuage the worries of international and local investors (Moyo 1995; 2000).

The Zimbabwean government left the dual property regime of land intact, a strategy followed by most post-Independence governments in the region (see Mamdani 1996; Cousins 2003). Land in the former European Areas, now renamed Large Scale Commercial Areas, was held as private property. The former Reserves, or Tribal Trust Lands, where the majority of the black farmers

---

[1] By 1998 4,000 mainly white large-scale commercial farmers retained 28 per cent of the land (11.2 million hectares) and over one million households were residing in the Communal Areas on 42 per cent of the land (16.3 million hectares). The 70,000 resettled households occupied 9 per cent of the land (2 million hectares) (Hammar & Raftapolous 2003: 8).

resided, were renamed Communal Areas, and land in these areas was held under communal tenure.

Despite positive experiences with resettlement of African farmers on former European Land (see Kinsey 1999), since the mid-1980s there had been a gradual shift in attention away from resettlement to what is referred to as 'internal resettlement' (Drinkwater 1991). The viability of communal land tenure was questioned and calls were made to implement land-use reforms that would render land-use in the Communal Areas more efficient. The assumption underlying the reforms was that improved efficiency and intensification of land-use could alleviate the pressures existing in most Communal Areas in Zimbabwe, and would reduce the demand for land in the former European Areas. The reforms and the ideas underlying them show striking similarities with the land reform policies the Rhodesian government had proposed for the Tribal Trust Lands in 1951 (see Drinkwater ibid.).

Not much was done from the mid-1980s onwards to acquire land for resettlement (Moyo 1995). The emphasis remained on internal land reforms in the Communal Areas, even after the Lancaster House Agreement expired ten years after Independence. At every election the government announced that it would expropriate land from white farm owners (Alexander 2003; Raftapoulos 2003), but little follow-up was given to these announcements. On the contrary, Alexander (2003) has described how since the early 1980s the government reacted with increasingly violent removal strategies to evict squatters on (abandoned) white-owned farms. Marongwe (2003: 164) cites the late Governor of Mashonaland Central Provice, Border Gezi, who in 2000 spearheaded many land invasions in his Province, telling squatters: 'What you have done is unlawful and the Government will not let you do that. Be prepared for eviction anytime (...)'.

In 1997 war veterans organised massive protests to demand compensation for their role in achieving Independence. They demanded compensation for their efforts in the form of pensions and land (see Alexander 2003; Hammar & Raftapoulos 2003). Pensions were paid and by the end of the year the government announced it had serious plans to solve the land issue. In 1998 a donor conference was organised to discuss these plans (Moyo 2000: 24-5; Hammar & Raftapolous 2003: 8-9), and a number of donors - including the UK, now accused of having sabotaged attempts to restore 'the stolen lands' - pledged substantial sums of money for the acquisition of white-owned farms. Again, despite these pledges, not much headway was made in the process of organising the redistribution of land between the Large Scale Commercial Areas and the Communal Areas (ibid.: 9), until March 2000, when the government lost the referendum on the introduction of a new Constitution that would further strengthen the position of ZANU(PF), the ruling party.

ZANU(PF)'s support for the spate of invasions of white-owned commercial farms is less likely to be related to the land issue than to the serious political threat the ruling party was experiencing for the first time since it came to power in 1980 (see Alexander 2003; Raftopoulos 2003: 229-32). A new political party, the Movement for Democratic Change (MDC), which had its roots in the trade unions, had been established in 1999, and unlike earlier opposition parties, attracted a large, countrywide following[2]. The farm invasions created chaos and a situation of lawlessness that drew attention away from the organised attacks on the political opposition. Western governments and the Western press focused mainly on the white farmers wounded or killed during invasions, and far less on the much higher number of black victims who were killed because they were associated with the MDC.

This does not mean that the land issue was a non-existent problem. Access to land has remained an important and emotionally laden political issue ever since the struggle for Independence, and there is a good reason why ZANU(PF) has chosen this issue for its political campaigns (see Moyo 2000; Alexander 2003; Marongwe 2003)[3]. Nor does the leadership of the MDC, or that of the Commercial Farmers Union for that matter, deny that the very skewed distribution of land between white and black farmers needed to be redressed. They are just not convinced that the invasions are the right way to address the problem, nor that the invasions will in the end benefit those who are most in need of land. Indeed, numerous land invaders have been evicted from confiscated farms to make way for high-ranking ZANU(PF) party members or their allies. The National War Veterans Association, which has led the invasions, several times even threatened to withdraw its support for the party if these evictions would not stop (Zimbabwe Independent 5 July, 2002)[4]. In other words, there is serious doubt whether the ruling party really wants to solve the land issue in favour of those who are suffering from land shortages in the Communal Areas. There have been ample signs in the first twenty years of Independence that government did not consider the communal farmers fit to take over the Large Scale Commercial Farms. The land reforms planned for the Communal Areas bear witness to this idea.

Zimbabwe is not unique in this. At Independence, most countries in Southern Africa were confronted with the legacy of a racially skewed distribution of land. As Cousins (2003) has recently pointed out, given this unequal ownership, it is not surprising that land redistribution featured prominently in the rhetoric of liberation movements and in the policies of post-Independence governments. However, in practice, Cousins continues, these governments have given far less

---

[2] The first opposition party, the Zimbabwe Unity Movement led by Edgar Tekere, captured 17 percent of the total vote in the general elections of 1990, and Tekere obtained 16 percent of the votes in the presidential elections (Raftapoulos 2003: 226). However, despite this success ZUM was disbanded before the next elections.

[3] Marongwe (2003) provides a highly interesting analysis of the actors involved in the land invasions and their motives.

[4] See for an analysis of the complicated relations between ZANU(PF) and the war veterans Kriger (2001) and Marongwe (2003).

priority to land redistribution than their manifestos would suggest (ibid.: 274). Among the reasons that Cousins cites are a dominance of neo-liberal policies with a strong emphasis on attaining foreign capital, and a '(…) widespread scepticism of policy makers about prospects for small-holder agriculture (…) (ibid.: 274)'.

This book is about the internal Communal Areas land reforms in Dande, in the Zambezi Valley in northern Zimbabwe, introduced by the Zimbabwean government with the help of the FAO and the African Development Bank. The reforms were symptomatic of the attitudes in government circles towards communal farmers in the first twenty years of Independence. The reforms were presented as a development project: the Mid-Zambezi Rural Development Project - hereafter referred to as the Mid-Zambezi Project.

Dande was an area of strategic importance during the struggle for Independence. Situated on the borders with Mozambique and Zambia, it was used by guerrillas of both the ZANU and ZAPU armed wings to enter the country. The population of Dande suffered a great deal during the war, being caught between the Rhodesian Forces and the guerrillas. After Independence the new government committed itself to bringing development to this marginal area. When this finally came in 1987, in the form of the Mid-Zambezi Project, many people of Dande did not react as gratefully as they were expected to. As a medium of a royal ancestral *Mhondoro* spirit in Dande whom I interviewed expressed it:

> We see it as war. Long way back people were shifting from where their homes were because of ants eating their huts or they were able to change their fields because they no longer were good. So (…) when these people were fighting during the war [of Independence] they said they wanted to live their traditional way (…) the Mhondoro looked after the boys [guerrilla fighters] well because in the bush there were lions, snakes, elephants, buffaloes and rhinos but none of them was injured because the Mhondoro were always looking after them. After the war we were expecting to live in our own traditional way. Then after the war they came saying they want to peg plots. (…) They said that people should shift and live along the road, but none of the Mhondoro is happy about this. (…) All the spirits are saying the war is not yet over and when it is over we will start seeing people practising the life of the old days.

Yet, instead of responding to local critiques, the planners and implementers of the project tended to denigrate the opposition to the land reforms as irrational and traditional, in the sense of backward looking. Unfortunately this is a rather common reaction among technocrats - and politicians as well (Ferguson 1990, Werbner 1997; 1998).

The fact that, in Dande, the mediums of royal ancestral spirits played an important role in expressing discontentment with the reforms only strengthened the planners and implementers in their opinion that local residents were clinging to their traditional way of life, resisting modern change. Apparently, many of them still adhered to the view that tradition is incompatible with modernity and conceived of traditional religious practices as a mark of this incompatibility.

They neglected the experimental and creative aspects of ritual practices, '(...) animated by men and women as they seek to make their worlds manageable and meaningful (...)' (Comaroff and Comaroff 1993: xxix).

This book aims to explore why the land reforms elicited so much resentment and resistance among the people of Dande. It seeks to analyse the clashes between local residents and project staff over development, modernity and tradition, and the role the spirit mediums played in these clashes.

Land reforms and land degradation narratives

Why did the government of Zimbabwe pursue these internal land reforms in the Communal Areas, when a similar programme initiated by the Rhodesian state had stranded because of widespread resistance? Given present-day developments in Zimbabwe it is easy to attribute all sorts of sinister motives to the introduction of the reforms. Yet, the government of Zimbabwe was not alone in thinking these reforms would help relieve the situation in the Communal Areas, therefore it did find donors prepared to assist in financing the Mid-Zambezi Project as a pilot project for the reforms.

A number of scholars have studied the rationales behind pre- and post-Independence land use policies in Southern Africa. Most explanations focus on the need for political and administrative control by governments over rural populations. On the whole, land reform programmes are based on the assumption that the land use practices of local - African - farmers are inefficient and irrational (see De Wet 1989; Drinkwater 1991; Keeley & Scoones 1999; 2000; Delius & Schirmer 2000). In his book 'Seeing like a State', James Scott (1998) suggests that local land-use practices are not so much irrational as 'illegible'. Farmers are often using their land for different purposes in different periods of the year and sometimes fields are used by different farmers at different periods of the year. All this makes it difficult for the state to know who is controlling which part of the land and who is residing where. Land reforms are one way of rendering the landscape more 'legible'; another way is the consolidation of villages or 'villagisation' that is and has been part of many of the land reform programmes implemented in Southern Africa[5]. Making the landscape legible entailed a simplification of local land-use practices. Scott supposes a strong link between state control and simplification: 'Indeed, the very concept of the modern state presupposes a vastly simplified and uniform property regime that is legible and hence manipulable from the center (Scott 1998: 35)'. Simplification of complex property systems is not always a bad thing; according to Scott, some degree is inevitably needed to develop an efficient fiscal system and

---

[5] Examples include 'betterment' programmes in South Africa (De Wet 1989; McAllister 1989), but also land reform programmes inspired by socialism, such as Ujamaa in Tanzania (Cliffe & Cunningham 1973; Cliffe & Saul 1975).

develop services and infrastructure (see also Sender & Johnston 2004). However, there is always a risk of oversimplification, which can indeed have disastrous consequences for those whose practices are subjected to it (Scott 1998: 30-5).

In Southern and East Africa, over time, a specific narrative (cf. Roe 1991; 1995; Adams & Hulme 2001) has been constructed to guide and justify land reforms or 'rationalisation' of local land-use practices: the land degradation narrative (Leach & Mearns 1996; Keeley & Scoones 2000; McKenzie 2000). This narrative has its roots in the colonial period and served to redefine a political problem - the increasingly distorted distribution of land between white and black farmers - as a technical problem. Decreasing agricultural production in those areas set aside for African farmers was construed as an environmental crisis caused by the farmers' lack of knowledge concerning 'proper', 'scientific' farming methods. This crisis justified government interventions. The form that these interventions took in the different settler colonies showed remarkable similarities: centralisation of scattered villages, conferring individual user rights, and separating grazing from agriculture (see Beinart 1984; Keeley & Scoones 2000; McKenzie 2000). Most colonial land reform programmes also involved the culling of cattle 'in excess of carrying capacities (see Scoones 1996)'. The goal of these interventions was to maintain a certain level of agricultural production in the Reserves, without allocating more land to African farmers. The similarities do not mean that there were no differences of opinion between and within colonial administrations about the intended results of the reform, for instance about whether only subsistence farming should be allowed or cash crop production as well, or about the role of 'traditional' authorities in the Reserves (see Hendrick 1989; Kramer 1997).

Keeley and Scoones (2000: 14) as well as Scott (1998: 342) argue that it is not only political control that drives states to simplifying and controlling property regimes, but also a sincere belief in 'modern', 'scientific' land-use practices. Scott adds another driving factor for land reforms, namely a powerful aesthetic dimension: 'High-modernist plans tend to "travel" as an abbreviated visual image of efficiency that is less a scientific proposition to be tested than a quasi-religious faith in a visual sign or representation of order (Scott 1998: 225)'. Scott suggests that it is these factors that lie at the heart of the striking parallels between colonial and post-colonial land-use reforms.

The new post-Independence governments were under pressure to do something to increase the standard of living of the African population and to assume control of countries that often underwent times of great turmoil before becoming independent. Keeley and Scoones (2000: 14) argue that establishing the new post-Independence state as a legitimate source of authority in rural areas meant identifying problems that required state intervention or state underwriting. The interventions that followed were to bring remote rural areas, with long traditions of suspicion towards the state, more firmly within reach (see also Munro 1995). Land reforms were, for reasons mentioned above, an ideal way to do this. Furthermore, many countries in Southern Africa gained Independence at a time when donors still frowned upon land redistribution (see Cousins 2003)[6]. Such interventions were presented as 'development', and this label functioned to deny that they served as instruments of political control. Ferguson refers to 'development' as an anti-politics machine, an instrument '(...) depoliticizing everything it touches, everywhere whisking political realities out of sight, all the while performing, almost unnoticed, its own pre-eminently political operation of expanding state power (Ferguson 1990: 254)'. McKenzie (2000: 716) argues that the depoliticisation effect of land reform programmes is facilitated by separating nature from society. Agricultural science is often based on the premises that it is possible to separate the different attributes of a crop and isolate variables in the interests of manipulation, replicability and control. This in turn allows for the proposal of '(...) universal solutions to what became defined as universal problems (...) (ibid.: 716)'.

Though land reform programmes are meant to reinforce the state's power over remote rural areas and contribute to the conservation of the environment, they are notorious for failing and leading to ecological damage (Scott 1998: 225; see also De Wet 1989). Scott argues that this is because there are limits to the extent state simplifications work. There are limits to the extent to which one can apply a standardised plan to a dynamic and variegated - natural - environment. Secondly, land reform plans often involve a standardised model of the farmers as well, assuming that they all have the same aspirations, and have the same inputs and labour available to invest in their production[7]. Most importantly, however, '(...) the efficiency depends on the response and cooperation of real human subjects. If people find the new arrangement, however efficient in principle, to be hostile to their dignity, their plans, and their tastes, they can make it an inefficient arrangement (Scott 1998: 225)'.

The continued 'illegibility' of local land-use practices stems from the fact that the farmers in the Communal Areas are continuously innovating and adapting their practices in response to the uncertain conditions in the dry marginal areas to which they have been relegated. They must do so in order to survive (see Scoones 1996; 2001; Reij & Bay-Waters 2001). Wynne argues that there is a distinct difference in the way local farmers respond to uncertain environments and the way natural scientists do: 'Ordinary social life, which

---

[6] In a recent article Sender and Johnston (2004) describe how the donor community has been 'converted' to land redistribution. While in the 1980s most donor countries were convinced that large-scale commercial farming was vital to the economies in southern Africa, they argue that subsidies and discriminatory pricing policies have rendered the large-scale farming sector inefficient. Small-scale farming is considered more productive and should benefit from land redistribution, provided that this redistribution is market-based.

[7] For studies repudiating the notion of 'standardised' communal farmers, see James (1985) and Cavendish (1999).

often takes contingency and uncertainty as normal and adaptation to uncontrolled actors as a routine necessity, is in fundamental tension with the basic culture of science, which is premised on assumptions of manipulability and control (Wynne 1992: 120)'. However, one can wonder whether this need for control is not something that is aspired to by local farmers as well, but impossible to attain. They are forced to accept uncertainty, forced to experiment in a 'haphazard' way and draw upon a body of knowledge that has been developed locally. They are often more successful because of their knowledge of the specific context in which they are functioning, but this knowledge may have been developed by trial and error. Science tries to replace 'haphazard' experimentation by controlled experiments that are context-independent and thus more widely applicable. This is why governments and development agencies have long favoured 'scientific' solutions, and, if they have become interested in local knowledge, often try to de-contextualise it by compiling 'best practices' that can be disseminated to other parts of the country or even the world.

Scoones attributes the failing of many land reform programmes, and other projects trying to render the landscape more 'legible', to distrust between local farmers and the 'purveyors of the scientific solution' (Scoones 1996: 51-2). It is not ignorance that engenders local farmers' reluctance to adopt the proposed practices, but a more fundamental disquiet about the technical rationale for the suggested solution under local circumstances and a suspicion about ulterior motives. Local farmers have preferred to follow their own informal and flexible alternatives in order to survive, and because changing their methods will disrupt their production (see also Scott 1998). The top-down approach to implementation limits the possibilities of exchanging perspectives and negotiating outcomes between local farmers and external agents. The result is the emergence of forms of resistance that are actively pursued, but perceived by outsiders to represent ignorance of the 'correct' solution, implying that people require education and persuasion (Scoones and Cousins 1994). The persistent perception that ignorance is at the root of resistance or non-compliance does not lead to questioning of the assumptions behind the intervention or a re-examination of its scientific premises (Scoones 1996: 52).

In this book I describe the development of the land degradation narrative in Zimbabwe, and analyse the way the narrative is reflected in the implementation of the Mid-Zambezi Project in Dande, which served as a pilot project for internal Communal Area land reforms envisaged for all Communal Areas in Zimbabwe. I will also analyse the way farmers in Dande reacted to the project, how these interactions influenced staff members of the project team that was to implement the land reforms, and whether this changed the latter's opinion about the validity of the land degradation narrative. As I will describe, the Mid-Zambezi Project resulted in increasing conflicts within the communities about land, but also in overt resistance to the project. Mediums of royal ancestral spirits, *Mhondoro,* played an important role in expressing resentment concerning the project.

The role of Mhondoro mediums

The evocation of ancestors and other images from the past has led many, development planners and scholars alike, to consider 'traditional' religions to be 'backward looking', as Thoden van Velzen and Van Wetering (1991: 399) remark: 'Particularly when searches for witches are organised or spirits called upon to legitimate political action, a society is diagnosed as being on the defensive, aiming at restoration of the social relations and values of the past'. They argue, however, that this is a misinterpretation, which fails to recognise the way in which the images of the past are simultaneously products of economic and political forces, as well as promises and visions of a future. They contribute to people's attempts to make sense of the present or even change present conditions (ibid.: 400-1; see also Comaroff & Comaroff 1993; Geschiere 1995: 23).

In similar vain, Strathern has urged scholars to move from 'nostalgic social theory' to a theory of nostalgia. She proposes two different modes of nostalgia: synthetic and substantive nostalgia (Strathern 1995: 110). Synthetic nostalgia betrays a yearning for a past that is found lacking in the present. The past is closed and has no further bearing on the present, but at the same time a process of estrangement from the present state of affairs can be recognised in expressions of nostalgia. The second form of nostalgia is an active attempt to create a sense of tradition and social memory that has a bearing on the present. The second form of nostalgia becomes a basic element in how societies or groups deal with their present predicament, how certain claims to power and interests are substantiated, and how certain subjective identities are realised (see also Battaglia 1995: 93). Strathern notes that in substantive nostalgia, the blending of older and later representations, signs and images, may be viewed as trajectories of personal and social empowerment (see for instance the work of Werbner 1991; 1996; 1998).

Van Dijk argues that cults like the *Mhondoro* cult in Dande offer a sacred - meaning 'ritually separate' - invocation of time to empower and transform the person or the community. They do not just operate with the flow of time 'as it is' but instead create their own temporality in which the past is represented as a source of empowerment. A conceptual frame is established in which it is crucial for the process of transformation and healing of the individual and the community to perceive and represent a past in such notions as ancestral spirits, former kings and important strangers, previous experiences, incantations, songs and rhythms (Van Dijk 2000: 136).

Van Dijk suggests that scholars should look not only at the way the past is presented in the present, but also at how the past is rejected, wilfully disempowered (see also Werbner 1998) or subjected to 'institutional forgetting' (see Douglas 1986; 1995; Shotter 1990). Scott states that many land reform proposals are point-by-point negations of local land-use systems. As I describe in this book, the mediums of the *Mhondoro* spirits present an image of the past that in turn is a point-by-point negation of the proposed land reforms, stressing that the image that they present reflects 'old traditions'.

The mediums of the *Mhondoro* spirits embodied the past that could serve to legitimate local challenges to state control over land. The ancestors, through their control over rain and fertility, and as ancient rulers over certain territories, were ideologically closely linked to land as a natural resource. In Southern Africa there are many ancestral cults that share these same characteristics, and there is an important body of literature about them. This literature focuses on a number of issues that are important to understand the role of the *Mhondoro* mediums in the reactions to the Mid-Zambezi Project. The link between land, other natural resources and the ancestors is one issue discussed extensively (see e.g. Schoffeleers 1978; Lan 1985). The importance of spirit mediums in political processes - related to the above-mentioned link - is another (see for example Garbett 1966a; 1969; 1992).

Various attempts have been made to group different cults together under the same banner. Werbner (1977) used the tributary relations between different spirit mediums and pilgrimage routes to argue that most local ancestral cults are in fact part of larger, what he has called 'regional cults'. Van Binsbergen (1995) has referred to the widespread utilisation of certain medical technology, the four-tablet divination, to demonstrate regional connections. Janzen (1992), whose work will be discussed below, has taken the region of Southern Africa as an organising principle, as well as the transformations that the mediums of the cults undergo.

Schoffeleers (1978) proposed the term 'territorial cults' to group together spirit medium cults that embody a strong relationship between ancestors, land, and political power. In the introduction to the volume 'Guardians of the Land', Schoffeleers argues that in Southern and Central Africa concern about ecological matters is dealt with through a number of religious institutions and ideas. In the first place there are the lineage cults, which are concerned with - among other things - the holding of land and stock, and therefore have an ecological dimension. Many professional cults, like the cults of hunters or fishermen, also have ecological dimensions. But the major focus of the volume is on '(...) a type of cult which functions for the whole of the community rather than for sections within it and which is at the same time profoundly ecological (1978: 2)'. Schoffeleers refers to this type of cult as a territorial cult: 'Characteristic activities of territorial cults are rituals to counteract droughts, floods, blights, pests and epidemic diseases afflicting cattle and man. Put positively, territorial cults function in respect of the well-being of the community, its fields, livestock, fishing, hunting and general economic interests. Apart from engaging in ritual action, however, they also issue and enforce directives with regard to a community's use of its environment (1978: 2)'. Schoffeleers argues that the basis of territorial cults is the principle 'management of nature through management of society'. Nature is upset when things are wrong in society, when crimes are committed or power abused. Schoffeleers points out that territorial cults have an important political dimension:

> Both the ecological and societal functions of territorial cults border on or overlap with functions usually associated with political institutions. When cult mediums exhort the population to plant a particular crop or employ a particular agricultural technique to the exclusion of other crops and other techniques, such actions, although essentially economic, may have political consequences (ibid.: 6).

Failure to comply with the directives issued by mediums is believed to cause droughts. Droughts and other climate disasters are interpreted by mediums as resulting from moral breaches and challenges of the socio-economic order, which can include the abuse of power by local leaders. One could therefore argue that the main principle of territorial cults could also be interpreted as 'management of society through management of nature'.

The political commentaries expressed through territorial cults are not confined to the local. The cults themselves, though stressing links between the ancestors and specific territories, are not confined to these territories. As Schoffeleers already remarked: '(...) territorial cults seldom function all by themselves. More usually, they form part of a wider organization which in various ways and to varying degrees establishes links between neighbouring communities (ibid.: 6)'. Since the 1970s numerous ethnographic studies have analysed the regional significance of cults like the *Mhondoro* cult. Werbner (1977) even considered this the main characteristic of such cults and referred to them as regional cults. For quite a number of years, the issue of regional political cults dominated the ethnography of the Southern African region of the Manchester School, elaborating on specific cultural issues that lent a specific 'regional' character to their production (see Fardon 1990: 5). In 1993 Ranger emphasised again how important these types of 'traditional' but regional cults were and still are in the engagement of local communities in wider networks and relations of exchange (Ranger 1993b).

Janzen (1992) has taken the focus on regionality a step further by grouping cults together on a regional basis rather than on the basis of constructs such as 'healing', 'divination' or 'fertility'. He describes a set of features and ritual practices that refer to any of these categories and joins them together under the banner of Ngoma. From comparing diverse healing practices that include drumming and are referred to as Ngoma in local settings, Janzen distils a list of characteristics that to a large extent are shared by all of them. These 'core features' are predominantly of an experiential nature and thus lead to a high level of shared recognition within the region. Ngoma, in other words, indicates a floating field of experiences that in a Foucauldian sense operates as a discourse from which local ritual practices 'emanate'. The ritual practice is produced through the language, the rhythm and rhyme within Ngoma.

My colleagues Rijk Van Dijk, Ria Reis and I have argued that although Janzen criticises classical approaches to Ngoma for their concentration on divination, possession and trance, he too chooses the same analytical unit: Ngoma as a therapeutic institution which transforms sufferers into healers. The seven formal properties or core features by which he defines Ngoma all pertain to this process of transformation. This is particularly clear from what Janzen calls 'the core ritual', in which all other features converge and without which we cannot speak of Ngoma: the therapeutic and initiatory Ngoma song dance in which the meaning of individual lives and suffering of the Ngoma practitioners is articulated and recreated (Janzen 1992: 86, 128, 174). In other words, Janzen's prime subject continues to be cults of affliction, and he limits the scope even further by focusing almost exclusively on the healers, ignoring lay participants in the cults. By focusing mainly on the 'doing' of Ngoma, the political aspects and the ideological core of many Ngoma institutions remain largely buried from view (Van Dijk, Reis & Spierenburg 2000: 5-7).

We have argued that Ngoma denominates a Southern African discourse of which the subject is the coming to fruition of life and of which the object is to ensure this fruition and to remove obstacles to it. As a discourse Ngoma may pertain to all spheres of life, be this the personal, the social, the political, the economic or the ecological sphere. In Ngoma healing power, that is, the power to counteract illness and misfortune, and political power, that is, the power to order and reorder social relations, are closely interwoven. Both powers draw on claims to specific relations with the spirit world. The boundary between healing and the (re-) ordering of social relations is often difficult to draw. Communal problems can be reduced to personal afflictions, or personal afflictions can be explained by referring to communal issues. Healing Ngoma can constitute a manifest political act and a political mode of transition. In healing, personal motives, experiences and fantasies can be 'channelled' into social ones turning healing into politics (ibid.: 5-7).

I believe that the involvement of the *Mhondoro* cult in the conflicts about the land reforms stems from its close connection to the land through its concern with rain and fertility, its inherent political character, which it shares with other Ngoma-type cults in the region, and its regional connectivity. Not only are the different *Mhondoro* mediums in Dande connected with one another; they also rely on the fame of some of the *Mhondoro* who are known nation-wide.

These 'national' *Mhondoro* as well as the political aspects of the *Mhondoro* cult have received ample attention in the literature on the cult. The major focus has been on the role of the *Mhondoro* cult in the two armed struggles against the white settlers, the first in 1896-97 and the second which led to Zimbabwe's Independence in 1980 (see e.g. Ranger 1967; 1985; Lan 1985; Daneel 1991). In this literature, a leading role is attributed to the *Mhondoro* mediums. They have been portrayed as the first to recognise the potential of armed resistance; consequently, they mobilised local support for the combatants and are even believed to have been involved in part of the planning of both wars. By contrast, there has been little concern for the role of the following of mediums. Occasionally, authors have hinted at the support mediums need from their adherents (e.g. Lan

1985: 66-7, 211), only to continue portraying the latter as passively following the mediums. Examine, for instance, this quote from Lan (1985: 222): 'Among the particular skills of the mediums that were called upon during the war was their ability to accumulate followings that crossed chiefly boundaries. These they put at the disposal of the nationalist leaders'.

Beach (1986) and Kriger (1988; 1992) have warned against overemphasising the role of the *Mhondoro* mediums. They convincingly showed that internal divisions within the local population have proved a more important factor in providing - or withholding - support to the combatants than statements issued by *Mhondoro* mediums. The concern of the authors was mainly the description of the armed resistance, rather than the *Mhondoro* cult itself. Consequently, they did not offer any suggestions about the influence of adherents on the *Mhondoro* cult itself.

For such suggestions one has to turn to the literature on the role of *Mhondoro* mediums in political succession (see e.g. Garbett 1966a; 1966b; 1992; Bourdillon 1979). Bourdillon has been rather outspoken about the influence of the adherents of the *Mhondoro* cult. He has described the involvement of *Mhondoro* mediums in a succession dispute that broke out in Dande after the death of a chief. The mediums changed their preference for one of the many candidates several times '(...) after much argument (...) (Bourdillon 1979: 177)'. Bourdillon concluded that 'spirit mediums depend for their status and their followings on their ability to assess and express public opinion (ibid.: 177)'. Yet, he does not clarify where or under what circumstances the arguments took place.

In this book, the influence of the adherents of the *Mhondoro* cult will be a second major theme. The involvement of the *Mhondoro* mediums in expressing objections to the Mid-Zambezi Project created a great opportunity to study the *Mhondoro* cult in more depth. Numerous authors have problematised the concept of 'community' (see e.g. James 1985; Cavendish 1999; Barrow & Murphree 2001), and it is fair to say that the community of (possible) followers of the *Mhondoro* mediums also constitutes a heterogeneous group of people with different aspirations as well as differential access to resources. Since the conflicts about land in relation to the project were being played out while I was in the field, I was able to study the interactions between the mediums and their different adherents in more detail, and develop some ideas about who was mobilising whom, and why rifts and conflicts concerning the involvement of the mediums occurred. These interactions and conflicts not only taught me something about the effects of the Mid-Zambezi Project, but also about the functioning of the *Mhondoro* cult.

Terence Ranger once remarked that 'the weight of recent scholarship on Zimbabwean religious experience has fallen, not on describing the "ordinary" in post-colonial Zimbabwe, but on narrating what happened during the "extraordinary" upheavals of the 1970s guerrilla war (Ranger 1991: 149)'. The period covered by this book is situated between the upheavals of the 1970s guerrilla war and the upheavals of the farm invasions, which started in 2000. Yet, to argue that this book deals with religious experiences in an 'ordinary' setting would hardly be correct. Even during this period the struggle for control over land did not cease, albeit that the parties opposing one another were different; this time it was - broadly speaking - the state versus communal farmers. Perhaps it is true that the *Mhondoro* cult becomes more visible and prominent at times of crisis. During crises, the mediums' pronouncements may acquire a more distinctly political character, and therefore perhaps provoke more discussions and rumours among the local population than in calmer periods, when the political is perhaps less visible in their pronouncements. It is also possible that because I was studying the cult and its adherents in the middle of the 'upheavals' caused by the land reforms, I ended up with a different picture of the role of the adherents than David Lan. Lan (1985) studied the role of the *Mhondoro* mediums during the war for Independence after the violence had ceased, and he and his interlocutors were reconstructing and interpreting what had happened. The result was a rather neat narrative that left out many of the complexities and contradictions that are harder to escape when the drama is unfolding right in front of your own - and your interlocutors' - eyes.

Struggles within the communities

The support for those *Mhondoro* mediums who were challenging the state's authority over land in Dande was not always unanimous. Just as different representatives of the state reacted differently to the mediums' challenges, so did members of the communities in Dande when pressure was put on them to accept the Mid-Zambezi Project and other projects that threatened to take away local control over land. This pressure took the form of bribing and scrutinising of *Mhondoro* mediums, and also of threatening the inhabitants of Dande with withholding the much needed and appreciated development of infrastructure and social services. I have tried to show the different reactions to these threats and their implications for the support of the counter-narrative forwarded by the *Mhondoro* mediums.

Villages, as anthropologists never tire to stress, do not constitute homogeneous communities, and this is particularly relevant when it comes to natural resource management, as Barrow and Murphree have emphasised again (2001: 25; see also Cavendish 1999). Apart from socio-economic status and gender, there was another distinction in the communities where I did my research that merited attention: the one between those who considered themselves autochthons and those considered - sometimes considering themselves - migrants. One of the questions I had set out to address when I started my research project was to study the impact of the internal land reforms on the position of the many migrants in Dande. I was also curious about the impact of the presence of a large migrant population on the position of the *Mhondoro* mediums.

The way in which participation in the *Mhondoro* cult is defined, namely simply by living and farming within the territory believed to belong to the *Mhondoro*, almost assures a heterogeneous body of - potential - adherents. Though the link between ancestors and a certain, bounded, territory may be used to stress autochthony and the right to control this territory vis-à-vis the state, this same link is used locally to incorporate both 'autochthons' and 'strangers'. All those living in, or more importantly, cultivating within the territory of a *Mhondoro* are supposed to honour this royal ancestor, and participate in the rituals devoted to the spirit. 'Strangers' are thus transformed into 'sons and daughters of the soil' (see also Lan 1985).

It appeared that the conflicts over land in Dande were being fought out at different levels. There were the confrontations with 'the state' and its representatives, in which the *Mhondoro* cult played an important role. The internal land reforms also resulted in conflicts within the communities over who would have the right to land if the reforms continued. These conflicts were rather fierce, as quite a large number of people would not be able to obtain land officially under the land reform programme, and would end up being classified as squatters. In the conflicts within the communities, notions of autochthony and strangerhood assumed importance. Just like notions of autochthony were used to claim control over land from the state, these notions were also important in the conflicts within the communities (see also Geschiere 1995; Geschiere & Nyamnjoh 2001). However, the *Mhondoro* mediums remained rather aloof in the latter type of conflicts. These conflicts were fought out in another but related part of the religious domain: witchcraft. As I will describe in Chapter Eight of this book, the same themes that crop up in the struggle with the state, came up in the witchcraft incidents related to internal conflicts over land: autochthony, modernity and tradition. Pertinently, the way these themes were addressed differed markedly.

Doing fieldwork in Dande

'Doing fieldwork' in Dande was a fascinating, but occasionally difficult experience. Dande is one of these famous 'hunting grounds' for anthropologists. Kingsley Garbett and Michael Bourdillon's work is based on fieldwork conducted in this particular area of Zimbabwe. If the spirit mediums of the area with their historical accounts of the ancestors conquering the area had not yet succeeded in doing so for many Zimbabweans, then it could be said that David Lan has 'immortalised' the area in the minds of many anthropologists with his magnificent book 'Guns and Rain'. This book has been a great inspiration for me, despite the fact that I disagree with some of Lan's conclusions. Ever since I read it, I dreamt of going there.

I was lucky to be able to travel to Dande several times, and twice I managed to stay in the area for a considerable period of time. The first time was in 1988-

1989, when I did fieldwork for a period of about half a year. Between 1992 and 1994 I was able to live in Dande for nearly two years. In between these two periods of extensive fieldwork, and since then, I have visited the area for shorter periods of time.

During a first period of fieldwork, which lasted till the end of April 1989, the focus of my research was on migration. My methodological approach at that time was much more restricted than during my later fieldwork. On the basis of a survey that had been conducted among migrants in different parts of the Zambezi Valley (Murphree, Murombedzi & Hawks 1989), I compiled a detailed questionnaire with open-ended questions. In two villages my research assistant and I interviewed thirty heads of households - though in practice in most cases other household members joined us for the interviews - who had migrated to Dande after 1980 and had participated in the above-mentioned survey. The idea was to obtain more detailed information than had been gathered for the survey on their motives for migration and how they had obtained their fields and homesteads, in the hope that certain patterns would become visible. Furthermore, we asked the heads of households to tell us their life histories. We also conducted a survey on - self-reported - agricultural production, land available for production, sources of income, livestock ownership and ownership of agricultural equipment. We compared these data with a similar survey we conducted amongst twenty-seven households in the two villages that were considered, and considered themselves, to be autochthonous. Apart from conducting the survey, I also interviewed staff of the Mid-Zambezi Project and local authorities about issues related to the migration movement to the Dande and the Mid-Zambezi Project itself.

During the second period of fieldwork my research was focused more directly on the consequences of and reactions to the Mid-Zambezi Project. I selected two main sites for my study; one village where the implementation of the Mid-Zambezi Project was quite advanced, and one where conflicts and resistance had caused considerable delays.

When I arrived the people in Dande were suffering from a serious drought that had affected the whole of the Southern African region. The 1991/1992 crop had failed completely and people were relying on food and money sent to them by relatives in town, and on drought relief distributed by the government. The fact that some people had had to move to new fields and homesteads because of the project made things worse. When I remarked that doing fieldwork in Dande sometimes was a difficult experience, I especially meant witnessing the plight of those suffering from the drought and the negative consequences of the land reforms without being able to really assist people other than on a very, very small scale and in a haphazard way. Starting fieldwork in this situation was not easy, as one can imagine, but for the people of Dande, trying to make a living, it was of course much worse. Fortunately, the 1992/93 rainy season started in time and was a good one, so people started planting their crops in the hope that soon they would be able to harvest the first green mealies to relieve their hunger.

Despite the fact that people had to work hard under difficult circumstances - temperatures soared to 48 degrees Celsius in the month before the rains started and most people had only one scanty meal a day - the people of Mburuma were still willing to accept me in their midst, perhaps because they already knew me.

The first time I had relied heavily on a pre-planned questionnaire. During my second stint of fieldwork my methodological approach was much more 'eclectic'. Levi-Strauss already concluded that every researcher engaged in qualitative research is in fact a bricoleur (Levi-Strauss 1966: 17). This I was indeed, collecting information from many different sources. I started my second fieldwork period with a second survey of (self-reported) agricultural production and semi-structured interviews on access to land. These were not only useful in terms of providing me with some of the data I needed - data I could compare with the survey I conducted in 1988/9 - but also legitimated my presence in the village of Mburuma, as well as in Mahuwe, the two main sites of my fieldwork. Going to see people, explaining my research and then actually 'collecting' data from them gave me a relatively clear role in the community: that was my work, that was why I was staying with them. 'Just' chatting away with people at random was not interpreted as work by my interlocutors. Yet, to me these 'chats' were just as valuable. I visited people in their fields when they were taking breaks during the hottest period of the day, spent many evenings in smoky kitchen huts chatting with the women while they were cooking, attended beer parties, weddings and funerals. I had asked permission to have my own homestead built close to the big baobab where all the village meetings were held, so I missed none of those. Nor did I miss any of the soccer matches, since the soccer field was right next-door as well.

Coincidence played an important role in my research (see Wels 2000: 51-9, 77-87 for a detailed discussion of coincidence and fieldwork). Though my appreciation of David Lan's book had launched a fascination with the *Mhondoro* mediums, I had not planned to study them in such a detailed way. However, it soon became clear that the *Mhondoro* mediums had become the spokespersons for the opponents of the Mid-Zambezi Project and that, in order to study the impacts of and reactions to the project, I needed to include the mediums in the study. The same had happened to David Lan, as he told me when he visited Zimbabwe about halfway through my second period of field-work. My research assistant and I tried to attend the mediums' meetings with project staff and other gatherings where they were asked to make statements about the project. I also decided to consult all mediums in Dande on the developments going on in Dande. We managed to meet all but three of the mediums who were practising in Dande at that time, and spoke to a total of fifteen mediums. Most mediums preferred that we talked to the spirits posses-sing them, rather than to the medium as a person. This required that we had to organise our work following the lunar calendar, since the mediums can only become possessed when there is sufficient moonlight, consequently they do not become possessed between last quarter and first quarter. We would first approach their assistants, asking if we could speak to the spirit. The assistant would then conduct a small ritual at the spirit's shrine to ask the spirit to come. We would spend the night in the village where the medium lived, and would be woken up by the assistant early in the morning when it was still dark, and led to the shrine where the medium would be waiting for us, already in a state of possession. Most of the time other villagers would be present, as well as people from neighbouring villages who also had matters to present to the spirit. As was custom, we would address our questions via the medium's assistant to the spirit, whose answer would be relayed back to us by the assistant. We recorded all but one of the spirit consultations, and my research assistant transcribed the tapes. Here my command of chi-Shona never reached the fluency to be able to translate all the subtleties, especially since the spirits express themselves in a rather archaic form of chi-Shona - they speak 'deep Shona', as my assistant would remark.

If there was one methodological guide that helped me deal with the sudden twists and turns that I felt my research was subject to, it was Van Velsen's method of situational analysis. His classical chapter published in 1967, as well as Mitchell's work on case studies (1983), reassured me that it might actually be a good idea to follow the meetings of the *Mhondoro* mediums on the project closely. These events brought most of the actors involved in the project together. They led to discussions that continued in kitchen huts, under trees in the field and at beer parties where dissenting voices could also be heard. The same applies to the witchcraft incidents related to internal conflicts over land.

By coincidence another project was introduced in Dande during the course of my fieldwork. Two irrigation schemes had been planned for in an area that had already been subjected to the introduction of the internal land reforms through the Mid-Zambezi Project. Again the *Mhondoro* mediums became implicated. This provided me with a second opportunity to study the role of the *Mhondoro* cult in conflicts over land, and I decided to spend some time in Chitsungo, where this second drama unfolded, to study the mediums' involvement more closely.

Outline of the book

This book is about the persistence of the land degradation narrative as a guide for Zimbabwean land use policies. This narrative, which has its origins in the colonial period, quickly replaced the narrative about the return of the stolen lands, and remained dominant in the period between the mid 1980s and the referendum on a new proposed Constitution in the year 2000. The book describes the influence of the narrative on the planning and implementation of the Mid-Zambezi Project, and the different reactions of the people subjected to this project.

The second chapter of the book will provide a description of the project area, Dande Communal Land, its location and climate. This chapter also provides a brief historical overview that focuses on migration and land-use. I describe how migration seems to have been a constant feature in Dande, and how the armed struggle for Independence also contributed to continued movement and displacement of people. Dande has been as a sort of 'overflow' area for the congested Communal Areas on the Plateau of Zimbabwe. The continued movement of migrants into the area has also led to calls to control this movement, more specifically, to control settlement and land-use patterns.

The second chapter also describes the pre- and post-Independence policies regarding the Communal Areas. Both periods show similar shifts back and forth in policies concerning three areas that are intrinsically related: land tenure, local government and decentralisation. Both periods have seen moves from promoting communal ownership of land to promoting a more individualised form of tenure and back again. Secondly, both periods have been characterised by inconsistent and contradictory policies concerning local government, sometimes reinforcing the powers of so-called traditional leadership, sometimes reinforcing 'modern' local government institutions - elected or not. Related to this are shifts between decentralisation and (re)centralisation. Neither pre- nor post-Independence governments have ever completely decentralised in the sense of devolving decision-making powers (see Ribot 1999), and often decentralisation policies served to extend the reach of central government into the Communal Areas (see Murombedzi 1992; Hammar 1998). As a result of contradictory policies the situation in Communal Areas, concerning which authority actually is responsible for allocating land, has become very unclear.

Chapter Three describes how, in this uncertain context, migrants have sought access to land in Dande. Since the 1960s the whole of the Zambezi Valley has experienced an influx of migrants looking for land to cultivate. This movement has continued since Independence. The majority of the migrants came from the congested Communal Areas on the Plateau. Farm labourers also looked to the valley when searching for land to set up a home for retirement. The Commercial Farms on the Plateau turned out to be linking pins, where migrants formed relations with people from Dande, using these connections to obtain land in Dande. Depending on their connections, they approached different authorities to ask permission to settle in Dande. Prior to the introduction of internal land reforms, the migrants were welcomed - sometimes even recruited - since they could contribute to further clearing the bush, driving away wild animals that could damage crops and kill people. Their hosts also hoped that with more inhabitants they would be able to promote claims for the development of infrastructure and services.

In Chapter Four I describe how the continued in-migration indeed drew the government's attention - as well as the attention of development and environmental organisations in the North. The result was the introduction of the Mid-Zambezi Rural Development Project, which served as one of the pilot projects for the internal land reforms that the government wished to introduce in all Communal Areas of Zimbabwe. The aim of the project was to restrict and control in-migration by limiting the number of new settlers. In this chapter I describe how the internal land reforms clash with local land-use practices, and how those subjected to the project reacted to the project.

Chapter Five describes the development of the ideas underlying the Mid-Zambezi Rural Development Project by looking at the history of the organisations involved in implementing the project. The establishment of these organisations is linked to the development of the 'land degradation narrative'. The political issues underlying the problems in the Tribal Trust Lands, now known as Communal Areas, were (re)interpreted as a technical problem, stemming from black farmers' lack of knowledge concerning proper land-use planning and agricultural methods. Their dearth of knowledge was believed to have caused the problem of declining soil fertility in the Communal Areas. 'Proper' land-use plans needed to be developed for these areas, and farmers needed to be trained in 'proper' farming methods. This narrative justifies the activities of the organisations implementing the Mid-Zambezi Project. In this chapter I describe the interactions of these organisations with local communities subjected to the project, and how these influenced staff members' belief in the narrative.

Chapters Six and Seven describe the involvement of *Mhondoro* mediums in expressing objections to the Mid-Zambezi Project and two irrigation projects implicating further land use reforms. The chapters provide an analysis of the development by the mediums of a counter-narrative to the 'land degradation' narrative. Furthermore, the case material presented in the chapters reveals the crucial role played by adherents in shaping mediums' pronouncements.

Finally, in Chapter Eight I focus on the divisions within the communities that were accentuated by the Mid-Zambezi Project. The project resulted in conflicts about who would have the right to land in Dande if the land reforms could not be stopped. I describe how in these conflicts witchcraft and witchcraft accusations played an important role. Debates on concepts like 'modernity' and 'tradition' as well as 'autochthony' took place in relation to the internal conflicts.

Setting the scene:
A brief history of Dande

Introduction

In this chapter I want to present the area where I conducted my fieldwork, Dande Communal Land. The aim of this chapter is to provide the reader with information about historical developments which I consider important to understand the chapters that follow; in other words, to provide a context against which to interpret my findings. Setting the context, however, is not an unproblematic exercise (see Kamsteeg & Wels forthcoming). Dande, though often considered a marginal Communal Land, has received considerable coverage in anthropological and historical works on Zimbabwe. What information does one select from all this? How far does one have to go back in history? How does one situate the history of Dande in the historical framework of Zimbabwe or Southern Africa?

Any selection is always a biased one, and depends very much on one's interpretation of the present. The historical background presented in this chapter focuses on a number of topics I consider to be closely related to my research. After a brief description of the location of Dande, I will discuss early migrations to and invasions of Dande. Migration seems to have been an important and continuous feature of life in Dande. The influx of migrants after Independence in 1980 therefore is not a new phenomenon, and earlier experiences may have influenced the way in-migration was dealt with by resident populations. The early migration histories are also important because some of them are remembered through and reflected in the *Mhondoro* - royal ancestral - cult, which played an important role in the expression of resistance against the land reforms that were introduced in Dande in 1987. Some aspects of colonial history are presented in this chapter as well. There are quite a number of similarities between the way colonial authorities and the present government regarded Dande; both considered it a marginal, empty area with room for 'excess populations' from the Plateau, and an area that needed to be brought under control. Controlling settlement patterns was one way of accomplishing the latter goal. Both colonial and post-Independence governments shifted back and forth between supporting communal tenure and trying to introduce some form of individual land tenure. This coincided with alternating movements; from reinforcing the positions of 'traditional' leadership, to strengthening 'modern', bureaucratic local government institutions. These shifts will be described in this chapter, as well as the local government structures that were present at the time of my fieldwork.

The struggle for Independence has an important place in this chapter as well. Since Dande was right on the frontline, many people there were severely affected by the war. As I will explain below, the war led to changes in settlement patterns and influenced expectations from the new government. The war also directed attention to the mediums of the *Mhondoro* cult as important actors within local communities, since they have been given an important role in the armed struggle. Given the importance of the *Mhondoro* mediums in this book, I will introduce them in this chapter, and will dwell on their being related to the war for Independence. First, however, I will give a brief description of the location of Dande within Zimbabwe and its administrational boundaries.

Location and boundaries

Dande is situated in northern Zimbabwe, in the Zambezi Valley. Reaching Dande requires a 240-kilometre drive north out of Harare, the capital of Zimbabwe. A few kilometres after Guruve, the road descends steeply into the valley. It was not until 1995 that the road from the Escarpment into the valley was tarred. Once you have arrived in the valley, however, the tar surface stops abruptly and a rutted, corrugated gravel road begins.

In the north, Dande borders on Zambia and Mozambique. The Zambezi River forms the border of Zimbabwe till it reaches Kanyemba, where the river continues into Mozambique and the border drops sharply leaving the land south of the river and Lake Cabora Basa to Mozambique. In the south, the boundary of Dande is formed by the Escarpment, in the west by the Angwa River and in the east by the Msengezi River (see also Lan 1985: 15).

Dande falls under the jurisdiction of Guruve District. Guruve District also contains a large area on the Escarpment and Plateau, referred to as Upper Guruve. It is here that the offices of the Rural District Council and the District Administration are located. At the time of my research, Dande was represented in Parliament by the MP for the neighbouring Centenary District. This MP was

Cde Border Gezi, who became Minister of Youth after the 2000 elections and established the notorious training centres for the ZANU(PF) Youth Brigades.

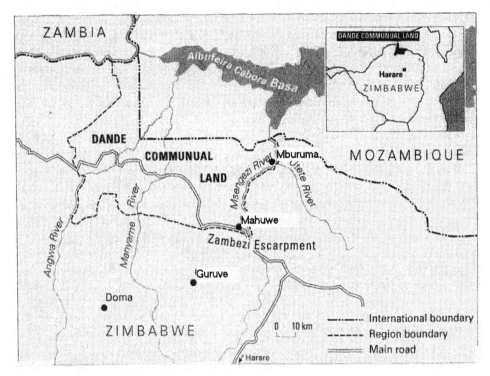

Map 1:   Dande Communal Land[8]

Pre-colonial population movements

Many family histories in Dande feature stories about (great-)grandfathers who came to Dande from elsewhere to hunt or trade, and many local notables like village headmen claim that their ancestors were not from Dande. Oral history as recounted by *Mhondoro* mediums and their adherents describes the long struggles for the control of rain and consequently land between invaders and autochthons - who, according to the same storytellers, also came from elsewhere. Dande seems to be an example providing evidence for the increasingly popular theory that in Africa migration, not sedentarism, is the 'normal' condition (see e.g. De Bruijn, Van Dijk & Foeken 2001).

---

[8] This map was kindly produced for me by Dick Foeken and has appeared before in Spierenburg (2001).

Mhondoro mediums frequently refer to the struggles between the children of Mutota, who invaded Dande, and Bangomwe, the 'autochthonous' ancestor. For a long time it was believed that these oral traditions could be linked to a population movement from the Plateau to the Zambezi Valley that took place in the fifteenth century (see e.g. Abraham 1959; Bourdillon 1970; Beach 1980; Lan 1985: 14-5). According to these traditions, Mutota set out from Great Zimbabwe in search of salt, trade and grazing areas. Mutota, or rather, his descendants, were believed to have founded a state in the early or mid-fifteenth century, stretching from the Zambezi to the Mozambican coast, while still retaining control over Great Zimbabwe near present-day Masvingo, from where many of the post-Independence migrants came. The capital of this state was believed to be in Dande. Historians thought that in the late fifteenth century the state lost control over the southern Plateau of present-day Zimbabwe, while the situation in the eastern part of the state remained fluid for some time. The oral traditions seemed to combine well with Portuguese documents from the early sixteenth century onwards. These documents provide detailed histories concerning the succession of members of a ruling dynasty to the hereditary Mutapa title, as well as the relationships between the Mutapa dynasty and its predecessors in the area. However, Beach (1994: 100-1) argues that in fact no close link exists between oral traditions and Portuguese documents earlier than 1629, and that the linkages after that are not very close ones either. Beach argues that this is partly because the people of the Mutapa state area have 'rewritten' their oral traditions, omitting rulers, condensing and altering events to make them fit the political needs of the day. Furthermore, it was not until the eighteenth century that the first oral traditions were collected. Nevertheless, Beach maintains that the origins of the Mutapa dynasty did lie in Great Zimbabwe and that members of the ruling class of Great Zimbabwe did build *zimbabwe*, that is, stone wall enclosures, in the Zambezi Valley. One of these was situated close to present-day Mahuwe, one of the villages where I conducted research, and I have visited its ruins several times. Portuguese documents suggest that the capital of the Mutapa State was located on the northern part of the plateau rather than in Dande, as oral traditions would have it. Yet, these documents do indicate that the Zambezi lowlands were indeed of importance to the Mutapa rulers (Beach 1994: 102).

Nowadays, there are three chieftaincies in Dande headed by chiefs who claim descent from the mythical Mutota. These chiefs are Kasekete, Chitsungo and Chisunga, and refer to themselves as Korekore. On the Plateau, bordering the Valley, there is another Korekore chieftaincy, headed by chief Chiweshe (Lan 1985). The name Korekore does not appear in documents up until the nineteenth century. Some believe that this name was given to the invaders by the people whose land they took. The name could be interpreted as a corruption of *kure kure*, which means 'far away' (Beach 1984; Lan 1985).

Lan refers to the people inhabiting the area before the arrival of the Korekore invaders as the Tande (1985). Nevertheless, I could not find any person who identified him or herself as a Tande, and most people I spoke to denied that such a group as the Tande ever existed. Chief Matsiwo, classified by Lan as a royal Tande, claims to be a 'true Korekore'. However, he does claim descent from Bangomwe, who is considered - also by him - as an autochthonous ancestor, and not one from Mutota. Chief Matsiwo heads the largest chieftaincy in Dande. Chief Matsiwo, as well as the 'other chiefs who call themselves Korekore', all claim that their clan is *Nzou Samanyanga* (Elephant, Keeper of the Tusks).

The vaDema or Mvura people are thought to have been brought to live in Dande during the later Mutapa period. Lan (1985: 17) says their mythology describes their incorporation in the Mutapa State as a result of military defeat. Some vaDema still live as semi-foragers in the Doma Hills in the southwestern part of Dande. Others have settled as agriculturists in the northwest of Dande (Lan 1985; Hasler 1992).

The wealth of the Mutapa state depended on agriculture, cattle herding, and trade in ivory, gold, salt and cattle (Beach 1994: 102 asf). In the fifteenth century, ivory and gold were transported via the Zambezi River and traded with Muslims who had settled on the Sofalan coast (in present-day Mozambique). Some of their African middlemen (who were often converts to Islam) settled in the interior along the river. In 1506, the Portuguese conquered the seaport of Sofala. By 1514, some Portuguese were actually living in the Mutapa State. Allegedly, their participation in succession disputes split the Mutapa leadership and contributed to its gradual decline from the late nineteenth century onwards (Beach 1980, 1994; Schoffeleers 1992).

The Portuguese were not only interested in trade. They also established large farms on the banks of the Zambezi River. To control their farm labourers and to defend the trade routes, the Portuguese established slave armies. The descendants of the slave soldiers as well as the descendants of Portuguese landholders who married members of the local (usually chiefly) lineages are known today as the Chikunda (Isaacman 1972; 1976). There is one Chikunda chieftaincy in Dande. The chief, called Chapoto, claims to be a descendant of the nineteenth century Portuguese landholder José Rosario Andrade.

The colonial period

In 1890, the settler-state of Rhodesia was established. Although the northern border between Mozambique and Rhodesia was drawn in 1891, trade with the Portuguese continued till the beginning of the twentieth century (Beach 1994). It was not until 1920 that the Rhodesian State finally established itself firmly in the Zambezi Valley. In the process, chieftaincies were reorganised by colonial administration and chiefs were appointed colonial officers (Lan 1985). The process of reorganisation continued up until Independence. Headmen loyal to the Rhodesian regime were appointed chiefs, and disloyal chiefs were demoted to the position of headmen. The Chitsungo chieftaincy - which features in

Chapter Seven - was created through this process (see Lan, 1985: 137-8). Its territory used to be part of the Mzarabani chieftaincy that was reduced to a headmanship. The Chitsungo chieftaincy was assigned to a branch of the Kasekete royal family.

Conditions for agriculture in Dande were (and are) not all that favourable. The climate is hostile, summers are hot and rainfall unreliable. Rainfall is concentrated in the period between October and April and averages 765 mm per year, but there are wide annual fluctuations and often dry spells often occur during the rainy season. The groundwater potential in Dande is low (GOZ/Euroconsult 1993). According to the consultants who did the feasibility study for the Mid-Zambezi Rural Development Project, the soils in the south of Dande, close to the escarpment, are quite fertile, but further to the north the quality of the soils deteriorates (African Development Fund 1986). This, however, is contested by local farmers, and it is not clear on which data the consultants have based their conclusions.

The collapse of the trade with the Portuguese, which had provided a reasonably secure income to supplement the unstable agricultural production in Dande, coincided with the imposition of taxation by the Rhodesian government (Beach 1980). In most literature, these developments are considered to have been the primary stimuli for - mainly young - men to move to the white-owned farms and mines on the Plateau to look for work (see e.g. Arrighi 1973; Palmer 1977; Phimister 1977/1983; Beach 1980; Stichter 1985). Pertinently, more recent literature suggests that circular labour migration cannot be attributed to political-economic contexts alone. Migrants' agency and the embedding of migration in socio-cultural patterns need to be taken into account as well (see Andersson 2001). Given the long history of involvement in long-distance trading, trekking considerable distances to look for work may not have been such a radical change as many authors have suggested. As I will show in chapter three, the migration practice from Dande to the Plateau of Zimbabwe greatly influenced migration in the opposite direction.

In view of the relatively adverse conditions for agriculture, and the harsh climate in the lowveld - with temperatures soaring to well above 40 degrees Celsius prior to the rainy season - the lands of the Zambezi Valley scarcely drew a second glance from the white colonists and virtually no land was alienated in Dande. This advantage was counterbalanced by the fact that the absence of a European farming area nearby (the closest being situated on the Plateau) made it difficult for the farmers of Dande to market their produce. Infrastructure in Dande was badly developed and services were poor.

Though land remained an abundant resource in Dande, in other parts of the country African farmers suffered from a serious shortage of this natural resource following the introduction of the Land Apportionment Act of 1930 and the resulting land alienations. Under this Act, more than fifty per cent of all arable land was allocated to the white settler minority. The areas allocated to African farmers were first referred to as Reserves, later they were termed Tribal

Trust Lands. These were often situated in less favourable climatological and ecological zones[9]. On the plateau in what is now Upper Guruve, black farmers were removed from their land as late as the 1950s to make way for white-owned, large-scale Commercial Farms. Most of these evicted people settled in Dande.

Dande has always been - and often still is - viewed as a wild and empty area. For a long time it was believed that the presence of tsetse flies constituted a serious constraint to agriculture there and contributed to Dande's 'underdevelopment' and an allegedly low density of human population. Tsetse flies are the most important vector of trypanosomiasis, which causes nagana in cattle and sleeping sickness in humans, both of which are potentially lethal diseases. Richards (1985: 128) states that many commentators during the early colonial period singled out cattle trypanosomiasis as a major cause of the 'backwardness' of agriculture in Africa and saw eradication of the fly as the first step towards a 'mixed farming revolution'. Even today, many agricultural scientists and demonstrators see the absence of the plough as the key limitation to farm size in Africa. Tsetse infestation was seen as a curse of the 'old Africa', which could and should be cured by colonial administration and science. Richards (ibid.: 129-37) convincingly shows that the opposite, namely, an increase in tsetse infestation as a result of early colonial settlement and agricultural policies, is a more likely hypobook.

Nevertheless, the fight against the fly has got a long history. In Rhodesia, it started in the early 1920s (Derman 1995: 10). The tsetse fly was regarded as one of the most serious threats, not only to agriculture in Dande, but to life in and the economy of the country as a whole. The major reason for tsetse eradication in the Zambezi valley was to prevent the spread of trypanosomiasis to the commercial cattle herds on the Plateau, but it was also seen as a move to permit farmers in the valley to introduce cattle for ploughing.

One of the earliest strategies employed to eradicate the fly was the killing of huge numbers of wild animals, which are its potential hosts. From the 1920s to the 1960s, between 20,000 and 40,000 head of wildlife were slaughtered each year. In the early 1960s, the Rhodesian government concluded that wild animal eradication would be more effective if it were combined with other control measures, including aerial and ground spraying with insecticides and the movement of human populations (see Barrett 1994; Derman 1995).

The Rhodesian government used - mainly African - farmers to open up tsetse-infested areas, on the basis of the - according to Richards - false assumption that intensified land use and increased human populations would lead to a decrease in wild animal hosts and thus would help combat tsetse flies

---

[9] There is an extensive literature on the history of the land apportionment and its consequences for the present agricultural situation in Zimbabwe: see e.g. Palmer 1977; Phimister 1977; Ranger 1985; Moyo 1986.

(Derman 1995: 11). The opening up of tsetse-infested areas also served another purpose. As more and more land on the fertile and tsetse-free Plateau was allocated to European farmers, the Native Reserves (later termed Tribal Trust Lands), which were set apart for African farmers on the Plateau became smaller and overcrowded. To provide more land, the Rhodesian government began to open up so-called Special Native Areas - of which Dande was one - in the Zambezi valley.

Although the Zambezi valley seems to have always attracted 'strangers', the large-scale in-migration of African settlers interested in agriculture began in earnest in the late 1950s and early 1960s. Some groups were actually ordered to move from the Plateau into the valley by the government, and were provided with transport. Most settlers, however, organised their migration without any help from the state. Driven by the increasing land scarcity in the Native Reserves/Tribal Trust Lands, they did not wait for the government to help them. The receiving local population welcomed the migrants, partly because it meant that wildlife, causing crop damage and endangering the lives of villagers, would be kept at bay.

One of the most persistent myths circulating among environmentalists is that the tsetse eradication campaigns caused large-scale migration to the Zambezi Valley (see e.g. Reynolds 1984). In fact, the primary motive of migrants was usually something else. As will be shown in more detail in the next chapter, the main 'pushing factor' of the migration movement to Dande - and to other parts of the Zambezi Valley - both before and after Independence, was the severe shortage of land in the areas set aside on the Plateau of Zimbabwe for small-scale African farmers. Regardless of the presence of the fly, quite a number of those farmers preferred the remote Zambezi Valley to the Plateau. Even if cattle could not survive there, a plot of land in the valley cultivated with a hand-hoe would still yield more than the small plots on the Plateau, even if the latter could be cultivated with the help of oxen. None of the migrants in the Zambezi Valley interviewed by myself, by Derman (1993) or by Murphree, Roland and Hawks (1988) ever mentioned anything about tsetse eradication as a motive for selecting the valley as a new home.

The earliest - gravel - road into the valley descended from Mt. Darwin (Centenary District) and was then extended across the valley floor. This meant that the eastern valley continued to be relatively inaccessible by motor vehicle until 1958-9, when the road from Guruve to Dande was built. Administrative tours in the valley had to be undertaken on foot, particularly in the west. A new paved road from Centenary to Mzarabani was completed in the mid-1960s. The roads facilitated greater administrative contact with the valley as well as the relocation of peoples. During the armed struggle for Independence, which started in the late 1960s, they were also used for troop movements (Derman 1995: 9).

The 1950s and 1960s saw a steady increase in human and livestock populations in the eastern valley. In 1961, the Native Commissioner estimated the population in the Dande Special Native area at 27,805 (Derman 1995: 15). In 1965, a Delineation Exercise was conducted which revealed that 6,237 households were residing in the area. Depending on the estimated average size of households, this adds up to a total population of somewhere between 30,000 and 37,000. Barrett (1994) says the cattle population in the eastern valley peaked in 1972 at approximately 23,000 head[10].

The 1960s also saw the establishment of two state farms, operated by TILCOR, in Dande. Experiments with cotton began at these farms, from which agricultural extension officers, who introduced the crop to the local farmers, worked[11]. Other crops grown in Dande were maize, sorghum and groundnut. Tractor ploughing was introduced around the same time. At first, tractors became available through the TILCOR estates from which they were rented out. Later a number of successful cotton farmers managed to buy their own tractors.

Land tenure under the Rhodesian State

Management of land in the Rhodesian state was characterised by a dual property regime. As described above, the Land Apportionment Act of 1930 divided Rhodesia into European Areas and Tribal Trust Lands. Land in the European areas was held under private property tenure. The tenure system that was encouraged by the Rhodesian state in the Tribal Trust Lands (TTLs) was essentially 'communal', although in effect the state had taken over ownership of the TTLs (Ranger 1985; Murombedzi 1990). A 'decentralised' system of local authorities became institutionalised from chiefs to village headmen to kraalheads,[12] who were to manage the land on behalf of the population in the TTLs.

Cheater (1990), Murombedzi (1990) and Ranger (1993) argue that the term 'communal', to describe the tenure system practised by African farmers before colonial interventions, was not only inappropriate but also the result of an ideologisation of the land issue by colonial authorities - and subsequently by post-colonial authorities as well. Several myths form the basis of the notion of communal tenure. Firstly, it is based on the idea that chiefs and headmen were guardians of the land and that no individual ownership of land existed. This implied that land had no exchange value and therefore was not subject to market forces (Cheater 1990; see also Mamdani 1996: 17). Nevertheless, Cheater

---

[10] It should be noted that the Shona of Zimbabwe do not make the distinction familiar in other parts of Africa between cattle-keepers and agriculturists. Cattle are mainly used for ploughing; cattle keeping is integrated in agricultural production and does not constitute a separate way of life.

[11] In May 1994, I met Mr. Mutero who had been employed as an instructor by TILCOR. He told me that the first village where cotton was grown was Mahuwe, and that the crop had been introduced there in 1967.

[12] Kraalheads are the headmen of small hamlets that administratively belong to a larger village, or the headmen of a neighbourhood of a large village.

(*ibid.*) found historical evidence of forms of tenure that resembled private ownership as well as land sales and exchanges. A second myth is that communal tenure represented an egalitarian form of land use. Ranger (1985; 1993) however, states that it was in fact the colonial state, through its attempts to prevent the emergence of peasant entrepreneurs in the TTLs that diminished existing disparities in land holdings and other productive resources. A third assumption was that communal tenure was mainly geared towards subsistence farming, while the existence of peasant entrepreneurs, as described by Ranger, again indicates otherwise (ibid.).

The 1950s witnessed a - albeit temporary - break with the ideology of communal tenure and indirect rule through chiefs and kraalheads. As more and more land was alienated from the African population, the TTLs became increasingly overpopulated and the soils rapidly deteriorated. Since a total collapse of agriculture would have had harmful effects on the Rhodesian economy, the government introduced the Native Land Husbandry Act in 1951 (Ranger 1985; Drinkwater 1991). Through this Act, the government sought to confer individual tenure rights to specific parcels of grazing or arable land, presuming that individual tenure would lead to more efficient land use. The right to allocate land in the TTLs was taken away from chiefs and kraalheads. Cogently, the implementation of the Act entailed a large cattle de-stocking exercise, allegedly to prevent overgrazing. Because of a great deal of opposition and resentment among the population of the TTLs, the implementation of the Act failed.

Following the Unilateral Declaration of Independence in 1965, a 'community' approach to the development in the Tribal Trust Lands marked a return to the ideology of communal tenure. This approach relied heavily on the co-operation of the chiefs, headmen and kraalheads who had their rights to allocate land restored (Thomas 1992; Government of Zimbabwe 1994). The underlying motive for this reversal of authority can be seen as an attempt to replace African nationalism with 'tribal government', which would be more controllable and would act as a buffer to grass-roots opposition (Ranger 1985). The government was also seeking to keep costs low by administering through the traditional institutions, including customary law (Thomas 1992). Though colonial administrators maintained that traditional election procedures should be followed in nominating chiefs, a number of chiefly dynasties were affected by government interference. The government could veto any candidate for the chieftaincy in favour of a more co-operative candidate, and the status of a chieftaincy could be lowered or raised (Bourdillon 1987: 119). I have already described the resulting changes in chieftaincies and headmenships in Dande above.

The effects of this development on the legitimacy of chiefs and headmen are heavily debated. Quite a number of authors argue that the policy of indirect rule seriously damaged their legitimacy, that any co-operation with the Rhodesian government was interpreted as collaboration (see e.g. Garbett 1966; Ranger

1982; Lan 1985; Thomas 1992). Lan even claims that many of the functions formerly performed by chiefs and headmen were transferred by their subjects to the spirit mediums, including the allocation of land. Bourdillon (1987) and Alexander (1995) argue that the role of chiefs and headmen in the pre-Independence period, especially during the war, has been oversimplified and misunderstood by many authors. Firstly, not all collaboration served only the chiefs' interests; there were many occasions on which they may have felt compelled to comply with the government's policy, for fear of losing the government's support for infrastructural developments and development projects (Bourdillon 1987: 119). Furthermore, they claim that there were also many chiefs and headmen who supported the freedom fighters, assumed party positions and co-operated with the guerrillas, citing several examples from Masvingo and Chimanimani Districts.

The armed struggle for Independence

Racial segregation policies - including discriminatory labour policies, the continuing alienation of land, land reforms and cattle de-stocking exercises in the Tribal Trust Lands exacerbated by heavy taxes - all caused considerable resentment among the African population of Rhodesia. In the 1950s, the growing discontentment led to the establishment of the first African nationalist movements (Ranger 1985). In 1961, the Zimbabwe African People's Union (ZAPU) was formed under the leadership of Joshua Nkomo. In 1963, Nkomo's opponents, among them Robert Mugabe, established the Zimbabwe African National Union (ZANU). Both parties were officially banned in 1964.

In 1965, Prime Minister Ian Smith issued the Unilateral Declaration of Independence (UDI) of Rhodesia, refusing to give in to pressures from the United Kingdom to share political power with the African population. In the same year, ZAPU sent small, armed units into the country and in 1966, ZANU launched its first armed attack against the white regime in Sinoia (Martin & Johnson 1981; Dabengwa 1995: 27). After this 'battle of Sinoia', which ended in a victory for the Rhodesian police force, all remained quiet for a while. But in the 1970s, the war intensified again, leading to Zimbabwe's Independence in 1980 (Martin & Johnson 1981; Lan 1985; Ranger 1985).

The Zambezi valley became a frontline. Both ZANU's Zimbabwe African National Liberation Army (ZANLA) and ZAPU's Zimbabwe People's Revolutionary Army (ZIPRA) were active in the area (Bhebe & Ranger 1995: 12; Dabengwa 1995: 28-30). Their fighters entered the valley from Zambia and Mozambique. In 1975 both armies briefly united into the Zimbabwe People's Army, but this alliance was only fleeting and, soon afterwards, both armed groups continued their struggle separately again.

Towards the end of the war, all residents of Dande were forcibly moved to so-called Protected Villages (locally known as 'keeps') close to the Escarpment.

The rationale provided for the 'keeps' by the Rhodesian government was that they were constructed to protect the villagers against any attack staged by the guerrillas. More likely, however, the 'keeps' were supposed to prevent people from supporting the guerrillas by providing them with food and information (Frederikse 1982; Lan 1985).

People living scattered in small hamlets were gathered together and forced to live in these large, completely fenced settlements, guarded by the Rhodesian forces. In 1978, the first, smaller, 'keeps' were established in Dande. In 1979, people were transferred from these smaller 'keeps' to one of the two big 'keeps' that were established in Dande; one at Mashumbi Pools, the other situated at Mahuwe. Only between sunrise and sunset were people allowed to leave the 'keep' to work on their fields or tend to their animals. For those living far away from the 'keep', this was impossible and many of them could not harvest anything and lost their livestock. Serious shortages of food occurred in the 'keeps' and mortality rates were high. As homes, fields and livestock were abandoned; large areas reverted once more to forest as they were left uncultivated. As a result, the wildlife populations increased again (see also Derman 1995: 15). The 'keeps' were dismantled only after the first elections in independent Zimbabwe in 1980.

The human population in the valley declined markedly during the war. Many residents left the area during this period, to avoid the fighting and the 'keeps'. In 1982, two years after Independence, a census was conducted which calculated that around 18,000 people were living in the former Dande Special Native Area, now Dande Communal Land. This figure probably contributed to the image of the valley as 'empty'. However, by 1982, not everyone who had fled from the valley during the war had returned. Furthermore, after Independence, migration to Dande slowly started up again, regaining serious momentum only after 1983.

Mhondoro mediums and the war for Independence

Here I would like to introduce the *Mhondoro* mediums briefly, since such an important role has been attributed to them in the war for Independence. *Mhondoro* are the spirits of royal ancestors, the great rulers of the past. All present-day chiefs of Dande claim to descend from one of the *Mhondoro*. The spirits are believed to continue looking after the territories they once ruled when they were still alive, by providing rain and fertility for the soil. In Dande, these areas have relatively clear-cut boundaries, which are known by most inhabitants; Garbett calls them 'spirit provinces' (1969; 1977). The land and all other natural resources in a spirit province ultimately belong to the *Mhondoro* of that province. The *Mhondoro* are thought to communicate with the living through a medium.

Some of the *Mhondoro* mentioned in this chapter have acquired national fame because of their association with the armed struggle for Independence.

Their reputation, and as a result the reputation of the *Mhondoro* cult as a whole, has benefited from this association. Much has been written about the involvement of *Mhondoro* mediums in the first rebellion against the white settlers in 1896-1897 - the first *chimurenga* - and the last struggle or second *chimurenga* which resulted in Zimbabwe's Independence. It is hard to find a book about the *chimurengas* that does not mention the *Mhondoro* cult, and very few publications about the *Mhondoro* cult do not mention the *chimurengas*. The main reason for the inclusion of this section is that the war literature, and the war itself, has affected the image of the *Mhondoro* cult. In my view it contributed to an image of strong, influential mediums and led to a neglect of the role of the potential adherents of the cult - which I will describe in detail in Chapters Six and Seven. Furthermore, the association between the war and the *Mhondoro* no doubt influenced the way the state dealt with and reacted to the cult.

After the battle of Sinoia, ZANU guerrillas embarked on a policy of mobilising popular support for the armed struggle. In 1971, ZANLA forces clandestinely entered Dande[13]. According to Josiah Tungamirai, who was the chief Political Commissar of the ZANLA forces, recruitment was facilitated by the participation and support of the spirit mediums in the area: 'With the help of the spirit mediums the guerillas were able to carry out their instructions to politicize the masses, to cache arms and to recruit would-be fighters in the Dande area'. (Tungamirai 1995: 41). He connects the involvement of *Mhondoro* mediums with the stories about the first revolt against the white settlers:

> (...) when ZANLA fighters arrived in the Dande area they discovered that the tradition of the spirit mediums Sekuru Kaguvi and Mbuya Nehanda, who had participated effectively in the first *Chimurenga* of 1896-7, was still alive in the 1970s and that the new generation of mediums was equally opposed to the oppressive system of the Rhodesian government (Tungamirai 1995:41).

The initiative of bringing the guerrillas into contact with the *Mhondoro* mediums, however, came from the local residents. Mayor Urimbo, leader of one of the first groups of ZANLA guerrillas operating in Dande, recalls: 'We spoke to the old people who said that we must consult the mediums. We were taken to Nehanda (...)' (cited in: Lan 1985: 136). The medium of Nehanda agreed to help the guerrillas. At first, Tungamirai felt somewhat uneasy about recruiting *Mhondoro* mediums. Later, however, he told Martin and Johnson (1981: 78): 'Mbuya Nehanda was ZANLA's most important and influential recruit (...)

---

[13] ZAPU had already mounted a campaign in the area in 1968 (Dabengwa 1995, 28-30) and remained active in parts of Dande afterwards. Nevertheless, little is known about the relations between ZAPU fighters and *Mhondoro* mediums. Brickhill (1995) maintains that ZAPU fought a secular war, in contrast to ZANU. However, Ranger and Ncube (1995) claim that ZAPU cadres and fighters maintained extensive contacts with officers from the Mwali cult.

Once the children, the boys and girls in that area, knew that Nehanda had joined the war, they came in large numbers'. ZANLA had war zones named after Nehanda and Chaminuka. Nehanda featured in many popular ZANLA war songs, which were sung at the all-night politicisation sessions (*pungwes*). Several mediums travelled with the ZANLA guerrillas; among them the mediums of Chipfene, Chiodzamamera, Chidyamauyu and Nehanda - the latter feature in Chapter Six of this book. In 1972, however, the Rhodesian army discovered the build-up of guerrillas in the northeast. Tungamirai (1995: 42) claims that the Security Forces mounted a manhunt for the spirit mediums. Fearing that the aged medium of Nehanda would be captured, the guerrillas decided to take her out of the country to a ZANLA-camp in Mozambique. At first she refused, but eventually she agreed. In mid-1973, she died in Mozambique. The three surviving mediums continued working with the guerillas (ibid.).

In his book 'Guns and Rain' (1985), David Lan also describes the co-operation of the above-mentioned *Mhondoro* mediums with ZANLA fighters. The central argument of Lan's book is that the support of the majority of the *Mhondoro* mediums for the guerrillas was a crucial aspect of the second *chimurenga*. During possession seances the mediums expressed the resentment many villagers felt against the white administration. Here, they proclaimed claims of the *Mhondoro* to the lost lands. Lan (1985: 146-53) says that the *Mhondoro*, the old warlords, had the authority to deal with war, even though their mediums had to avoid witnessing actual bloodshed. When the guerrillas arrived, they were strangers to the people in Dande. It was ZANLA's policy not to send guerrillas to fight in their home area where they might become involved in local power struggles. The *Mhondoro* mediums explained to the villagers that the guerrillas were not foreigners from Zambia and Mozambique as announced in government propaganda. Through participation in rituals and by adhering to the ritual restrictions imposed upon them by the *Mhondoro* mediums, the guerrillas were, Lan argues, ritually transformed from strangers to 'sons of the soil'. The *Mhondoro* mediums provided the guerrillas with '(...) the set of symbols with which [their] moral authority was expressed (Lan 1985: 220)'. According to Lan, this was important for obtaining popular support in Dande. In his 1995 article in 'Soldiers in Zimbabwe's liberation war', Tugamirai fully agrees with Lan's analysis:

> They [the mediums] told the *povo* [Portuguese for 'people'] why the guerrillas had come ... They went further to remind the *povo* that this was what Nehanda meant when she had said, '*Mapfupa angu achamuka*' (my bones shall rise from the dead) (1995: 42)[14'].

---

[14] Perhaps the most extreme opinion on the role of spirit mediums during the second *chimurenga* is expressed by Martinus Daneel in a paper he presented at a conference in

Bourdillon (1987b) has questioned Lan's analysis and has argued that perhaps the celebration of the mediums as war heroes after Independence (see below) contributed more to the popularity of the mediums than the fact that they contributed to the popularity of the freedom fighters. Nevertheless, as I will show in Chapter Six and Seven, in the pronouncements on the Mid-Zambezi Project, the image of the spirits and mediums as major actors in the bringing of Independence crops up many times and seems to legitimise the critique of the post-Independence government.

The post-Independence government has demonstrated a rather ambiguous attitude towards the *Mhondoro* mediums. Ranger argues that the Zimbabwean state simultaneously claimed to be the heir of African tradition and of colonial modernity, 'the custodian of proletarian ceremonial (the invented May Day parades), of national glory and of rural customs' (1983b: 106). The *Mhondoro* cult has played an important role in attempts to create a new Zimbabwean identity. The new government tried to transform the Shona ancestor, Nehanda, into the (grand-)mother of the new nation, Zimbabwe. In the Parliament of Zimbabwe, on the imposing staircase, which sweeps down from the ministerial offices, a statue of Nehanda has been placed. Actually, the statue depicts Charwe, the medium of Nehanda who was hanged after the first *chimurenga* was lost, as she can be seen in a picture taken while she was held in prison. The same picture is copied on numerous flags and banners, which decorate the National Stadium every year at the celebration of Independence. At every Independence celebration, the ancestors (as well as God) are praised for their help during the struggle for Independence. After Independence, all over the country army barracks, streets, schools and even a few local newspapers (controlled by ZANU/PF) were (re-)named after Nehanda (see also Lan 1985; Weiss 1986). Not only the state kept the memory of Nehanda alive. In the cities as well as in the rural areas, newly established local co-operatives and savings-clubs were named after Nehanda by their founders. In Dande, almost every local group involved in local development activities bears a name that refers to Nehanda, her praise names or significant events derived from the myths about her life and activities.

Utrecht in 1991, as well as in his novel 'Guerilla Snuff' (published under the name of Mahfuranhonzi Gumbo). Daneel assigns an important active military role to the *Mhondoro* and their mediums. He claimsthat 'Traditional religion (...) inspired the guerrilla fighters, in many cases informed and *even gave direction to strategic operations* at the war front and contributed greatly to close cooperation between rural communities and fighters (1991: 12, my italics)'. Daneel says many ex-combatants believed in a spiritual war council, a *dare rechimurenga*. This council was presided over by Mwari and consisted of the super-*Mhondoro* Nehanda and Kaguvi, as well as local *Mhondoro*. Daneel claims that '(...) in the spirit world the final authority behind the ZANLA and ZIPRA high commands, and probably more effectively in charge of the entire war effort throughout the country, was the *dare rechimurenga* (ibid.:13)'.

In Zimbabwe, Nehanda's image is pervasively present in public life. A strong connection is made between Nehanda and the Independence of Zimbabwe. There is even a rather strong connection made between President Mugabe and Nehanda. Numerous stories circulate, even today, about how Nehanda advised President Mugabe during the war and about the promises he reputedly made to (the medium of) Nehanda before she died.

Although the great *Mhondoro* of the *chimurenga* have become eminent national heroes, according to Ranger and Bhebe there has been no continuation of what they call the wartime alliance (1995: 24). After Independence, the government tried to end the *Mhondoro*'s political role. It allocated an exclusively healing role to their mediums by, as Ranger and Bhebe describe it '(…) lumping them together with n'angas as members of the Zimbabwe National Traditional Healers Association (ZINATHA) (ibid.: 24)'. In 1981, the Traditional Medical Practitioners Act, was passed as law (Lan 1985). The purpose of this Act was to establish a Traditional Medical Practitioners Council and to give legal standing to the Zimbabwe National Traditional Healers Association (ZINATHA). The function of the Council is to supervise and control the practice of traditional medical practitioners and to foster research and development of knowledge. All traditional medical practitioners have to be registered by the Council, including spirit mediums. Individuals who make use of the official title of Spirit Medium (or Traditional Medical Practitioners if no spirit possession is involved) even though they are not registered, are liable to a fine of Z$ 1000.- or imprisonment for two years (Lan 1985:220). Mediums who do not measure up to the standards of the Council can be expelled. Through the Council, the government is actually claiming the ability to declare who is and who is not a legitimate and authentic spirit medium. The possible political implications of such an agency have been noticed by others, as can be deduced from the formation of an independent Zimbabwe Traditional Healers Association by an ambitious politician (The Herald, 17-11-1992).

Independence and the return of the stolen lands

In 1980, Zimbabwe became independent. The first post-Independence elections were won by ZANU and Robert Mugabe became Prime Minister and later President of Zimbabwe. ZANU has stayed in power ever since. In 1987, ZANU and ZAPU merged into ZANU(PF) and Joshua Nkomo became vice-president, which he remained until his death in July 1999[15].

---

[15] The reconciliation between ZANU and ZAPU was preceded by a long period of hostilities. The ZANU-dominated government cracked down hard on any supposed ZAPU-related opposition and many people were killed (Catholic Commission for Justice and Peace 1997; Werbner 1998; Alexander, McGregor and Ranger 2000; see for a family history of that period Werbner 1991).

As I mentioned in the introduction, the new post-Independence government promised the return of the stolen lands to the African farmers and developed plans for an ambitious resettlement programme. The first post-Independence development plan envisaged the resettlement of 162,000 families onto former European Land before the year 1986, but by 1991, only about 48,000 families had been resettled (Palmer 1990; Blanckenburg 1994: 30). The availability of land for resettlement was a problem, as the rights of property owners had been guaranteed for ten years under the Lancaster House Agreement. As mentioned earlier, despite its supposed Marxist orientation, the government seemed to protect the Commercial Farming sector, which generated much-needed foreign currency. In 1988, the government even reduced its land acquisition budget by nearly two-thirds (Moyo 1995: 116).

In the mid-1980s, the government shifted its focus from the re-distribution of land to internal land reforms in the Communal Areas - which was the new name for the Tribal Trust Lands. The plans (re-)surfaced in response to a period of serious droughts, which lasted from 1982 until 1984, and to problems experienced with the acquisition of land from the large-scale Commercial Farming areas for resettlement. The assumption underlying the land reforms was that improving the efficiency and the intensification of land use could alleviate the pressures existing in most Communal Areas in Zimbabwe and would reduce the demand for land in the former European Areas. The reforms are discussed in more detail in the section below.

In 1992, after the Lancaster House Agreement had expired, a Land Acquisition Act was adopted that facilitated the expropriation of land by the state. The Act seemed a move back to land redistribution between Communal Areas and the former European Areas, as it allowed the government to acquire land compulsorily even when it was fully utilised. Pertinently, the Act stated that land would be bought at a 'fair price' instead of ruling market prices - as had been specified in the Lancaster House Agreement. Nevertheless, little happened in the period between 1992 and 1997, only about a hundred farms were designated for redistribution in this period, and only a few of these were actually confiscated.

The year 1997 was marked by violent protests by war veterans, demanding compensation for their efforts during the struggle for Independence in the form of pensions and land for resettlement. In November of that same year, a list of 1471 Large-Scale Commercial Farms designated for resettlement was published in the Government Gazette. This was criticised by the Commercial Farmers lobby, the private sector and the donor community, which claimed that it was not clear how the government would use the designated farms and expressed its fear that the plan would seriously undermine the commercial farming sector and investors' confidence in the country. Partly in response to this criticism, the government organised a donor conference in September 1998 at which a draft policy entitled 'Land Reform and Resettlement Programme Phase II' was presented (Hammar 2003: 8). During the conference, the government agreed with the other parties - donors, commercial farmers and representatives of the private sector - that the land reform programme should start with an inception phase during which 118 farms would be designated for resettlement. The donor community promised 17 million Z$ to assist the government in acquiring farms and providing reasonable compensation to the owners. Despite this agreement, the Minister for Lands and Agriculture signed acquisition orders for over 800 farms. Around the same time, several senior government leaders stated that more farms would be confiscated and that owners would receive compensation only for farm improvements, not for the land itself. However, again practice diverged from rhetoric and in reality only a part of the designated farms were confiscated and fair market value compensation for the land was paid.

Twenty years after Independence, the land issue flared up again. In the run-up to the general elections in June 2000, a new Constitution was drafted. Apart from strengthening the position of the ruling party, ZANU-PF, and the sitting President even more, the proposed Constitution was also marked by far-reaching possibilities to confiscate land for resettlement, obliging the former colonial government to pay for the land while the government of Zimbabwe would only pay for land improvements. The Draft Constitution was the subject of a referendum in February 2000 and was rejected: government spokespersons argued that this was *because* of the radical land reform proposals; the opposition claimed that *despite* these proposals a majority had voted 'no'. The leadership of the opposition party MDC has never denied that the land issue was a pressing one, but maintained that for the majority of the voters, the reinforcement of the powerful position of the ZANU(PF) leadership was more important than the proposals for redressing the unfair distribution of land. The rejection of the new Constitution was followed by a spate of farm invasions, led by the Zimbabwe National Liberation War Veterans Association. The Association has a somewhat ambiguous relationship with the government, in many cases its actions coincide with ZANU(PF) objectives, but as I have briefly mentioned in chapter one, there have also been occasional conflicts, as well as rumours that the party leadership feared the Association's leadership to become too powerful. The farm invasions were accompanied by plenty of violence against members of the opposition. Despite this violence the opposition won 58 of the 120 seats contested in Parliament. The farm invasions[16] and the violence intensified in the run-up to the presidential elections in May 2002 and continue even today.

---

[16] The former Governor of Matabeleland, Welshman Mabhena, had the honour of being the most prominent black commercial farmer to have his farm invaded, in early July 2000, after the elections had taken place.

Post-Independence land use policies in the Communal Areas

Although the struggle for redistribution of land between the Large Scale Commercial Farming Sector and the Communal Areas seems to dominate the political scene, land reforms in the Communal Areas themselves were at least as significant to ordinary Zimbabwean farmers. Prior to the post-2000 land invasions, these areas made up 42 per cent of all land in Zimbabwe and harboured 57 per cent of Zimbabwe's population (Moyo et al. 1991: 58; Weiner et al. 1991: 147). Consequently, they remained economically as well as politically important. Plans for the Communal Areas have been numerous, often contradictory and have had great impact on the lives of people who inhabit the areas. Most policy contradictions revolve around three key issues that are intrinsically related: 1) ideas concerning the viability of the principle of communal tenure itself; 2) the form of local government: 'traditional' versus 'modern' local government structures; and 3) how much control should be devolved to local government structures: decentralisation versus central government control.

After Independence, the land property regime was officially 'de-racialised', but not, as Mamdani (1996) calls it, 'de-tribalised'; the dual property regime continued. As mentioned earlier, during the first twenty years of Independence, the former European Areas were left largely untouched and were renamed Large Scale Commercial Farming Areas. For the majority of Zimbabwean farmers, access to land remained dependent on their membership of a group, as subjects of a chief. The Tribal Trust Lands were renamed Communal Lands.

The Communal Lands Act of 1982 states that authority over land in Communal Areas is vested in the President who holds all Communal Lands in trust for the people. The Ministry of Local Government, Rural and Urban Development was made responsible for administering Communal Land through the District Councils (Thomas 1992; Government of Zimbabwe 1994:22). The act stated that Councils shall '(…) have regard to customary law relating to the use and allocation of land (Government of Zimbabwe 1994: 23)'.

The installation of District Councils in the Communal Lands this soon after Independence and before a new administrative structure had been officially introduced, caused considerable resentment among local residents (Alexander 1995: 181). Untill then, the local administration had been in the hands of either the former support committees that had helped the ZANU-related ZANLA-forces during the war (Lan 1985: 209-10) or of the local branches of the ZANU party, sometimes in co-operation, sometimes in competition with traditional leadership (Alexander 1995: 181).

The establishment of District Councils indicated an attempt to re-establish a powerful state bureaucracy in the rural areas, mostly by the Ministry of Lands and the Ministry of Local Government. Decisions concerning development policy and land reform were taken at the national level, and the channelling of state resources to rural areas was controlled by the ministries, with little sensitivity to bottom-up demands, as noted by Alexander (ibid.: 183). Continuities from the past were evident and the Presidential directive, which allowed the appointment of Africans in any section of the public service if the President on the advice of the Prime Minister deemed it necessary in order to redress past imbalances, did not bring any change to the prevalent modernising and authoritarian ideology of the civil servants (ibid.: 180; see also Drinkwater 1991).

In 1984, the Prime Minister issued a directive, outlining the institutional framework for development in Zimbabwe, which completely excluded chiefs and headmen. Democratically elected Village Development Committees (VIDCOs) were to be the basic planning unit in this new system of local government. Each VIDCO would represent about a hundred households. The VIDCO was to submit its development plans on an annual basis to the WARD Development Committee (WADCO), which would represent about 600 households. The WADCO would co-ordinate the plans from all VIDCOs under its jurisdiction. It would then submit the ward plan to the District Development Committee (DDC). The DDC would incorporate the ward plans into an integrated district plan submitted to the District Council for approval. The District Council would comprise all Ward Councillors, that is, the chairpersons of the WADCOs. The Ward Councillors would be assisted by a District Administrator (DA) - who also served as the Chief Executive Officer[17] - appointed by the Ministry of Local Government, Rural and Urban Development. The District Development Committee, which was to develop the district development plan, was to be entirely composed of district heads of central government ministries and departments, together with representatives of the state security organisations, and chaired by the DA. The District Development Committee was therefore a central government committee. Once the District Council had approved the district plan, it was to be submitted to the Provincial Development Committee (Murombedzi 1992; Thomas 1992).

---

[17] Still, there are cases, e.g. in the Guruve District Council, in which the two functions are executed by two different people.

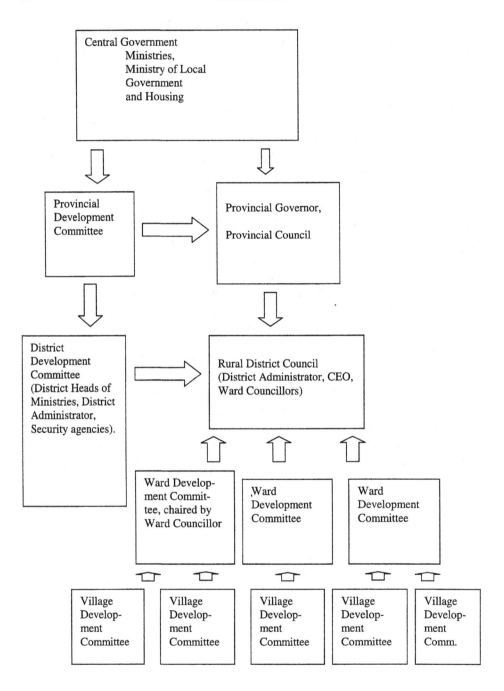

Figure 1:   Local Government Structure (Source: author's own material)

The Prime Minister's directive officially constituted an attempt to decentralise government and promote community participation in developing development policies. In practice, however, District Councils tended to be dominated by the government officials serving on them. Furthermore, the fact that development plans had to be submitted to the District Development Committee before being submitted to the District Council did not help either (Thomas 1992: 10). Yet, many Councils lacked both the expertise necessary to formulate development plans, and the resources to implement them. District Councils were almost entirely dependent on grants and on resources and expertise provided by sectoral ministries (Alexander 1995: 183). Plans to train VIDCOs and WADCOs in administrative skills proved over-ambitious because of a lack of sufficient financial and human resources (Thomas 1992:12). Where training was provided, the emphasis was on implementing central government policies rather than on training VIDCOs and WADCOs to develop their own development policies[18].

Though the operation and recognition of VIDCOs and WADCOs differs from area to area, there have been complaints about the lack of local support and participation within these structures[19]. Alexander (1995: 183) argues that the alleged weakness of VIDCOs and WADCOs can be attributed to the arbitrary nature of the units. VIDCOs and WADCOs were not built on previous communities and affiliations but simply on the figure of 100 and 600 households (see also Government of Zimbabwe 1994: 25). However, in some instances local amendments have been made; figures were reduced or enlarged to create some overlap with existing communities[20].

Apart from the lack of decentralisation of authority and resources to VIDCOs and WADCOs, there were also problems with their representation. The Commission of Inquiry into Appropriate Agricultural Land Tenure Systems concluded:

In practice, VIDCOs have no *modus operandi* allowing regular elections or other recognisable characteristics of democratic governance. Some, if not most, have had only one election since 1984. There was evidence of autocracy and manipulation (Government of Zimbabwe 1994: 24).

---

[18] A Ward Councillor in the area where I conducted my research showed me the training material he received and the notes he took during the training he attended in 1994.

[19] In 1989 the Minister of Local Government Rural and Urban Development made the following statement: 'What is however disturbing is that in some areas there is an unacceptable level of participation in the planning process by residents at the village and ward levels. Reports reaching my ministry suggest that people are not sufficiently involved or active in the village and ward development committees'. (MLGRUD 1989, quoted in Murombedzi 1989: 22).

[20] Quite a number of VIDCOs and WADCOs in Dande did not contain the specified number of households, but were delineated in such a way that they more or less overlapped with existing villages or neighbourhoods.

Derman and Murombedzi have discussed the domination of ZANU(PF) in local government institutions in the Zambezi Valley: 'The provincial governors and district administrators are political appointees and well-placed in the party. It is an unspoken assumption that to be on the District Council one has to be a member of ZANU(PF) (1994: 122)[21]'.

Although 'communal tenure' had been maintained in the Communal Areas after Independence, at the same time this form of tenure was considered unproductive. As described above, plans to introduce land reforms in the Communal Areas (re-)surfaced in the mid-1980s. Many authors, among them Drinkwater (1991), Alexander (1995) and McGregor (1995), have pointed out the similarities between the land reforms and the Rhodesian Native Land Husbandry Act of 1951.

The reforms were officially introduced in the first Five Year Development Plan of 1986, but in fact had already been prepared when the Communal Land Amendment Act passed in 1985 (Thomas 1992: 15). The amendments facilitated the intention of the government to introduce the demarcation of arable and grazing lands, and areas for rural housing construction. In contrast to the Prime Minister's 1984 directive, which apparently sought to promote 'grass-roots' development, the Communal Land Amendment Act authorised non-elected governmental officials of the District Development Committees to prepare and adopt development plans of their own volition (Thomas 1992: 15)[22]. No mention was made of any consultation of local people, other than the fact that when a plan had been prepared and approved by the District Council, a copy had to be sent to the chairman of every VIDCO of the Council affected by the plan (Section 4 (5), cited in Thomas 1992:15), who would have thirty days to consult local inhabitants and report back any objections to the council, together with *the identity of the objectors* (Section 4 (6), cited in Thomas 1992: 15, his italics).

In the end, the Ministry of Local Government Rural and Urban Development took direct control over land allocation in those Communal Areas that were subjected to internal land reforms. In these areas land allocation was carried out by its Department for Rural Development, and not by the District Councils (Government of Zimbabwe: 1999).

In 1988, the Rural District Councils (RDC) Act was adopted, though it was implemented only in 1993. In theory, this Act provided a deepening of the decentralisation process, but in practice it firmly established the authority of the state at the local level (Hammar 1998: 25-6). The purpose of the Act was to

---

[21] In one district in the Zambezi Valley it was more than an unspoken assumption. In Nyaminyami, before the 1988 unification of ZANU and ZAPU, ward councillors who were elected but were members of the ZAPU were not permitted to serve on the council (Derman & Murombedzi 1994: 122).
[22] Communal Land Amendment Act Section 4 (1), cited in Thomas 1992: 15.

establish a single type of rural local authority through amalgamating two previously separate types of councils: the District Councils, that served the Communal Lands, and the Rural Councils, that served the Large Scale Commercial Farming Areas. The resulting Rural District Councils were empowered under the Act to be the land allocation and land conservation authority (ibid.; Roe 1992). The act supposed a considerable devolution of power and resources to elected local authorities. Nevertheless, as had been the case with the District Councils, the Rural District Councils enjoyed very little autonomy from the centre - either in terms of resources or in terms of decision-making powers - and served in fact to reassert the power of the central state over the rural areas.

In the second half of the 1990s, the objectives of decentralisation changed. As part of the economic structural adjustment programme, the government undertook a reform of the public sector. Decentralisation and devolution were supposed to help reduce the role of the public sector as well as the costs of government operations. More and more ministries started to decentralise funds and devolve responsibilities to the local level. To co-ordinate these efforts more effectively, a Committee of Ministers on Decentralisation was set up. Lack of local resources and capacities, the latter especially among the elected Rural District Councillors, had been identified as the main obstacle to decentralisation. In response, a nation-wide RDC Capacity Building Programme was launched in 1996, with financial support from a number of European countries as well as from the World Bank. Training and the deployment of resource persons were to foster institutional and human resource development. Furthermore, each Rural District Council received a considerable development grant to effectuate projects and activities that could serve as test cases for newly developed skills, accountability and local democracy (Government of Zimbabwe 1999b). This programme was to continue in the year 2000, but with recent changes in Government and the political upheavals that preceded and continued after the general elections in 2000 and the Presidential elections in May 2002, its future is uncertain.

Meanwhile, significant changes in the position of 'traditional leadership' had taken place. Though the 1984 directive excluded chiefs and headmen from the new institutional framework - they could only participate if elected into either VIDCOs or WADCOs - and though they were attacked by technical planning ministries as anachronisms who stood in the way of progress, there were also voices in the new government defending them. Immediately after Independence, former employees of the Ministry of Internal Affairs lobbied for a continuing role of chiefs and headmen, on the grounds that their exclusion from local government could lead to confusion, even anarchy, in the Communal Areas (Alexander 1995: 186). In many districts, chiefs were soon to be invited as *ex officio* members to the meetings of the District Council. Already in 1982, a Chiefs and Headmen Act was passed, which recognised the institution of the chiefs, stating their right to a government stipend well in access to the stipend of

awarded to ward councillors (Alexander 1995: 182, 187). Pertinently, the act
did not, however, recognise the institution of the headmen, nor did it provide a
restoration of the chiefs' power over land allocation or court matters (Government of Zimbabwe 1994: 25). Since Independence, the courts presided over by
chiefs and headmen had been transformed into Community Courts, operating
under the Ministry of Justice. In 1992, civil jurisdiction was restored to chiefs in
all matters except land issues (Government of Zimbabwe 1994: 26).

Despite increasing recognition of chiefs, in practice legislation continued to
limit their role significantly, on the ground, however, that both chiefs and
headmen still played an important role in matters relating to land. The Commission of Inquiry into Appropriate Agricultural Land Tenure Systems concluded:
'Inhabitants of Communal Areas however, still refer most land matters and
requests to traditional leaders (1994: 24)'.

Alexander cites two reasons for the re-emergence of traditional leadership.
Once the war ended '[b]acked by a strong pressure for a return to "normality"
after the trauma of war, traditional leaders - and male elders in general -
reasserted their power (1995: 179)'. Another factor constituted what she refers
to as the authoritarian and modernising ethic of the development bureaucracies.
Especially the land reforms introduced in some of the Communal Areas and the
plans to eventually implement them in all Communal Areas contributed to an
increasing local respect for chiefs and headmen (ibid.: 187). In the light of these
developments and because of the structures in which they operated, VIDCOs
and WADCOs were gradually perceived to be instruments of local administration, essential implementation units for plans that continued to be developed in
a 'top-down' fashion (Thomas 1992: 12). Alexander argues that by formulating
an agenda based on a popular revival of 'tradition', traditional leaders were able
to draw on a constituency that found itself threatened by the new agricultural
policies. The traditional leaders certainly did not reject all aspects of 'moderni-
sation', but reacted to the authoritarian implementation policies and the loss of
local control over land. Traditional leaders invoked a version of the past in a bid
to challenge the authority of the state and local development bodies.

Due to the confusing amount of contradicting acts and legislation, the
situation with respect to land tenure became increasingly unclear. In reaction to
this, the government established a Commission of Inquiry into Appropriate
Agricultural Land Tenure Systems. On the basis of extensive interviews and
discussions, the commission concluded that all local government institutions,
from DCs to VIDCOs, claimed authority to deal with land issues (Government
of Zimbabwe 1994: 23). The Commission added that in practice chiefs and
headmen were found to have illegally reassumed their former role in land
allocation. The Commission concluded that '[t]his profusion of overlapping and
incongruent local organisational structures, each with its own boundaries and
drawing on different sources of legitimacy, has thus created weak and disparate
local institutions (ibid.: 26)'. In its recommendations to the government, the

Commission advised the latter to restore the role and powers of both chiefs and headmen in matters of land:

> While traditional leaders are clearly not mentioned in the land laws, the requirement in the law that land administration is done with regard to customary law in itself implies some role of traditional leaders, given their status as executors of customary law (ibid.: 24).

The problem, however, is the great deal of differentiation in the Communal Areas. Though the re-emergence of traditional leadership seems to be widespread, not everybody may feel that local chiefs and headmen represent their interests (see Chapters Three, Six and Seven).

According to Hammar, the draft policy 'Land Reform and Resettlement Programme Phase II', which had been presented at the donor conference in 1988, attempted to resolve earlier contradictions concerning the role of traditional authorities in land allocation, but with limited success (1998: 21). The draft policy proposed to use local plans and involve chiefs, headmen, traditional assemblies, the Rural District Council and the District Administrator without providing any articulation of how this would work in practice (ibid., 21). A new Act concerning traditional leadership that was presented early 2000 did not provide much clarity about this either. The Act proposed the establishment of Village and Ward Assemblies consisting of all adult village and ward inhabitants. The Assemblies are to be chaired by chiefs and headmen. The office of village headman will be officially re-instated. Village headmen will be given the task of collecting the development levies for the RDC and in return will be able to 'keep' a certain percentage of the levies for themselves in lieu of a salary.

VIDCOs will become 'sub-committees' of the Village Assemblies and will be chaired by the village headmen as well. Problematically, the position of the WADCOs vis-à-vis traditional leadership is less clear. WADCOs will continue to be chaired by the Ward Councillors, who will still represent the Wards in the Rural District Councils (Government of Zimbabwe 1999). The draft policy presented at the donor conference in 1998 also proposed the establishment at the national level of a part-executive, part-advisory land board. Furthermore, it brought up the issue again of a reorganisation of the Communal Lands (ibid.: 24). Hammar concludes that the draft policy '(…) retain sufficient, and by-now familiar ambiguity with respect to land authority in Communal Lands […] to allow the state to play its cards in many possible ways (ibid.:21)'.

Post-Independence developments in Dande

The importance of the valley to the struggle for Independence committed the post-Independence government to pursue the development of the area (Derman 1995: 14). Shortly after Independence, initiatives were taken to increase the

number of schools and clinics in Dande. Furthermore, the Grain Marketing
Board, as well as the Cotton Marketing Board established depots in the area.

In 1982, the Agricultural and Rural Development Authority (ARDA)
commissioned a study of the possibilities for developing the area. One of the
main recommendations made by the consultants was to 'rationalise' land-use
planning. The authors of the study report (Hawkins and Associates, cited in
Derman 1995: 19) suggested that the agriculturally poor northern and western
zones could be used for the development of wildlife resources for safari operations and game ranching. Agriculture was to be the main economic activity in
the more favourable zones. The consultants also concluded that the re-emergence of tsetse fly infestation posed a serious threat to the agricultural development of the Zambezi valley.

Following another consultancy study in 1983, the European Economic
Community funded the establishment of a Regional Tsetse and Trypanosomiasis Control Programme to investigate the best methods to control and eliminate
the fly belt in Zimbabwe, Zambia, Malawi and Mozambique. At that time,
eradication of the fly was still seen as an unquestionably good move. The EEC
financed aerial spraying of the whole length of the Zambezi valley. The
spraying programme was only stopped in 1988 because of the development of
alternative cost-competitive techniques (Barrett 1994).

The anti-tsetse spraying campaign, however, met with a wave of protest
from environmental organisations in Europe, who feared that tsetse eradication
would lead to uncontrolled settlement of farmers in the Zambezi Valley.
Eventually, this would seriously damage the allegedly 'fragile ecology' of the
valley (Derman 1993)[23]. Calls were made to control the influx of new settlers,
through 'proper land use planning'. As I will show in the next chapter,
migration to Dande was not linked to tsetse control, but nevertheless, the EEC
commissioned the FAO to develop a land use plan for the mid-Zambezi Valley
area. Subsequently, the Mid-Zambezi Rural Development Project was one of
the projects suggested by the consultants and its practical development was
carried out in co-operation with the government (African Development Fund
1986).

The project was officially introduced in 1987, covering virtually all of
Dande except the area west of the Manyame River. The African Development
Fund assisted in funding the project. The actual implementation was the responsibility of the Department of Rural Development (DERUDE, a department of
the Ministry of Local Government and Rural and Urban Development of the
Government of Zimbabwe) and Agritex (the national agricultural extension
service). The guidelines for the project were in accordance with the internal
land reforms the government wished to introduce in all Communal Areas of

---

[23] Without 'fragile' being clearly defined, however. See for an expression of such fears
Reynolds (1984).

Zimbabwe (see Government of Zimbabwe 1985; 1985b; African Development Fund 1986).

Initially, the Mid-Zambezi Project was designed to resettle 3000 families from overpopulated Communal Areas on the Plateau in the project area. It was assumed that 4600 households were already living in the area. The 3000 new families were to be placed in 130 newly created villages. The families already resident would have their villages reorganised. All arable land was to be (re-)distributed on the basis of plans and maps developed by Agritex (African Development Fund 1986). Soon after the introduction of the project it was discovered that already more than the 7600 households catered for, were living in the project area. No new families were brought in, but the project went ahead transformed into a purely internal land reform and village consolidation or villagisation project.

Originally, the project was scheduled for completion in 1992. However, owing to technical and organisational problems, but perhaps even more importantly, to increasing resistance by the local population, the project lingered far behind schedule. In 1992, project funding was extended for another three years. In 1995, when the extension expired, project staff was withdrawn from Dande and DERUDE ended its activities. The remaining tasks were devolved to the District Development Fund.

Another development project I need to mention in this chapter is the irrigation projects planned in the Chitsungo Ward of Dande. The Mid-Zambezi Rural Development Project had already been implemented in this ward, when, in 1993, the inhabitants were confronted with these two new projects.

The national agricultural extension agency Agritex, which had been involved in the implementation of the Mid Zambezi Project, had also planned an irrigation project in Chitsungo Ward. Using water from a dam already built on the Plateau of Zimbabwe, 1000 hectares were to be irrigated and redistributed into small plots among local farmers. This would mean the redistribution of land that had already been redistributed under the Mid-Zambezi Project. Agritex had already obtained funding for its project and started its activities early 1994. This led to a wave of resentment and resistance among the populations of Chitsungo and in 1995 the project was abandoned (see Chapter Seven).

However, the Agricultural Development Authority (ADA) also had plans to implement an irrigation scheme in the same area. ADA wanted to construct a dam on the escarpment, in Upper Guruve, on the Dande River. ADA had inherited the two TILCOR estates situated in Dande, one of which is situated in Chitsungo Ward. The main objective of the dam construction plans was to provide water for the irrigation of the ADA state farm in Chitsungo Ward. Probably in order to secure donor funding, a 'community component' was developed, involving plans to create 1500 to 2500 irrigated small-scale farm units, which would be distributed among the local population. Implementation of this scheme would likewise lead to the redistribution of land that had already been redistributed land under the Mid-Zambezi Project.

A feasibility study was completed and the African Development Bank agreed to fund the implementation of the project[24]. In 2002, construction work on the dam commenced.

The Zambezi Valley was, and often still is, viewed as underdeveloped and backward. Therefore, both government and donors have invariably assumed that virtually any development activity would be welcome (see also Derman: 1990). For example, the Appraisal Document of the Mid Zambezi Project states:

> (...) the Mid-Zambezi Valley is recognised to have been a neglected area requiring development. The need has also been appreciated to extend the rural development programme [the resettlement programme] to the communal areas. Thus the risks frequently associated with the start up and implementation of this type of project[25] are though to be minimal (African Development Fund 1986: 43).

With the implementation of the Mid Zambezi Project and the irrigation plans, local control over the land has been greatly reduced. Communities have no say as to where villages, land for cultivation and grazing areas will be situated. This has generated palpable tension in the area. The projects have sparked off a plethora of internal conflicts over land in the local communities, and conversely also concerted resistance to their implementation.

The area near Mzarabani was one of the first where new fields and residential stands for the Mid-Zambezi Project were demarcated. When the people in the area saw the metal demarcation pegs appear they feared the worst. A protest march to the District Administration Office was staged. The protesters carried the pegs which they had removed and dumped these in front of the office. Unfortunately, news about a possible protest march had already reached the then Provincial Governor. He managed to organise a group of soldiers to come down to the office. As the soldiers pointed their guns at the protesters, the governor asked if there was anyone who wished to complain about the project. Intimidated by the presence of armed soldiers, the protesters returned home. Bullied but not cowed, this did not mean the end of their resistance. It continued, but no longer always as openly as in the beginning. This book is about the continuation of the struggle over land and the grievances of those who have been subjected to the Mid-Zambezi Project and the irrigation projects.

Research locations

In order to study the effects of the Mid-Zambezi Project, I chose two villages in Dande in which to conduct my fieldwork. Both villages were located within the project area, but were affected differently by the project. One was among the

---

[24] Kinsey, personal communication.
[25] Probably a reference to the critique on other resettlement and villagisation projects implemented in Ethiopia and Tanzania.

first villages in Dande in which the project was implemented, in the other village people resisted implementation quite successfully.

The first village was Mahuwe, 'Where the sun always shines', according to a billboard that has been put up by the project manager of the Mid-Zambezi Project. Though, from a climatological perspective, this statement is not far off the mark, some villagers removed the billboard shortly after the project staff left the area. Mahuwe is situated at the foot of the Escarpment. It is the first village one encounters when taking the road from Guruve down to the valley, right at the point where the tarmac road ends and a so-called dirt road begins.

In fact, Mahuwe consists of two villages, named after their headmen: Fume and Chawasarira. In the late 1960s, when cotton was introduced to Dande, a number of families from both villages moved to the present location of Mahuwe, to be closer to the new road to the Escarpment. Their headmen followed later. Since then, the populations of the villages have increased considerably. During the war, Mahuwe was the place where one of the two main 'Protected Villages' or 'keeps' was located, as well as the site of a Rhodesian Forces' army camp. After Independence, a large number of people who had been interned at Mahuwe decided not to return to their more isolated villages and built new homes in Mahuwe. Furthermore, the villages attracted a host of migrants from elsewhere in Zimbabwe. Consequently both villages expanded to the extent that it became difficult to see where the one ends and the other begins. The name Mahuwe stems from the official name for the business centre that was established near the villages (see below).

Since Independence, Mahuwe has fallen under the Bazooka (sometimes spelled Bazhuka) Village Development Committee, a name that is a clear reminder of the war. Until 1994, it was part of Matsiwo B Ward, after the re-organisation of the wards in Guruve District it became part of Ward 7. It has a police station, a depot of the Cotton Marketing Board, a depot of the Maize Marketing Board, an office of the Veterinary Service, an Agritex office, a small primary health-care clinic, a primary school and, since 1997, even a secondary school. It has a 'business centre' with several grocery shops and two 'bottle stores' where bottled beer can be bought. Several bus companies run daily bus services to and from Harare. There is no electricity in Mahuwe. Before the implementation of the Mid-Zambezi Project there were water pumps at the business centre and next to the clinic; since then several more boreholes have been drilled in the village.

Agriculture is the main economic activity for the inhabitants of Mahuwe, but not their sole source of income. The majority of households also receives income from members engaged in wage labour. The government services mentioned above provide local job opportunities. Nevertheless, quite a number of households have members working temporarily in the towns and on Commercial Farms on the Plateau of Zimbabwe (see Chapter Three for more details).

When I first arrived in Mahuwe in 1988, the Mid-Zambezi Project management staff had just set up camp in the old abandoned Rhodesian Forces' camp.
Demarcation of residential stands and fields had started and I arrived just after
the protest march had been staged. I stayed for six months, until April 1989.
When I returned for a couple of weeks in 1990, the village looked different.
People had begun to move from their scattered homesteads surrounded by
fields, to the newly demarcated residential stands, some having to walk long
distances to their fields, which were situated on the outskirts of the residential
area. Fences had been erected everywhere. When I returned in 1992 for a period
of almost two years of fieldwork, the implementation of the Mid-Zambezi
Project was nearing completion, except for the fact that a large number of
households that had not managed to obtain a residential stand and field in
Mahuwe and were still living in the village, refused to leave. They had moved
to the officially designated grazing areas, to the riverine zones where cultivation
was forbidden, or shared a plot with a family that had obtained one.

The second village in which I conducted fieldwork was Mburuma. This
village, also in the Matsiwo chiefdom, was established sometime in the
1920s. The first inhabitants moved their village several times, sometimes
moving closer to the river in order to escape the missionaries' attention, then
back to the gravel road leading to the mission station again. This village has
practically no facilities. In 1989, a borehole was drilled and a handpump was
installed, but the pump is broken most of the time, so the main source of
drinking water remains the Musengezi River. One of the villagers has tried to
set up a shop several times, but every time has had to give up his efforts after a
few weeks. In 1988, two classrooms were built, but the school was never
finished and never operated. The nearest school is situated ten kilometres away
at Masomo, which is too far away for the youngest children. Villagers are still
trying to persuade the Rural District Council to send teachers and to use the
existing classrooms to teach the youngest children, but so far to no avail. In
1995 a clinic was opened at Masomo, which meant that people in search of
medical aid no longer needed to cross the river to Musengezi or, in the rainy
season, undertake the 40 km trip to Mahuwe. In the dry season the bus to and
from Harare passes once every two days, but in the rainy season the road
becomes impassable.

Mburuma falls under the Fungai (which means 'think!') Village Development Committee. Until the re-organisation of the wards it was part of Matsiwo
B Ward, since then it has become part of Matsiwo A, which was renamed Ward
5.

The main economic activity in Mburuma is agriculture. As in Mahuwe, a
majority of households also receives income from members engaged in wage
labour. However, in contrast to Mahuwe, local job opportunities are almost non-
existent. In the cotton-picking season, jobs can be found on the ARDA estate in
Muzarabani, just across the river, but most job-seekers move to the towns and

Commercial Farms on the Plateau of Zimbabwe (see the next chapter for more details).

When I first went to Mburuma in 1988, there was not yet a sign of the Mid-Zambezi Project. When I returned in 1992, the metal pegs demarcating the new residential stands and fields were in place, but had not yet been allocated. In this part of Dande, there was stiff resistance to the Mid-Zambezi Project and project staff was having a difficult time getting people to comply with the project requirements. I spent most of my time in Mburuma, where I had my own home-stead allocated to me by the village headman and the chairman of the Village Development Committee.

Though the Mid-Zambezi Project affected the two villages in different ways, it had a profound influence on daily life in both of them. In both villages, many people felt that the proposed land-use reforms were unfair, and this apprehen-sion created severe insecurity about land. The project resulted in serious conflicts over land, both between the state and local communities and within the communities themselves. The latter often involved disputes between 'autoch-thons' and 'immigrants'.

In the next chapter, I will describe pre-project land-use and allocation practices, with the aim of contributing to a better understanding of why there was so much resentment against the Mid-Zambezi Project. I will also provide more information about the position of migrants in the villages prior to the introduction of the project, to illustrate the profound changes that have occurred in local attitudes towards them.

Strangers and land: Land-use before the Mid-Zambezi Project

Introduction

The attempts by both the Rhodesian and the post-Independence governments to control access to land and land-use practices have not been very successful. As the previous chapter shows, problems having to do with control over local populations have led not only to shifts back and forth between centralisation and decentralisation, but also between communal and more individual tenure-ship, though no permanent title deeds were ever issued in the Communal Areas. This situation is not unique for Zimbabwe. In her seminal book 'No Condition is Permanent: The social dynamics of agrarian change in Sub-Saharan Africa', Berry (1993) describes similar attempts elsewhere in Africa and concludes that neither colonial nor post-colonial governments have been able to control the conditions under which farmers gained access to land or the ways in which they used it. James Scott (1998) argues that such attempts are likely to be doomed because they fail to take into account the complexities of local land allocation and land-use systems which in some cases allow parcels of land to be used at different times by different people for different purposes. This kind of multiple use and ownership does occur in Dande, as will be shown below. But perhaps the complexities go even deeper. In a recent article on the concept of communal tenure, Pius Nyambara asks the question: 'But what if tradition meant competing struggles for power, land and access rather than codes of conduct, however malleable they might be?' (2001: 772). He agrees with Berry that rights to land are often ambiguous and subject to ongoing interpretation. Berry states that the politicisation of tenure is evident from multiple, overlapping and sometimes internally inconsistent sets of rights and means of access (1993: 24).

Nyambara (2001) problematises the concept of communal tenure on the basis of the research he conducted on how migrants in Gokwe - also located in the Zambezi Valley but in the western part - gained access to land in the period 1963-1979. He suggests that 'communal tenure' must be located '(...) at the junction of different ideologies including those of state-posed legal codes and of the various interpretations of "custom", which individuals advanced in defence of their claims'. (ibid.: 773). He argues that conceptual gaps existed between the legal paradigms and 'customary' practice, and that this situation created an arena in which both legal and 'customary' paradigms were manipulated by various groups of people who manoeuvred to acquire land through various channels. He claims that very little research has been done regarding the actual practices by which land was acquired either in the past or today (ibid.: 773).

I started my research in Dande by looking at the same question as Nyambara did, but initially I focused on migrants who had settled in Dande shortly after Independence. I do not claim that my research demonstrates what 'tradition' looked like. I am not sure such any attempt to do this would in the least be feasible, but as I conducted my study, a fierce struggle about the control over land unfolded itself, resulting from the implementation of the Mid-Zambezi Project, which deeply influenced peoples' ideas about 'traditional land tenure'. In this struggle different parties involved in the conflict presented diverse visions on 'customary' land tenure. The Mid-Zambezi Project (as well as the larger programme for land reforms in the Communal Areas of which the Mid-Zambezi Project formed part) was based on certain ideas about 'customary communal' tenure. It endorsed some parts of these and rejected others, its purpose being the 'rationalisation' of land-use in Dande. The people subjected to the Mid-Zambezi Project recounted another story about 'traditional' land-use practices, which presented a system that was 'fair' and more responsive to the needs and capacities of people. In this story the chiefs and their headmen were presented as those who should be responsible for land allocation. The Commission of Inquiry into Appropriate Agricultural Land Tenure Systems (Government of Zimbabwe 1994) accepted this version and advised the government of Zimbabwe to involve these 'traditional' authorities in land allocation in the CAs of Zimbabwe. What I hope to show in this chapter is that the same manipulations of the legal and customary paradigms that were identified by Nyambara, were going on in Dande. The narrative about pre-Mid-Zambezi Project land allocation that was put forward by people opposing the land reform programme, did not coincide completely with their accounts of how migrants obtained land in Dande before the Mid-Zambezi Project was introduced. From this it follows that the Commission's call for a return to 'traditional' land tenure may not have been very realistic.

This chapter also contributes to the expatiation on a topic raised by Blair Rutherford in his book 'Working on the Margins. Black Workers, White Farmers in Postcolonial Zimbabwe' (2001). Quite a number of migrants in Dande are former farm labourers, often of Mozambican or Malawian origin (see also Murphree et al 1989)[26]. Nyambara (2001) discovered the same in Gokwe. Rutherford argues that Commercial Farm workers in Zimbabwe are generally '(...) imagined through a dualistic space, now called commercial farms and Communal Lands. This divide *is* rural Zimbabwe for many policy-makers, development experts and academics (Rutherford 2001: 3)'. He maintains that the (predominantly white-owned) Commercial Farms and the Communal Areas smallholder farms are thought of as operating and existing in two different spaces. Pertinently, official commentators and decision makers base their analyses, administrative structures and development interventions on this assumption. Furthermore, farm labourers, who are considered neither Commercial Farmers nor 'African peasants', have a more or less liminal identity, and have been largely excluded from development policies, social programmes and political rights. They have had very limited access to (government) schools, and until 1998 were unable to vote in local government elections (ibid.: 4). Rutherford describes how farm labourers have been marginalized, but also shows how they have put up against the processes of marginalization. One of the ways by which farm labourers contested their marginalization was by trying to 'become a peasant', and obtain land in a Communal Area.

The problematisation by Rutherford of the 'spatial order of things' (cf. Pigg 1992; Malkki 1995), the crude division of the rural areas of Zimbabwe into Large-scale Commercial Farm Areas and Communal Areas, is mirrored by Van Binsbergen's (1999) and Andersson's (2002) calls to problematise the rural-urban divide. The Mid-Zambezi Project, as well as the resettlement programmes, has been designed to separate the 'real' fulltime farmers from urban (and farm) labourers. Both Potts (2000) and Andersson (2001) explain that this is impossible. Andersson's case study shows how labour migrants from Buhera create social networks that encompass both rural and urban territories. People's social security is not spatially situated - in agricultural production in rural areas - but socially situated in the rural-urban (or Communal Area - Commercial Farm) network (ibid.: 71-2). In this chapter, I will illustrate that such networks not only facilitate (temporary) out-migration; they do the same for in-migration into the Communal Areas. I disagree with Andersson when it comes to the importance of kinship as the organising principle of such networks. The networks connecting those staying in Dande, those moving out and those moving in do incorporate 'strangers' who are symbolically incorporated through so-called *sahwira* relationships (see also Chapter Eight). Furthermore, in my view, Andersson underestimates the productive value of land. Perhaps his conclusion that struggles over land have little to do with the economic value of land but are politicised territorial struggles mainly between village headmen may be valid for Buhera. However, in Dande conflicts about land are related to issues of social security and the economic value of land.

---

[26] See for the history of migration patterns in Southern Africa Potts (1992); on migration from Mozambique see Adamo, Davies & Head (1981); Newitt (1995).

Migration to Dande

When I first came to Dande in 1988, it was to study the motives and origins of migrants who had settled there. Previous research had shown that shortly after Independence a rather substantial migration movement to the Zambezi Valley had begun, and this was generally attributed to renewed attempts to eradicate the tsetse fly in the valley, as well as to the ever-increasing pressure on land in the Communal Areas on the plateau of Zimbabwe. A number of socio-economic surveys had been conducted among new settlers in the valley (Murphree, Murombedzi & Hawks 1989; Cutshall 1989; 1990; 1991) and I set out to do a more in-depth study among migrants in two villages in Dande.

Over time it became clear that the influx of migrants into Dande was not something new and that there was no relation to tsetse eradication campaigns (see also Derman 1995). In fact, defining who was a migrant and who was autochthonous turned out to be rather difficult. At the time I started my research, however, the term 'migrant' was mainly used to refer to people who had settled in Dande after Independence, and sometimes to families who had arrived between the second half of the 1960s and the early 1970s. In-migration had been interrupted during the struggle for Independence, but even during that period there were people moving back and forth between the plateau and Dande.

As I already described in Chapter Two, population censuses show a steady population increase in Dande in the 1960s. The population grew from roughly 27,800 to somewhere between 30,000 and 37,000 (Derman 1995: 15). The census data, however, indicate trends; the figures cannot be taken as absolute since labour migration was taking place continually, with individuals or households moving away but retaining land rights in Dande (see below). In the 1960s the Rhodesian government stimulated migration to the Zambezi Valley, and actually relocated quite a number of households there. Yet, even in those days many migrants moved to the valley on their own initiative and using their own means. The 1982 census showed a decline with around 18,000 people still residing in Dande. This was probably due to the fact that not all people who had fled the area during the war for Independence had returned. In 1985 numbers had increased again; Guruve District Council listed 24,000 people living within the area where the Mid-Zambezi Project was to be implemented (which did not cover the whole of Dande Communal Land) (Derman ibid.: 15).

Initially I wanted to concentrate my study on people who had been defined and defined themselves as migrants, and who had arrived in Dande after 1980, the year of Independence. This was the same group Murphree, Murombedzi and Hawks (1989) and Cutshall (1989; 1990; 1991) had focused their surveys on. In 1988 and 1989 I interviewed thirty members of migrant households in Bazooka VIDCO (Matsiwo B Ward) and Rutendo VIDCO (Matsiwo A Ward) who had participated in the survey conducted by Murphree et al. (1989), as well as twenty-seven members of 'autochthonous' households I had selected myself. I also conducted a survey of agricultural production amongst all selected house-holds. In the survey conducted by Murphree et al. (ibid.), the heads of the migrant households had reported they had moved to Dande after 1980. Yet, I discovered that in fact, a third of the selected migrant households had already arrived before Independence, one household as early as 1969. In all of these cases the male household heads had come to Dande after 1980, but their wives had arrived earlier to set up the farm.

Murphree et al. (1989) had found in their survey that 13 per cent of the migrant households in Lower Guruve came from Large-scale Commercial Farms where they had worked as farm labourers. Among the people I interviewed, 39 per cent came from the Large-scale Commercial Farm Areas, and 57 per cent from other Communal Areas in Zimbabwe. Especially among the migrants interviewed in Bazooka VIDCO, a high percentage came from Commercial Farms: 55 per cent. The reason for this may have been that this VIDCO is situated close to the escarpment, along the road leading up to the plateau. Several buses per day leave for and arrive from Harare and Chinhoyi. Since most of the migrants coming from the farms were elderly people who depended on the support of their children who still worked as farm labourers, Bazooka VIDCO may have been a better choice than many of the other VIDCOs farther into in the valley. But there may be yet another explanation. During my second period of research in Dande, I discovered that the question of where migrants came from was, again, not such an obvious one either. Most migrants had come through Commercial Farms on their way to Dande, including those migrants who still held land rights in other Communal Areas of Zimbabwe. So some people may have responded to the question of where they came from by referring to the last physical place in which they resided before coming to Dande, whereas others may have interpreted the question in a broader sense and replied by referring to the place 'they originally came from'.

Nevertheless, generally speaking, two different groups of migrants can be distinguished which differ markedly from one another in terms of motives, aspirations and production. One group of migrants is constituted of former farm labourers who held no (or no longer) rights to land in other Communal Areas of Zimbabwe. The other group did hold land rights in other Communal Areas of Zimbabwe; some came directly to Dande from their home area, others came through a Commercial Farm. I encountered very few migrants who had come directly from a workplace in town to Dande, though a number of the former farm labourers did at one stage hold jobs in town.

Former farm labourers migrating to Dande

One of the first migrants I interviewed in Chawasarira was Mr Furukay. He was an elderly man, who walked with a stick. Since it was raining he invited me inside the cooking hut where a fire was burning. He apologised for the poor condition of his cooking hut; through the holes in the roof drops of water spattered on our clothes, leaving blackish stains caused by soot from the cooking fire. During the interview his granddaughter, wearing a tattered school uniform, came in with a jar of water. His wife and grandson were at the fields. When I asked Mr. Furukay where he came from and how he had ended up in Chawasarira, he started telling me his life-story in a nutshell. I will paraphrase his story, which I wrote down in my notebook.

I was born in Mutarara, Mozambique. I do not know exactly when, but my identity card says I was born in 1922. When I was still young I was forced to work for the Portuguese in Beira, they took me away from home. After some years I managed to run away, but when I returned home my parents had died. I stayed with my brother for a while, but I could not get along with him, so I left. I came to Rhodesia in 1945. I did not want to work for the Portuguese, and the Rhodesians were recruiting labourers. I walked two days to get to a registration point. There we were given food. When I was registered we were taken to the railway station, and put on a train to Salisbury. My first job was with a tobacco-selling company. One of the farmers who came to sell his crop asked me to work on his farm, because he saw I was a good grader. The farm was in Glendale. Working conditions were good and I was paid well. After five years I wanted a change and I moved to another farm, in Guruve. There I worked for two years as a foreman. At first I was the only foreman working at the farm, but then another man became foreman as well. This man had used magic to get the job. I was afraid of the man and left. In 1955 I found work at a farm in Centenary. There I worked as the third foreman. The manager wanted to make me first foreman because I was good at tobacco planting and grading. One of the other foremen used magic against me, sometimes when I woke up in the morning I could not see. I then found work at another farm in Centenary where I worked for ten years as a foreman. It was at this farm that I met my wife. We had four children together. After ten years I left, I felt I was growing older and I no longer wanted to be foreman anymore because of all the conflicts this created with my fellow-workers. I found work as a general labourer at another farm in Centenary, where I stayed until after Independence. Then the owner of the farm fired me because I had become too old for the work. The farm owner told me that now that the country had become Independent and I had received my Zimbabwean citizenship, I would be able to live wherever I wanted. I was sent away without any bonus or pension. I stayed with one of my sons on another farm. But my son was no longer given food rations by his employer, so we had to use our money to buy food. That is why I decided to go and look for a place to farm. I wanted to retire, find a place to establish a musha [a home with a field] and grow my own food. One of my son's colleagues told him that Chief Hwata had visited a Commercial Farm in the area to ask people to come and live in his chiefdom. But when I took the bus to Muzarabani, I was told by the village headmen that I could not get a plot there. I was told to go to Mahuwe, where I met sabhuku [village headman] Chawasarira, who told me I could obtain a plot of land in the village. I also asked permission to settle in Chawasarira from the village chairman and the VIDCO chairman. The VIDCO chairman allocated me a field (...) I then returned to my son to fetch my wife. We came to Chawasarira, accompanied by two grandchildren. We cleared our field and built huts. Then I went back to Centenary to the farm where one of my two surviving children was working. I was employed as a seasonal worker for a year. Then I went to join my wife in Chawasarira, and have not left the village since. My two children continue to work on Commercial Farms and sometimes send me money. I cultivate three acres, where I am growing maize and sorghum. My wife is younger and does most of the work, together with the grandchildrenwhen they return from school.

Mr. Furukay's story was quite representative of those of other former farm labourers I interviewed. 75 per cent of them were born outside of Zimbabwe, in Mozambique, Malawi, and a few in Zambia. Yet, almost all of them had Zimbabwean citizenship, and a third of them were married to a Zimbabwean citizen. Half of them came to Zimbabwe when they were children. All but one already had relatives living in Zimbabwe when they arrived.

The male household heads were generally older than those of migrant households from Communal Areas: they were between forty and seventy-six years of age, the average age being fifty-nine. Almost all of them said they had come to Dande to find a place to spend their old age, or 'to retire', as they themselves called it. More than a third indicated that they had also come to establish a farm for their children who were still working as farm labourers, and to grow food for them. Those who were relatively young had come to establish a home, a *musha*, to prepare their 'retirement', and to grow food for those household members remaining at the workplace. Of these households, it was often the women who would move to Dande, bringing with them the youngest children, to set up a farm. The households from Commercial Farms were often smaller than those from Communal Areas, with an average size of 6.2 members. The majority consisted of a couple with their youngest grandchildren, while their children and older grandchildren would remain on the Commercial Farms as labourers. A quarter of the households were headed by women. In half these cases the women had husbands who were still employed at farms or in town. The other female household heads were either divorced or widowed.

Generally speaking, the former farm labourers received very little education; only one of the interviewees had finished primary school. Yet, only a small minority of the men had been general labourers. The others had worked as tobacco graders, foremen or as tractor drivers. In most cases both husbands and wives worked at the farms. The wives usually worked as seasonal workers, and were mainly employed during harvests[27]. Most ex-farm labourers, like Mr. Furukay, had a history of moving from farm to farm, looking for better wages and improving their working conditions. Yet over half of them (64 per cent) had once or twice worked for more than ten years at one and the same farm (with some working as long as thirty years for one employer), often the last farm they worked at before coming to Dande.

---

[27] This is consistent with Rutherford's findings, which indicate that women could not acquire permanent jobs at Commercial Farms, only as domestic servants (2001: 7).

Wages earned in the period before Independence reportedly varied considerably, some reporting the equivalent of 3 Z$ a month, others up to the equivalent of 25 Z$; the average reported wage was the equivalent of 10 Z$. Almost all ex-farm workers reported receiving food rations before Independence, or a small plot of land on which to grow food. All reported that after Independence their wages had been increased, but that food rations had been abolished. The abolition of food rations played an important role in many of the stories provided by ex-farm workers when asked about their motives for migration. It also appears in Mr. Furukay's story. Though the main motive for migration to Dande was that the migrants felt they had become too old for the work at the Commercial Farms, their negative attitude towards the idea of having to spend money on food was often reported as something that triggered them into thinking of establishing a *musha*, where they would be able to grow food for their children who continued to work as farm labourers. Many migrants reported that after Independence, farm owners were not keen on keeping elderly workers employed, though only one migrant reported that he was actually fired because of his age; they were equally loath to keeping retired farm labourers on their farms.

Rutherford (2001) describes the changes in policy towards Commercial Farm workers after Independence that may have stimulated migration to the Communal Areas of Zimbabwe. He describes how during the war for Independence farm labourers had been regarded with suspicion by the freedom fighters. They were closely associated with the white farmers, though it was recognised that they were often exploited, and were often seen as 'foreigners'. After Independence the Ministry of Labour initiated labour regulations and set minimum wages for farms more or less annually (ibid.: 43). Farmers were urged to stop providing food rations but pay better wages instead. The initial enforcement of the laws came from ZANU party activists more than from the government. Shortly after Independence the ruling party established Party Cells, which were also referred to as Village Committees in the Communal Areas. ZANU established worker committees on Commercial Farms (ibid.: 44). Many farmers reacted to the new regulations by illegally firing workers and downgrading permanent workers to a seasonal or casual status (ibid.: 44). The new government granted citizenship to anyone who had been in the country for a specified number of years. Government and party officials went from farm to farm granting citizenship cards to 'foreign' workers and informing them of their right to vote (but only in national elections) and obtain land rights in a Communal Area in the district in which they were registered (op.cit.: 44-5). During the colonial period, law prohibited foreign labourers from settling in the Reserves/Tribal Trust Lands. None of the migrants I have interviewed mentioned the active promotion of migration to the Communal Areas, and since at the time I was not aware of the above-mentioned policy, I did not ask where and how migrants of foreign origin obtained their citizenship. But, as I mentioned previously, most did have citizenship. Many people did refer to Independence as a motive for migration, saying that after Independence people could live wherever they wanted. Migrants from other Communal Areas often also reported this, so I did not relate it to specific events in the Large-scale Commercial Farm Areas. Nevertheless, even if these events had created an *increase* in migration from Commercial Farms, they were not the sole cause. In-migration from Commercial Farms had already started before Independence. In his study on migration to Gokwe between 1963 and 1979, Nyambara (2001: 774) also found quite a number of former farm labourers of foreign origin who wanted to 'retire' to the land[28].

When I asked people why they had opted for settlement in Dande and not some other Communal Area, almost a third (27 per cent) of the former farm workers I interviewed said that they had relatives living in Dande. In two cases the relatives were the close kinsfolk of the women, who were 'from the area'. But in most cases it concerned relatives who had already moved to Dande in the 1960s and early 1970s. The majority, however, had had colleagues from Dande who had informed them that there was land available there. Two people told me that Chief Hwata had visited their farm to tell farm workers about the possibilities of settling in Dande. When I met the chief he confirmed that in 1982 and 1983 he had indeed visited several Commercial Farms in Upper Guruve to ask people to settle in Dande (below I will explain why he and others from Dande were recruiting people for Dande). Two migrants, who worked on farms in Upper Guruve, had taken the bus to the nearest Communal Area, which happened to be Dande Communal Lands, to ask around if they could obtain a plot of land.

The elderly former farm labourers said that all they wanted was a place where they could 'retire'; it did not really matter which place. The younger migrants, especially the women who had come alone while their husbands had continued to work on a Commercial Farm, said that they had opted for Dande because they had heard that the soils were fertile and that it was a good place for growing cotton.

The stories of women who moved to Dande to farm while their husbands continued working were a little different. They too had a history of moving from farm to farm before settling in Dande. In their case they opted out before

---

[28] Over time, however, the power of the workers and village committees weakened because the government and the party gave them less support to avoid disruptions in the farming industry (Rutherford 2001: 46). Workers' access to government schools or clinics hardly improved. Relaxation of state control over the commercial farm sector was also part of the IMF-informed and World Bank-supported Economic Structural Adjustment Programme. Government and party officials' attitudes to the desirability of farm labourers applying for land in resettlement areas or even Communal Areas became more and more negative during the 1980s. Farm workers were depicted as people who '(...) were only used to being supervised and they cannot supervise themselves (MP Mutoko, cited in Rutherford 2001: 56)'. Frequent references were made to their 'foreignness', as a sign that government had less responsibility for them (ibid.: 56).

they became too old to start a productive farm. Nyambara speaks of the 'booking of land' by wage labourers who leave their wives and children behind in the rural areas (2001: 776), but this denies the role of women as farmers in their own right. The women I interviewed did not just want 'a home', but wanted to establish a productive farm that would not only produce food for the family, but also cash crops for the market. All the women I interviewed indicated that part of their husbands' wages was invested in the farm, to buy agricultural inputs and to hire labour to help them weeding and harvesting.

One of the women I interviewed was Mrs. Mbware. Her situation differed clearly from that of Mr. Furukay. When I visited her she invited me into her house. She and her children were living in two-room brick house with a corrugated iron roof. The house was freshly painted, and the living room contained a couch and armchairs, a dining table with six chairs and a wooden cupboard with glass doors. Mrs. Mbware's daughter served us tea in china cups. Mrs. Mbware had been elected chairperson of the ZANU(PF) Women's League local branch. She was also the treasurer of the local branch of the Salvation Army. When I asked her where she came from and why she had settled in Dande, she told me a story with a beginning quite similar to that of Mr. Furukay, but with a different ending.

I was born on a Commercial Farm near Banket, where my parents worked, in 1944. My parents had grown up on this farm and remained there until the owner died. Then they found jobs on another farm, in Mapinga, where my father died. My mother later moved to Dande with me. When I was old enough, about fourteen, I also started working on the farm, mainly during the picking season. It was at the farm in Mapinga that I met my husband. He was also born on a Commercial Farm. His grandfather originally came from Mozambique, but his father had been born in Rhodesia. After our marriage we spent about four years in Mapinga, then found jobs on a farm near Southton mine. We stayed there for seven years. My husband was trained as a car mechanic at the farm, and he was earning quite well. After seven years we moved to another farm. After a year the farmer moved to another farm, and we did not want to follow him. We then found jobs on a farm in Mutorashonga [Upper Guruve]. Soon after our arrival the farmer sold his farm and started a road construction firm. He employed my husband as a driver. I lost my job when the farm was sold. I then decided it would be a good idea to find some land to start farming for myself. I had been putting pressure on my husband for some time to establish a musha so we would not have to buy our food. I thought it was better to look for a place before we would be told to leave our jobs because we had become too old. When I lost my job my husband finally agreed with me. That was in 1980. My sister got married to a seasonal worker from Chikafa [also in Dande]. My sister and brother-in-law had returned to Chikafa to grow cotton, that is how I knew that Dande was a good place to grow cotton. On my way to my sister, I had to change buses at Mahuwe. I decided that Mahuwe was a better place to settle because it had better bus services, and it would be easier to travel from there to my husband's working place.

Mrs. Mbware and the other younger (former) farm labourers were doing better than the elderly migrants were. The elderly migrants were barely able (and sometimes not able) to make a living. The financial support they received from family members engaged in wage labours was spent on buying food and other necessities. The younger migrants were able to sell some of their (food) crops every now and then. Only Mrs. Mbware, however, was able to grow cotton as well as maize. Her husband was better paid than most other absent husbands, and Mrs. Mbware had enough money to invest in the more expensive inputs needed to grow cotton. When she arrived in Mahuwe, she had been able to use part of the savings from her husband's wages to hire some people from the village to help her clear her fields and build her huts.

Migrants from Communal Areas

The second group of migrants that can be distinguished consists of people who, prior to settling in Dande, held (or still hold) rights to land in other Communal Areas. None of the migrants I interviewed, however, had moved directly to Dande from these Communal Areas. In fact, there were quite a number of similarities between the stories told by migrants from Commercial Farms and those from Communal Areas. Migrants from Communal Areas also showed a highly mobile career history in many different workplaces - often Commercial Farms - before settling in Dande. In many cases, this mobility did not stop once the move to Dande had been made. Often only part of the family settled in Dande, while other members continued to move from place to place in search of work. Rutherford's (2001) conclusion that the spatial and conceptual separation of Large-scale Commercial Farm Areas and Communal Areas needs to be questioned is confirmed by the stories told by the migrants.

The majority of migrants from other Communal Areas whom I interviewed in 1988/9 indicated that they had selected Dande because they had relatives living in the area. However, when I returned for a second period of fieldwork in 1992, I also interviewed these relatives and found out that most of them (60 per cent) had learnt about the possibilities of settling in Dande from colleagues on the Commercial Farms where they had worked, who were natives of Dande. One of the 'second generation' migrants I interviewed actually mentioned this. Mr. Mukaro was a man in his early forties. He spent most of his time in Chitungwiza, the satellite-city of Harare, where he had a job with the Town Council. I had asked his wife if I could interview her, but she told me her husband was around for his holidays and preferred that I would speak to him.

I was born in Gutu in 1952. I attended primary school in Gutu, where I completed Standard 3. I moved to Hwata [also in the Zambezi Valley, just across Msengezi River] with my parents in 1965, where I completed Standard 6. In 1974 I started working on Gota Farm in Upper Guruve, where my father had been working. This is where he got the idea of going to Hwata. There were people from Hwata working at

Gota Farm, and my father became their sahwira [see below for an explanation of this type of relationship]. I left the job after only two months, because I did not like the work. I wanted to go to Centenary to start a farm there, but because of the war I could not go. In 1977 I went to Salisbury, where I worked for the council of the location [high-density suburb, township]. I still work for Chitungwiza Town Council, where I clean the markets. In 1978 I got married. My wife lived with my parents in Hwata most of the time.

My parents had fields in Gutu, about 6 acres. They grew maize, groundnuts and rice. Every year they would sell about two bags of rice, but it was not much. In Gutu my father was a messenger of the chief. My parents moved to Hwata because the soils are much better there.

My parents came to Rutendo VIDCO in 1980. They had been moved to the keep at Masomo, that is how they got to know the area. They saw it was better than Hwata. There are fewer depressions in the fields, so you do not have so many problems when it rains. My wife and I got our fields in Gera [Rutendo VIDCO] in 1987.

The Commercial Farms seem to be linchpins in the migration process. Here, people learned from colleagues about the fertile soils of Dande, and some of the chiefs from Dande went here to recruit migrants. Commercial Farms were not the only sources of information though; other workplaces were also mentioned by some (18 per cent) of the 'first generation' migrants I interviewed in 1992. Yet, the farms feature more prominently in migration stories. Perhaps because they are places where large numbers of workers from all over the country - and from abroad - gather, ideal venues for gathering information about other places in Zimbabwe that might offer better opportunities for farming than one's home area.

The migration networks that connect Dande to the Commercial Farms seem to be somewhat different from the networks described by Andersson (2002). First of all, the networks described by Andersson are mainly based on kinship. The Dande networks also tie in 'strangers'. Friendships with these 'strangers', often formalised in *sahwira* relations, seem important. *Sahwira* relationships explicitly unite 'strangers'. Among the Shona, when a person dies, the deceased's body cannot be washed or buried by someone from the deceased's own family, nor even by someone from the same clan. 'Strangers' are needed to bury the dead and each family has a special relationship with one or more families that belong to a different clan to take care of each other's deceased. The members of these families refer to one another as *sahwira* (Bourdillon 1987: 61). *Sahwira* relations can be formed between people who belong to different ethnic groups; nor is difference in nationality a barrier. In theory the *sahwira* relationships extend to following generations, they are inherited patrilineally. In the village of Mburuma, all migrant households had developed *sahwira* relations with 'autochthonous' families. In most cases (71 per cent) the relationship had been established outside of Dande, at the workplace. The *sahwira* relations involved both ChiShona-speakers from other parts of Zimbabwe and former farm labourers of Mozambican, Malawian or Zambian origin. This does not mean that kinship is of no importance in migration networks. As was described above, most of the migrants who came to Dande *after* Independence were invited by relatives who had preceded them to Dande in the 1960s. Furthermore, as we have seen above, marriage also plays a role in attracting 'strangers' to Dande.

Secondly, the networks described by Andersson (2002) seemed to involve the movements and connections between more or less fixed places: between Buhera and certain neighbourhoods in town. The networks involving 'autochthons' and migrants connected Dande with numerous Commercial Farms as people travelled from farm to farm. Relatives and friends informed each other about available jobs and tried to secure jobs for each other. Nicknames given to farms and farm owners provided information about the working conditions on certain Commercial Farms. The networks played a role in securing access to land, both for those who did not yet have a *musha* and for those who already had one elsewhere.

Yet, apparently there are limits to the degree of mobility of and within the networks. Though the networks contain many ex-farm labourers of foreign origin, the migrants who held land rights in other Communal Areas before settling in Dande nearly all came from roughly the same geographical area: the Communal Areas surrounding Masvingo. Nyambara discovered a similar pattern of geographical concentration; most of the migrants who had held land in one of the Tribal Trust Lands before coming to Gokwe came from Gutu and Bikita, close to Masvingo (2001: 774-5).

There were also a few people who had heard about Dande in ways other than through information from relatives or colleagues. In the first group of people I interviewed, there were three ex-freedom fighters, two of whom had fought in Dande and decided to return after the war. The third one had followed his brother who had also fought in Dande. His brother had managed to be elected Ward Councillor for Matsiwo A Ward. When I arrived in Dande, however, the brother had been jailed for poaching and another Ward Councillor had been elected. I interviewed the remaining brother about their choice for Dande:

> I was born in Bikita. I went to school from 1964 to 1967. In 1968 I went to work at Triangle. I was working on Hippo Valley, a sugar cane plantation. I left Triangle because the wage was not enough. In 1969 I went to Empress Mine near Kadoma where I was working as a general labourer. I worked there for nine months. Then I had to leave because I did not have a juvenile certificate [official pass certifying that the holder had reached the minimum wage at which wage labour was allowed]. From Kadoma I went to Chatter sawmill in Chimanimani. I worked there for one year. Then I left to join the freedom fighters because life was very hard for us black people, we were earning very little. I joined them in 1975. I was living in the bush near Mutoko for five years. During the cease-fire I was transferred to Hoya Assembly point where I was trained as a Presidential Guard. But later I did not want to be a guard [anymore], so I left. I signed demobilisation papers and was paid well. When I

returned to Bikita I found out that my father had died. That is why I left the army; I had to look after my mother and my brothers and sisters. Masvingo was over-crowded, we only had four acres for the whole family and it was impossible for young people to get a field. That is why we came here; here there is plenty of land. I am from a family of ten. Five children were still at home when I returned. Two of my brothers, who were married, also used the four acres. We harvested very little, because the soils were overused. We had to buy maize from the demobilisation money and brew beer for sale.

I came here in 1981. By then I was married and I was still working as a Presidential Guard. But I had to leave because I had to clear the fields, build the huts and bring our cattle from Bikita to this place. Here we have seven acres of good soil. We are doing well, we can sell crops and pay the school fees for my brothers and sisters. One brother is handicapped, he is now in Bindura. We can live from the farm, I do not have to work.

We were well received by the people here, there are many ex-combatants here. Some of the ex-combatants came from this place, that is how I knew about it. As well as from my brother who fought in this area when he was a freedom fighter himself. He was so well liked by the people that they elected him a Ward Councillor.

Most ex-combatants who had fought in Dande and had returned as migrants recounted that they had been well received. They had been given assistance with the clearing of their new fields from neighbours and food to bridge the period until the first harvest. The Ward Councillor's relations with at least some of his neighbours had deteriorated, since they had reported his poaching activities to the police. It is interesting that none of the ex-combatants had even considered applying for land in a resettlement scheme on a former Commercial Farm - I specifically asked them about that option - though they often justified their choice of migration by saying that after Independence people could live wherever they wanted.

Despite important similarities in the migration stories, there were also some notable differences between migrants from Commercial Farms and migrants from other Communal Areas in Zimbabwe. A much larger percentage of the latter households were female-headed (44 per cent, against 25 per cent of the migrants from Commercial Farms); most had husbands who were still engaged in wage labour, although some were widowed or divorced. The average age of household heads was lower, forty, and in general they were better educated than the retired former farm workers were (average level of education: Standard 5). The usual size of the households was quite similar: 6. As was the case with the former farm workers, there were virtually no polygynous households among the migrants from Communal Areas, and few extended families.

About 44 per cent of the migrants from Communal Areas could be consid-ered landless: they did not have their own fields but were sharing fields with their parents. They came to Dande to have their own fields. Just over half of the migrants (56 per cent) were not landless; they did have their own fields in their home area. They reported having left their home area because the soils were exhausted. They came to Dande with the aim of growing cash crops. Very few reported having been able to sell crops in their home area, but all but two had cattle, ranging from seven to fifteen animals. As will be shown below, migrants from Communal Areas were generally more successful in farming than the elderly former farm labourers.

Access to land for migrants

One of the questions I asked was how the migrants had gained access to land. At the time of the first survey, the implementation phase of the Mid-Zambezi Project had just started. This project was to change practices and perspectives concerning access to land drastically (see Chapter Four). The people I interviewed had all arrived before the start of the project, but this does not mean that their answers to my questions were not influenced by the project. The implementation started with the demarcation of fields, and when the first pegs appeared people began to form some idea of the changes this would bring along. Information and rumours started to circulate about how the fields would be distributed and this aroused great concern among migrants about whether they had followed 'the right procedure' for obtaining land in Dande, and would consequently be allowed to stay.

Since 'the right procedure' was the subject of so many debates and so much anxiety, I tried to find out what the 'official version' of this procedure was by asking the then District Administrator, who had given me permission to do research in Dande. He said that the 'official' procedure for migrants to prepare for their move was the following. Any person desiring to migrate and obtain land in a district other than his home district should obtain a letter from the VIDCO of the community he originated from - the 'he' is used deliberately here, since according to the DA only men could obtain such letters - stating that the VIDCO agreed with the decision taken. Then the VIDCO of the community where the migrant would like to settle needed to issue a letter stating the preparedness of the community to receive the migrant, and giving an indication that there would be enough land available for new settlers. With these two letters the future migrant would have to approach the District Council of his home district, in order to obtain the Council's permission to leave the district. Then a final letter would have to be obtained from the receiving District Council, indicating acceptance. This rather complicated procedure, which required plenty of travelling, was repeated to me by the DC's Executive Officer and several of the Resettlement Officers working on the Mid-Zambezi Project, but I never found it back in any of the official government documents on land. The above-mentioned Commission of Inquiry also concluded that the texts were not clear, and argued that there is no legal basis for the role of the VIDCOs in

land matters (Government of Zimbabwe 1994: 27). Apart from this complication, the descriptions still did not make it clear who would actually allocate the
land to migrants, but most officials thought that that would be the task of the
Ward Councillor who would have to consult the District Council, including the
government officials serving on the Council. The procedure as described by the
various government officials, however, showed a remarkable resemblance to the
procedure described by the DC Gokwe in 1973, cited in Nyambara's article on
Gokwe (2001: 775).

The majority of the migrants had not followed the procedure set out above.
Just over a tenth of the migrants had passed through the DA's office to ask for
official transfer papers. Over half of those had done so only after they had
already settled in Dande, to make sure they would have the right papers to
obtain land under the Mid-Zambezi Project. This confirms the conclusion of the
Commission of Inquiry that local government institutions had little control over
land-use practices in Communal Areas (ibid.: 26).

Most migrants had followed different routes to obtain permission to settle in
Dande and obtain land. Contrary to what Nyambara (2001) describes for
Gokwe, it appears there are no separate migrant villages in Dande, though in
some villages migrants do constitute a large part of the population (see also
Derman 1995). All had settled in existing villages, and though some started by
sharing fields with relatives who had already migrated to the villages, all had to
ask permission to settle. All but two of the migrants I interviewed had
approached the village headman, the sabhuku[29], for permission to settle. Half of
the migrants had also approached the chairman of the Village Development
Committee, the VIDCO, and a quarter had approached the chairman of the
Village Committee as well. The chief of the area was not mentioned at all. A
notable difference between the two VIDCOs where I interviewed people was
that only in Rutendo VIDCO, located in Matsiwo A Ward (later Ward 10) a
considerable number of migrants (29 per cent) had approached the Ward
Councillor (the ex-combatant who later was jailed for poaching). In Bazooka
VIDCO hardly anyone had approached the Ward Councillor. The actual allocation of fields was done by the *sabhuku* (37 per cent), the VIDCO chairmen (27
per cent) or by both these local authorities in co-operation (36%). The order in
which people approached these authorities varied and depended on their
personal circumstances and convictions. Migrants tended to first approach the
authority through whom they thought they stood the best chance of obtaining
land. These would then take the prospective migrant to the other local authorities to support their case. For instance, Mrs. Mbware, whose story was
presented above, had been a chairperson of the ZANU(PF) Women's League,
which influenced whom she approached in Mahuwe:

---

[29] Sabhuku means owner of the book, the book being the tax-book. Village headmen
were responsible for collecting taxes under the white settler regime.

Since I already had been chairperson of the Women's League when I was living in Mutorashanga, I decided to approach the ZANU(PF) party chairman in Mahuwe. The party chairman took me to the headman. When I returned with my husband, the headman showed us three plots we could choose from. The party chairman advised us to register at the DC and the DA's office.

Mr. Furukay had been told he could not obtain land in Hwata, and then proceeded to Mahuwe where:

I met sabhuku [village headman] Chawasarira, who told me I could obtain a plot of land in the village. I also asked permission from the village chairman and the VIDCO chairman to settle in Chawasarira. The VIDCO chairman allocated me a field, at the edge of the village in the bush. Together we showed the plot to the sabhuku, who agreed I could cultivate it. The sabhuku put a first peg in the ground where my huts were to be built, and clapped his hands to ask the Mhondoro to look after me.

A third common option in the procedure to obtain land in Dande was explained to me by the ex-Ward Councillor's brother. Despite them both being ex-combatants for ZANLA, he and his brother did not approach the ZANU-established village committees that were still operating in 1981, when they arrived, but:

My brother and I went first to the sabhuku, then to the Chief, then to Guruve DC, then to the DA. Then we went back to Masvingo to get the transfer letters. It was very easy to get these letters once you were allocated land and had papers from the DC. The sabhuku performed chiumba, by moulding mealie [maize] meal and leaving it in the field after clapping hands to the spirits. I paid the sabhuku a fee for the spirit medium, mari yemukhokho.

Obtaining official transfer letters became an important issue after the introduction of the Mid-Zambezi Project, and many people mentioned trying to obtain such letters after they had already had been allocated fields and homesteads by the *sabhuku* or VIDCO chairmen.

Nyambara (2001: 776-7) reported that divorced women had great difficulties obtaining land in Gokwe, and were considered social misfits. Rutherford (2001: 202) remarks that most female farm labourers saw access to land in a Communal Area as being dependent on their fathers or husbands. Nevertheless, the divorced or widowed female migrants I interviewed had all had land allocated to them in their own right and did not report any difficulties in obtaining land. I have no idea why the situation in Dande would be different for women; perhaps village headmen and other local authorities in Dande felt a greater need to see that the land was occupied and the number of inhabitants augmented than did their counterparts in Gokwe. As I will show in the next chapter, the implementation of the Mid-Zambezi Project would greatly reduce women's access to land.

In their stories of how they obtained land many migrants referred to the *Mhondoro* or to their mediums. In contrast to what David Lan (1985: 166-175) describes, the mediums did not actually allocate land to migrants. Migrants seldom approached them for permission to settle in Dande; only two of the migrants I interviewed had actually asked permission from a *Mhondoro* medium him/herself. Most migrants (71 per cent) mentioned that the *chiumba* ritual was performed by the *sabhuku* for which a fee, the *mari yemukhokho,* had to be paid. Two forms of *chiumba* were mentioned, one for asking permission from the *Mhondoro* to establish a homestead, the other for asking permission to cultivate a field. Before establishing a homestead the *sabhuku* would clap hands [sign of respect] for the *Mhondoro* while uttering words of praise, and drive a symbolic first peg in the ground. The ritual concerning the allocation of fields involved 'mealie meal', maize meal. The *sabhuku* would mix mealie meal with cold water and mould it into the shape of a shell. This shell would be placed in the field allocated to the migrants by the *sabhuku,* while the *sabhuku* would utter words of praise to the *Mhondoro* and ask the spirit to show his approval or disapproval. The next morning, if the shell was still in one piece the migrant could start clearing his or her new fields, if the shell had cracked the *sabhuku* would have to look for a new field. Only two people reported having had both forms of the *chiumba* performed for them. The fee paid for the rituals varied from Z$ 2.50 to Z 4.- (at that time the Z$ was about 0.1 US $).

Rutherford also discusses the fees, or 'token gifts' paid to village headmen by farm labourers acquiring land in a Communal Area near Karoi (2001: 213). He says that the business of asking fees was rather lucrative. In Dande the *sabhuku* claimed that the fees were handed over to the mediums of the *Mhondoro,* but as we will see later (Chapter Eight), the mediums themselves complained that this was not what was happening. Yet, none of the migrants I interviewed reported having had to pay the *sabhuku* or VIDCO chairman to register their plots, which according to Rutherford (ibid.: 216) was common practice in the Communal Area near Karoi.

Most migrants were allocated fields on the edge of the villages, fields that still needed to be stumped and cleared. Only one person obtained already cleared fields from a household that was leaving Dande, and he paid 30 Z$ per acre for his field. Others rented cleared lands for roughly the same price to be able to plant a first crop before clearing their own, new fields. The rented fields sometimes belonged to households that were leaving Dande temporarily looking for work on the Plateau. Some migrants also rented several acres from households that had one or two acres to spare. Those who had relatives living in the same village would often share the fields of their relatives to get a first crop.

Most of the villages in Dande are located close to rivers or streams that provide drinking water. Furthermore, the banks of these watercourses are highly valued for the cultivation of food crops, since they could yield two harvests a year. As the influx of migrants continued, however, it became increasingly difficult for migrants to obtain such fields. None of the migrants whom I interviewed and who had arrived after 1980 had been allocated riverine fields, or *mudimba* as they were referred to locally, though many reported cultivating *mudimba* which they borrowed or rented. I will discuss the allocation of riverine fields in the next section.

'Autochthons' and access to land

Since so many migrants had come to know about Dande through former colleagues on Commercial Farms or in town, it will come as no surprise that those who consider themselves 'autochthons' of Dande were highly mobile as well. Many made the same journeys from farm to farm as were described by the migrants quoted above. Some were born on Commercial Farms where their parents worked and spent years on the Plateau before coming down to Dande to (re-)claim land. And when they did, they did not always return to the village from which their parents claimed to have come. This was the case for instance with Menira Black. I interviewed Menira, whom I estimated to be between fifty-five and sixty years of age, at her homestead:

> I was born in Chinhoyi, but I do not know when. I am the youngest in a family of twelve. I never went to school. I was born on the farm where my parents worked. My father was a guard. My parents are from the area around Mashumbi Pools [in Dande], but they moved to Chinhoyi before I was born. I met my husband when he came visiting a friend on the farm where we lived. He was working on another farm, somewhere between Mvurwi and Concession. When we got married I moved to the farm where he was working. My husband was a tobacco grader. He worked on that farm from 1952 till 1986. We have seven children; three are still going to school. I also worked on the farm, with my eldest [children]. That is how we could pay the school fees. But after Independence we also had to buy food. Some of my relatives were living on nearby farms; others were still living in Dande. Some were killed during the war. [M.S.: Why did you return to Dande in 1986?] Before 1986 we were still interested in working. We had a good life on the farm. We were living in brick houses, we had water from a tap, and the schools were nearby. I also attended church there. But now we are old, my husband has health problems and we wanted to have a home. Now we can work at our own pace, nobody will tell you you are lazy if you take a rest. My eldest [children] are still working, they help us. [M.S.: Why did you not go back to Mashumbi Pools?] I no longer know anybody there anymore, some of my relatives were killed during the war and the others went to the 'keep' at Mahuwe. They never went back. This place where we are staying now is my sister's. She went back to Mvurwi to work and she asked us to look after her place. [M.S.: did you ask permission to stay here?] No, we just took my sister's place. [M.S.: Did you see the sabhuku?] No, the sabhuku knows we are here. I am related to the sabhuku, so there is no need to ask. But we did register with the village committee to get a twelve-acre plot [through the Mid-Zambezi Project].

Mrs. Black's husband originally came from Zambia. A large number of people from Dande met their husbands or wives at their place of work, and took these 'strangers' with them to Dande. Mrs. Black's husband had paid a bride price when he had married her. But in Dande the practice of bride service continued for a long time. Men who could - or would - not pay a bride price were required to move in with their parents-in-law and help them cultivate their fields. The period of the bride service could extend to no less than ten years. Often, upon ending the service the couple would decide to stay in the village of the wife's parents.

The story of Mrs. Black vividly indicates that the struggle for Independence caused displacements. Many inhabitants of Dande left the area because of the fierce fighting that went on between ZANLA and ZIPRA, which opposed the Rhodesian Forces. Yet others left their workplace, especially if they were working on Commercial Farms that were targeted by the guerrillas, to return to Dande. The last two years of the war, all inhabitants of Dande were placed in camps guarded by the Rhodesian Forces, the so-called 'keeps'. After Independence when the camps were dismantled, not everybody returned to the place where he or she had lived before being moved to the camps. In some cases whole villages were relocated to some other part of Dande by their headmen, as was for instance the case with Masomo village. The map I had of the area was based on old Rhodesian Forces' staff maps, and every now and then I got lost because villages were no longer located where I thought they were.

The high mobility rate among the inhabitants of Dande as well as the constant influx of 'strangers' is clearly repeated in the myths of the founding ancestors of Dande, as well as in the stories of how the village of Mburuma/Chikuku was established. I will discuss the founding myths in Chapter Eight. Here I will present *sabhuku* Mburuma's version of the history of the village of Mburuma.

My grandfather got married in Gonono, in the village of Chauti. He lived with his parents-in-law. Because he was always fighting, people were afraid of him. Sabhuku Chimanga also was a fighter, so my grandfather's in-laws thought it would be good idea if my grandfather went to live at Chimanga village. But they were always troublesome these two, so sabhuku Chimanga thought it would be better to give Mburuma his own village. So he took him to the Native Commissioner and Mburuma registered as a new sabhuku. Then Mburuma moved close to where I am living now. Soon afterwards he moved closer to the river. He moved three times between this place and the river because the people were afraid of the white missionaries. They did not want to be seen by the missionaries when they travelled to Msengezi. Then in 1948 they moved to the other side of the road, where you had your hut when you came here the first time. I was born in 1947. In 1948 I went to Banket with my parents, where they had found jobs. In 1950 we came back, and in 1951 I went up there [on the Plateau] again to look for work. I only returned in 1981. In 1951 I was working at a farm in Guruve. In 1957 I went to Bindura to work for the postmaster. When the postmaster moved to Harare I went with him. I stayed with him till 1960. Then I went back to Harare where I remained till 1964. From there I went to Mvurwi. In 1964 I married my first wife. We had seven children together, some live in Mutare, Rusape, one in Harare, one in Mvurwi. When we were divorced my wife went to Kadoma. She took the last-born with her. One of our children is living here with me. I came back here in 1981, after Independence. When I was visiting my uncle I met my second wife and I decided to come and live here. While I was living here I married my third wife. My father's brother gave me some land. No, my uncle was not the sabhuku then, his elder brother was. My grandfather had three wives; he had ten sons and three daughters. They exchanged the post of headman within the family until the war. Then the person who held the post left for a Commercial Farm because of the war. He then gave the post to the old man, from the other house; this man held the post until two years ago. When this man became old and ill he gave the post to me because he did not have any sons of his own. That was two years ago. I am now the acting-sabhuku; when the old man dies we will decide who will become the sabhuku. I do not expect any problems, but if there will be problems we will have to see Chivhere [the Mhondoro of the area].

My mutupo [clan] is Gushungo Ngonya, the mutupo of my second wife is Nzou Samanyanga, and the mutupo of my third wife is Tembo mazvimba kupa. [M.S.: I have not yet heard of Gushungo Ngonya, where does it come from?] The original area of the Mburuma family is somewhere in Zvimba [near Karoi, on the Plateau]. My grandfather came here to hunt, that is when he met his wife and decided to stay here.

So even the 'owner' of the village of Mburuma turned out to be the grandson of a migrant.

The continued influx of migrants over time, but also the introduction of cotton led to some changes in land-use practices. As I already remarked above, most of the villages in Dande were established on the banks of the many rivers that flow from the escarpment into the Zambezi River. The founding families of the villages all have riverine fields. These *mudimba* are of crucial importance; researchers from WWF have concluded that without riverine cultivation there will be no food security in the area (see Lynam et al. 1996). This was confirmed in the household production survey I conducted in 1992/3, just after a major drought. Only those families who had access to riverine fields reported having harvested anything at all. The same WWF researchers, however, conclude that the tenurial regime under which the *mudimba* are managed is unclear, and this, they argue, would threaten the ecological sustainability of *mudimba* in the Zambezi Valley. I would disagree with this. In Dande the riverine fields are of such importance that the regime under which they are managed resembles private ownership. Once a family has been allocated riverine fields, these will always be considered their property, whether the family is cultivating the fields or not. They are inherited and subdivided among sons, but even after long absences from the village returning 'originals' could always reclaim them. Many migrants borrowed or rented *mudimba* from families that had left the village to find work on the Plateau. This borrowing and renting produces a complicated picture when one asks who has access to which part of the riverine fields. Below I present a map that my research assistant sketched when we were walking in the riverine fields with some of the farmers working there. We had asked who was farming the *mudimba* and the result was this patchwork of small fields, the boundaries of which were frequently a topic of discussion amongst the farmers accompanying us.

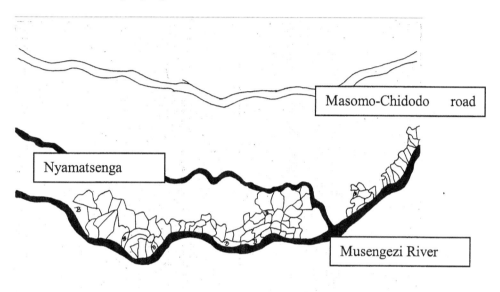

B = Bush
Map 2. Cultivated Riverine fields at Mburuma village between Nyatsengwa Stream and Musengezi River.

However, when we later asked who controlled the *mudimba*, the map was greatly simplified [see Map 3 below]. Only a few families were said to own the *mudimba*. These families were considered the *mugari wemuno*, which was translated as 'originals of this area', by the people in the village who spoke English.

In wintertime the picture changes again as the riverbeds are parcelled out and each family in the village, migrant or autochthonous, establishes a vegetable garden, which is watered with water from shallow wells dug in the riverbeds[30].

---

[30] Most rivers in the valley are not perennial, drying up in wintertime. The soils, however, will remain moist, and shallow wells provide sufficient water. Such wells are not only used for watering the gardens, but are also the main source of potable water in the dry season.

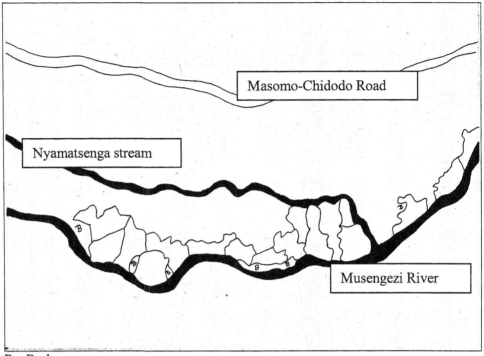

B = Bush

Map 3.   Riverine fields owned by families in Mburuma village.(idem)

There are many restrictions on what crops can be grown on the *mudimba*, issued by the mediums of the *Mhondoro* cult. Only food crops are allowed, farmers are prohibited from using inorganic fertiliser or pesticides in the *mudimba*, and trees growing on the riverbanks may not be cut down. While I was staying in Mburuma, one farmer was seen violating these regulations. His case was reported to the spirit medium and the farmer had to pay a substantial fine.

With the introduction of cotton in Dande in the 1960s farmers also started to use upland fields. The riverine fields continued to be used for food crops. The upland fields could be allocated to other families once abandoned, without any possibility for those who had cleared the fields to reclaim them, though sometimes the new user would have to pay a fee for the clearing done by the former user. It is very likely that in other parts of Zimbabwe, land was not so readily handed over to other users. Until the introduction of the Mid-Zambezi Project land was not considered scarce in Dande, with the exception of the *mudimba*. As will be shown later, ideas about the ownership of upland fields changed as a result of the project.

The extension of upland fields by 'originals' for their children or the subdivision of their riverine fields was reported to the *sabhuku*, and sometimes to the VIDCO chairman. These were decisions taken by the male heads of the household, sanctioned, but not effected, by the local authorities. Only new migrants settling in an existing village would actually have their fields allocated to them by village headmen or VIDCO chairmen.

The clearing of new fields by migrants was much welcomed before the introduction of the Mid-Zambezi Project. When I asked Chief Hwata why he had travelled to Commercial Farms to invite migrants to Dande he said:

> When we were in the keeps we lost a great deal. We lost a lot of equipment. We lost our cattle. Our fields reverted to bush again. Now there are many elephants in the area. They came here during the war. We need more people to clear the area so we will not have so many problems with wild animals. Also, the people down here do not have as many schools and clinics as those up on the hill. We need more people so we can go to the DC and the DA and tell them: look, there are now many, many people here; you have to give us schools and clinics.

Sabhuku Mburuma said that before the war many villagers had planted banana plants. After Independence people stopped replanting them because the plants attracted elephants, a problem they had not experienced before they were moved to the keeps: 'So we need more people, so we will have fewer elephants'.

Agricultural production

To give some idea of how the allocated land was used I will present data from the surveys I conducted on agricultural production. Despite fears that the continued influx of migrants into the Zambezi Valley would lead to environmental damage, the District Administrator, the Chief Executive Officer as well as most agricultural extension officers took a more sanguine attitude towards migrants - provided they came from other Communal Areas, not from abroad - than they did towards the 'autochthonous' population (see also Dzingirai 1995). Migrants were considered to be people who showed initiative, were better educated, and were importing 'modern' agriculture into the Zambezi Valley, whereas the original inhabitants were considered very 'traditional', in fact, a little backward. Migrants were considered more efficient farmers, better producers. These attitudes will be discussed in more detail in Chapter Five. Here I will show that the survey I conducted in 1988/9[31] did not confirm preju-

---

[31] The figures on acreage in all the tables presented below, including those based on the 1992/3 survey, represent estimates made by the farmers interviewed. Though I visited the fields of the farmers interviewed, I did not have the equipment to conduct precise measurements. The data are hence to be treated as estimates and not precise data. Yet, they arc interesting in terms of (crude) comparisons they allow between the different groups of farmers. Given the allocation procedures followed by the Mid-Zambezi project team (see Chapters Four and Five), the perhaps ensuing pressure to overestimate the number of acres under cultivation was likely to be felt by all farmers interviewed.

dices concerning low productivity of 'autochthonous' farmers. In fact, of the three groups of farmers that could be distinguished, the most productive one was the 'autochthonous' group. This may have been because the 'autochthonous' households were generally larger (average 9.4 members compared to 6.4 for migrant households) and thus had more labour available. 'Autochthonous' households were more likely to cultivate riverine fields, which in good years can yield two harvests. Migrants had a disadvantage because starting a new farm required the initial investment of an amount of labour in activities that did not immediately result in agricultural produce, like clearing fields and constructing housing. It often takes a few years before a new farm becomes fully productive. The survey of 1988/9 showed that the least productive farmers were the retired former farm labourers, which was not surprising considering their generally advanced age.

Table 1. Data on self reported cultivation and production 1988/9 season (Bazooka and Rutendo VIDCO)

	Migrants from CFs N=11	Migrants from CAs N=19	'Autochthons' N=27
Average acreage cultivated	2.9	5.5	10.3
Maize Percentage cultivating	94%	88%	100%
Average acreage	1.65	2.04	3.2
Average yield (bags)	2.2	4.3	18.3
Percentage selling	0	0	30%
Sorghum Percentage cultivating	19%	19%	22%
Average acreage	1.4	1.4	1.1
Cotton Percentage cultivated	36%	81%	89%
Average acreage	1.5	2.3	6.3
Average yield (bales)	2.25	5.4	13

At the start of the agricultural season 1992/3 I conducted a survey in Mburuma only, which revealed a different pattern. I only recorded the acreage cultivated, since the 1991/1992 harvest had been particularly bad. This time 'autochthonous' farmers were cultivating fewer acres than migrants. Yet, during the drought more 'autochthonous' farmers had managed to harvest maize, probably because they had more riverine fields available. They reported that they had planted fewer acres at the start of the season, since they wanted to save seed for a second crop on their *mudimba*, in order to recover from the drought.
Migrants from Commercial Farms in Mburuma cultivated as many acres as migrants from other Communal Areas, and many more than appeared from the

1988/9 survey, that was conducted in both Bazooka and Rutendo VIDCO. A possible reason for this was that the migrants from Commercial Farms who settled in Mburuma were younger than those who had settled in Bazooka VIDCO - which included Mahuwe. Mburuma is a pretty isolated village, much more difficult to access by public transport. Migrants who were older and less able to cultivate may have chosen to live closer to the roads so that their children on whom they depended could visit them more easily.

Table 2. Self-reported acreage cultivated in Mburuma 1992/1993

	Migrants CF N=7	Migrants CA N=13	'Autochthons' N=55
Acreage cultivated (total)	6.4	6.4	5.4
Acreage wetlands	0.2	0.6	1.1
Acreage maize	2.5	2.5	2.4
Arcreage sorghum/millet	2.1	2.4	1.6
Acreage cotton	1.8	1.5	1.3
Percentage farmers who harvested in 1992	71% ·	75%	83%

Table 3. Livestock ownership Bazooka and Rutendo VIDCO, 1988/9

	Migrants from CFs	Migrants from CAs	'Autochthons'
Percentage of households owning cattle	0%	69%	19%
Average number		8	4
Percentage of households owning goats	9%	31%	19%
Average number	7	8	6
Percentage of households owning poultry	82%	75%	78%
Average number	9	9	16

Migrants from Communal Areas possess more cattle than 'autochthonous' households. Many took cattle with them from their home area. I only report the data from the 1998/9 survey, since the data from the 1993 showed a similar pattern, though overall numbers were lower, probably because of the drought.

The higher incidence of cattle ownership among migrants from Communal Areas is one of the reasons why they are considered better farmers. Cattle can be used for ploughing. However, many 'autochthonous' households use tractors for ploughing. Before the war quite a number of cotton farmers owned their own tractors, but most lost these during the war. At the time of the first survey, the Lutheran World Federation operated a tractor renting service, which was used extensively by autochthonous households. Later, the Lower Guruve Development Association, a local NGO, was established. This Association, which received funding from foreign donors, including the Dutch organisation Novib, also set up a tractor scheme.

Table 4.   Mode of tillage, renting of labour and farming equipment

	Migrants from CFs	Migrants from CAs	'Autochthons'
Mode of tillage			
Tractor	9%	19%	70%
Cattle	0%	69%	15%
Hand	91%	13%	4%
Combining methods	0%	0%	11%
Percentage of house-holds hiring labourers	18%	63%	41%
Percentage of house-holds hiring tractors	9%	19%	67%
Percentage of house-holds hiring cattle	0%	0%	7%

Only a few ex-farm labourers were able to hire local labour to help them weed and harvest. Those who could do this were younger women whose husbands were still working, who used their husbands' income to pay for the hired help. Migrants from Communal Areas hired local labour more frequently than 'autochthonous' households, since they generally had less family labour available.

Lastly, 'autochthonous' households reported having more additional sources of income alongside agricultural production, which may explain why they were able to hire tractors.

Less than a fifth of the elderly ex-farm labourers reported receiving financial assistance from children who continued to work on the commercial farms they had left. Since most of these children were employed as general labourers, they could only contribute small amounts at irregular intervals. Nevertheless, the retired farm labourers were often accompanied by some of their grandchildren who could help their grandparents on the farm and at the same time were able to receive an education in Dande, where education is relatively cheaper than in the Commercial Farm Areas. The younger, female, former farm labourers received, as I already mentioned above, financial assistance from their husbands who were still at work. Their husbands, however, were not employed as general labourers, but had more specialised, hence better paid, jobs such as driver, foreman or mechanic.

Table 5.   Additional sources of income

Percentage of house-holds receiving income from members engaged in:	Migrants from CFs	Migrants from CAs	'Autochthons'
Wage labour	27%	38%	40%
Performing labour on other people's fields	9%	26%	31%
Making baskets/mats ·	0%	0%	44% ·
Brewing beer	0%	0%	22%

The percentages of households receiving financial support from members engaged in wage labour did not differ much between migrants from Communal Areas and 'autochthonous' households. The distribution amongst different categories of wage labour did not vary much between the two groups either. About a third of the households received income from members employed as general farm labourers, often on temporary contracts. When crops threatened to fail, households would send members they no longer needed for weeding and harvesting to look for work in the nearby Commercial Farm area. Another quarter benefited from household members working as domestic servants. About a third of the households had members working in more specialised jobs such as foremen, tobacco graders, drivers, mechanics or skilled construction workers. Slightly less than ten percent of the households (both migrant from Communal Areas as well as 'autochthonous') were supported by relatives who were employed as nurses, teachers, policemen and in one case, as the manager of a small branch of Zimbank in a suburb of Harare. The bank manager fell into the category of 'autchothons'.

In conclusion, the prejudicial feeling - to which I will return in Chapter Five and Eight - that 'autochthonous' farmers were not doing as well as migrants from other Communal Areas has to be reviewed. While immigrants may have had more cattle at their disposal for ploughing, 'autochthonous' farmers had more labour available, and more often used tractors for ploughing. Overall, the elderly ex-farm labourers seemed to be worse off, though some of the younger ones who settled in Mburuma did manage to cultivate a substantial acreage.

Concluding remarks

Migration seems to be a key feature of life in Dande. As a result it is difficult to make a clear distinction between immigrants and 'autochthons'. As the story of the headman of Mburuma village confirms, even 'traditional' authorities such as headmen may have their roots outside of Dande, and as the founding myths recounted in Chapter Six will show, so may chiefs. Many people who are nevertheless considered autochthons move away from Dande for considerable lengths of time, sometimes with, sometimes without their family members. Their stories, as well as those of more recent newcomers testify to the need perceived by Rutherford (2001), Potts (2000) and Andersson (2002) to problematise the rural-urban divide as well as the sharp division that is often made between Communal Areas and Large-scale Commercial Farm Areas. From the migration stories, a picture emerges of Commercial Farms as the linchpins in the migration process. It was here that workers from different parts of Zimbabwe met, gathered information about farming possibilities, formed enduring relations that facilitated access to land and in some cases, and managed to save money to invest in new farms.

How migrants obtained land and how they were able to organise agricultural production, varied considerably from household to household. Still, when it came to production it appeared that distinctions could be made between newcomers who prior to migration held land rights in other Communal Areas of Zimbabwe, and former farm labourers who did not hold land rights before coming to Dande. Among the latter, especially the elderly, who had continued to work for wages as long as possible, had the greatest difficulties in making a living of their new farm. Migrants from Communal Areas often had some production assets, such as cattle, which they brought with them to Dande. They reported faring quite well in their new homes. The survey data did not lend justice to the prejudice so often expressed by local government staff and members of the Mid-Zambezi Project team that 'autochthonous' farmers were rather unproductive.

The data presented in this chapter do support the conclusion by the Commission of Inquiry into Appropriate Agricultural Tenure Systems that land allocation procedures in the Communal Areas were very complex and that many authorities were claiming the right to deal with land. Yet, their further conclusion that there was a need to hand back the authority to deal with land issues to the chiefs and headmen seems rather problematic. In Dande the relations between traditional authorities and the VIDCOs and WADCOs differ from village to village. In many cases, headmen co-operate with VIDCOs and WADCOs. Traditional leaders themselves are rarely elected as members of the VIDCOs and WADCOs, but their close relatives sometimes are. There are villages, however, where some tension and competition exists between headmen and VIDCOs. When migrants form the majority of the village population, they may come to dominate the VIDCOs. In such cases, migrants, who may feel the headmen do not adequately represent them, may only approach the VIDCOs with their requests. As has been shown in this chapter, the personal position and history of migrants definitely influenced which local authority they approached first to ask for permission to settle in a village and obtain land. We have seen that both VIDCO chairmen and village headmen were involved in land allocation. Some migrants received land from headmen; others from VIDCO chairmen, and again others had their new fields allocated to them by both working in co-operation. Metcalfe (1993) also concludes that because of the many shifts in authority over land back and forth between 'traditional' structures to 'modern' local government structures, a return of power over land to 'traditional' authorities has become virtually impossible.

In Dande this issue was made even more complicated by the introduction of the Mid-Zambezi Project, which will be presented in the next chapter.

4

The Mid-Zambezi Rural
Development Project

Introduction

In Chapter Two some of the developments which led to the introduction of the Mid-Zambezi Project were already described. Several factors and actors influenced the perceived need for the project, its goals, and the way it was operationalised. There was the government's need to do or at least appear to be doing something to contribute to the development of Dande, as it was a former frontline area. Then there was the EEC-funded programme to eradicate the tsetse fly; the insect that was considered a major obstacle to development in the area. Environmental organisations assumed a link between this programme and the influx of migrants - whose access to land was described in the preceding chapter - and demanded proper land-use planning (see e.g. UNEP 1986). This demand coincided with the government's move away from land redistribution in favour of internal land reforms and villagisation.

In 1984/5 the EEC responded to the calls for proper land-use planning and commissioned the FAO to identify and prepare an integrated rural development project for the Mid-Zambezi area. The proposed project was mainly based on the government's plans for the implementation of land-use reforms in the Communal Areas throughout the whole of Zimbabwe. The main difference was that a resettlement component was added which foresaw the in-migration of about 3000 households from other parts of the country. The African Development Fund agreed to finance the project, which was now called the Mid Zambezi Rural Development Project (ADF 1986).

The implementation phase of the Mid-Zambezi Project started in 1987. The project was supposed to be completed in 1992, but the implementation turned out to be a much more difficult task than anticipated. In 1992 government received funding for a three-year extension. Still, even these extra three years were not enough to complete all project activities.

Right from the launching of the project, staff experienced problems attributable to the lack of information they had concerning the area and its inhabitants, as well as to the sometimes conflicting aims of the project. One of these aims was to rationalise local land-use and render it more efficient. In a nutshell, the assumption underlying the project was that local farmers did *not* use their land in an efficient and rational way. The flaw was that this assumption was not based on detailed studies of local land-use practices, but on rather general ideas on what 'communal tenure' looked like. By adopting these ideas as a basis for the land reforms, the post-Independence government returned, as it were, to the Rhodesian way of interpreting the problems in the Communal Areas. The project was designed to promote 'scientific' land-use planning, yet the allocation procedures were based on an interpretation of 'traditional' land rights. This interpretation allowed neither for possible regional differences nor for the dynamic character of 'tradition', which entailed changes in ideas about who had rights to land.

Secondly, the project was designed both to control in-migration to prevent environmental degradation *and*, paradoxically, to bring in 3000 more households. Soon after the implementation phase had started, project staff discovered that the project plans were based on outdated information concerning the number of people already residing in the project area. Detailed maps had been prepared with limited numbers of fields and homesteads in those areas that the project planners considered arable. These numbers did not take into account the in-migration of an additional 3000 households. Worse, they did not even coincide with the number of households already present in the area. This observation did not lead to any changes in the plans, except that no new families were allowed to come to Dande. The land reform project went ahead, regardless of the plight of all the families that would not be able to secure fields and homesteads, and would become officially landless, labelled 'squatters' by the government.

In this chapter I will describe how project staff tried to implement the project. Less attention will be paid to the ideological underpinnings of the project. These were introduced in the first chapter, and I will return to them in more detail in the next chapter. Here, the focus will be on the procedures and practicalities of the land reforms. I will also describe how the land-use planning exercise clashed with local ideas and practices concerning land-use, and with the way local farmers have sought to cope with the changes brought about by the project.

The project area

The project area covered virtually all of Dande except the area west of the Manyame River. The Msengezi River formed the eastern boundary of the project area. Seven Wards were included in the project area: Matsiwo A and B, Chitsungo, Neshangwe, Chisunga, Chiriwo and Mzarabani. The latter did not fall under the jurisdiction of Guruve District Council, but under Centenary District Council.

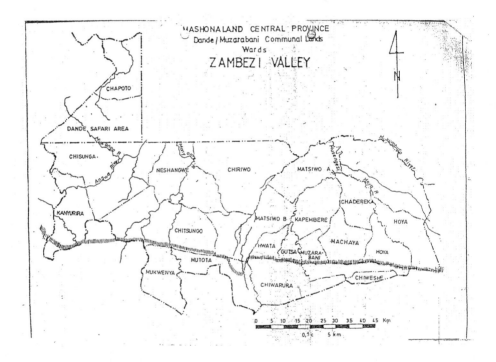

Map 4.   Wards in Dande Communal Land.
          Source: Zimbabwe Trust, Report on the CAMPFIRE Programme:
          The Guruve/Dande experience.

Goals and objectives of the Mid-Zambezi Project

The main goal of the project was to prevent environmental degradation of the Mid-Zambezi area by controlling spontaneous in-migration to Dande, limiting the number of new settlers to 3000 families, and by 'rationalising' land-use practices of those already present in the project area (ADF 1996: 1, 39). The original plan proposed to place the new settlers in 130 newly created villages. On the basis of the 1982 national census, it was estimated that approximately 4600 households were already living in the project area prior to implementation. These people would have their villages reorganised and their arable fields redistributed (ibid.: 25-30).

As I already remarked above, there seems to be an inherent contradiction between the goal of protecting the environment in the project area through controlling spontaneous in-migration, and the objective of settling 3000 new families in the area (see also Derman 1995). The environmental goal was probably dictated by the donor organisations, which paid for project preparation and implementation. It is also likely that the government wanted to use the area as an 'overflow' for the Communal Areas on the plateau. The policy move away from the redistribution of land between the Large Scale Commercial Farming Areas and the Communal Areas described in Chapter Two also entailed a change in objectives with regard to the development of marginal areas like the Zambezi Valley (see also Barrett 1994: 31). Land for the land hungry was to be found by opening up these marginal areas and through 'rationalising' and intensifying land-use in all Communal Areas. This may be considered as a break with early post-Independence policy and as a return to Rhodesian policies (Derman 1995: 23). The Mid-Zambezi Project involved both policy elements; it proposed an internal land reform exercise that would facilitate the relocation of farmers from overpopulated Communal Areas on the Plateau to the 'marginal' Dande Communal Land.

'Rationalising' land-use practices in fact came down to the abolition of multiple use of the land, either for various purposes or by different owners, which was common practice in Dande prior to the introduction of the Mid-Zambezi Project. This involved the physical separation of land used for the cultivation of crops, land used for grazing and land used for habitation. Furthermore, scattered landholdings were to be consolidated. In this, the Communal Areas Land reform programme in general and the Mid-Zambezi Project in particular showed a very close resemblance to the activities under-taken in relation to the 1951 Native Land Husbandry Act (see Drinkwater 1991).

Land was to be (re-)distributed, with households receiving a single plot of twelve acres of arable land and a one-acre residential stand in a reorganised village. Households would not obtain a permanent title deed for the land, but would be given temporary user rights. These permits could be revoked if residents did not conform to project guidelines, which, as Derman (1985) argues, was consistent with the view that central government owns the land in Communal Areas and has the right to set the conditions under which it can be used. In the southern part of the project area each household would also be allocated the right to graze four to six cattle units (depending on the quality of the soil) on communal grazing lands (ADF 1986: 20-25). For Matsiwo A, the Agritex

Planning Branch proposed the creation of fenced paddocks within these grazing areas, which would allow rotational grazing (1993: 23-25). The ADF appraisal report (1986) only mentioned the designation of communal grazing areas, but did not point out explicitly whether rotational grazing in paddocks should be practised.

Originally, land-use in the northern zone was to be based upon game utilisation. In fact, the planners foresaw that the Natural Resource Management component funded by the project should be seen as a pilot scheme for CAMPFIRE (see Derman 1995: 26). The old, dilapidated game fence running through the project area was to be replaced by an electric fence to separate game from cattle and to protect the agricultural zone from wildlife damage. Further fencing was to be installed around farmers' fields. Cattle keeping would not be allowed north of the fence. A tractorisation programme was planned to solve the problem of draught power. The project was to provide fifty tractors and help establish tractor co-operatives. Several water points would be built for wildlife.

In the whole of the project zone farmers already resident would be expected to move away from 'non-arable' land, that is, riverine fields. This objective was based on the assumption that streambank cultivation causes erosion and siltation. State intervention in streambank cultivation dates back to the colonial era. The Water Act of 1927 (amended in 1976) states that: 'No person shall conduct any operations which interfere with the bed, banks or course of a public stream or any swamps or marshes forming the source of a public stream or found along its course without permission'. This act was followed by the Natural Resources Act of 1942, which introduced regulations prohibiting streambank cultivation within 100 feet (now often interpreted as 100m) of a streambank. In the 1960s the ban was lifted in the European farming areas, and not reinstated again when these areas were renamed Large Scale Commercial Farm Areas after Independence. To this day, though, farmers in the Communal Areas remain bound to the old water acts (see Murombedzi 1991). It should be noted, however, that prior to the implementation of the Mid-Zambezi Project local state officials never actively enforced the ban on riverine cultivation.

In addition to the land reforms, the Mid-Zambezi Project was to provide improvements in infrastructure and services. The project document initially envisaged: the upgrading of roads, the construction of two new Rural Service Centres (RSC) to supplement the existing three RSCs, the construction of clinics and staff housing at each of the five RSCs, the construction of twenty additional classrooms plus teachers' houses, the provision of village water supplies (through the drilling of boreholes), and the reconstruction of the old game fence (ADF 1986: 25). In terms of services the following was anticipated: the establishment of a branch of the Agricultural Finance Corporation at Mahuwe to extend access to credit and loans, and an increase in the number of Agritex assistants from five to ten (in order to have one assistant for every 760 households). The latter were to assist local farmers with on-farm development, natural resource management and co-operative development. Furthermore, two additional veterinary health assistants and an animal health officer were to be employed, and two animal health centres and two additional dip tanks be constructed.

The project was to run for five years, with a budget of Z$ 25.23 million, which at the start of the project was the equivalent of about 11 million US$. The government of Zimbabwe was to contribute 3.28 million Z$, mainly in terms of salaries for project staff members. It is not clear from the project document whether this included salaries of teachers and health workers who were to be employed at the new schools and clinics.

Implementation

The actual implementation of the Mid-Zambezi Project was the responsibility of the Department of Rural Development (DERUDE, a department of the Ministry of Local Government and Rural and Urban Development of the Government of Zimbabwe, as the Ministry was called at the time) and Agritex (the national agricultural extension service). A project team was established, consisting of a Project Manager - a Senior Resettlement Officer - appointed by DERUDE, and seven Resettlement Officers, also working under the authority of DERUDE. The land-use planning was the responsibility of the Provincial Agritex Planning Branch, which would send teams to the project area to demarcate the arable and residential plots. The task of the seven Agritex local Extension Officers (in fact only two extra officers were employed) was to educate local residents about the project, and to hone agricultural techniques and conservation measures, as well as to lend assistance to the demarcation teams.

The land-use proposal for Matsiwo A Ward states that the land-use planning was carried out 'using the Agritex methods' (Agritex Planning Branch 1993: 33): Aerial photos were interpreted to delineate crests and drainage patterns and determine non-arable and potentially arable land. Non-arable land was defined '(…) as areas closely dissected with streams, areas of extensive gravel outcrops, and the verges of rivers and streams'. The report specifically states that checks on the ground were employed to confirm photo interpretation. This included soil coding through the digging of pits and augering. Carrying capacity estimates were done '(…) randomly in fallow and virgin lands'. (ibid.: 33), but the methodology section of the report offers no clues concerning the basis for these estimates. The data acquired in this way was used to draw up detailed maps with individual residential stands, individual arable plots and communal grazing areas. The local Agritex Extension Officers helped by collecting socio-economic data from VIDCO Chairmen, Village Community Workers, Environmental Health Officers and Veterinary Officers.

Whether this methodology was followed in all land-use plans for the project area is not clear. The Project Manager once told me that he thought that the first land-use plans were based solely on aerial photo interpretation, without verification on the ground. The many complaints about plots that had rocky patches or depressions in them that got waterlogged during the rainy season suggest that this was indeed the case. The Matsiwo A land-use plan also mentions 'awareness meetings' with villagers (ibid.: 33), but these were never held in the other Wards prior to the demarcation exercises.

Once the maps were drawn, teams of Agritex officials moved into the project area and started demarcating fields and stands with metal pegs. It was these Agritex officials who were responsible for designing cultivation plans for the twelve-acre plots. A standard pattern is mentioned in the ADF appraisal report: 2 ha of cotton, 0.75 ha of maize, 0.5 ha of sorghum, 0.25 ha of millet, leaving 0.5 ha fallow to facilitate crop rotation (ADF 1986: annex 13). The Matsiwo A proposal offered a different pattern, suggesting that half the plot be left uncultivated for rotation, but the Agritex Extension Worker in charge of the Ward advised people to follow the ADF proposal (see next chapter).

On the basis of the 1982 census, the Project Appraisal (ADF 1986) stated that approximately 19,000 people, similar to about 4600 households, were already residing in the project area prior to the implementation of the Mid-Zambezi Project. Thus 7600 plots were designated for these plus 3000 new households. This also seems to indicate that the detailed exercise described for Matsiwo A, which mentions 1046 households living in Matsiwo A Ward alone, had not been carried out in the other Wards. For some reason, the overall plan made no use of census data that were available at the Guruve District Council in 1985, listing 24,000 people living in the project area (Derman 1995: 15). And even these figures were outdated by the time the Mid-Zambezi Project was implemented, as spontaneous in-migration continued after 1985.

Resettlement Officers employed by DERUDE were charged with selecting new settlers and allocating so-called 'arables' and 'residentials' to local farmers. They soon discovered that far more people were already living in the project area than were catered for by the plans. The goal of moving new settlers to the area was abandoned, but all those already present were supposed to conform to the new land-use patterns. Given these circumstances, the project became an internal land reform or villagisation project only. The maps with new villages and fields for the southern project zone were not adapted and the number of fields and residential plots to be allocated there remained the same. Adaptations were made in the plans for the northern zone, however, when it became clear that there was insufficient land for the proposed number of settlers in the southern zone. The idea of reserving the northern zone for wildlife utilisation was abandoned (see Derman 1995).

In order to receive a residential stand and a twelve-acre field, local farmers had to meet a set of criteria similar to those created to select farmers for resettlement projects on former European land. To qualify for a plot of land, farmers had to have Zimbabwean nationality, no source of income other than farming, and be a married male. Women could not obtain land within the project area. The exclusion of women was justified by referring to 'traditional' land rights (see Government of Zimbabwe 1985: 16). However, as we saw in the previous chapter, widowed and divorced women did have land allocated to them in their own right by 'traditional' village headmen in Dande. Below I describe how some of these headmen tried to prevent women from losing their land. The allocation criteria also show that the government tried to separate 'the real farmers' from those combining farming with wage labour, thereby trying to create a separate class of 'real labourers', as it is explicitly mentioned in the Communal Lands Development Plan of 1985 that first introduced the land reforms (ibid.: 46)[32]. It should be noted, however, that the criterion relating to sources of income was never seriously applied[33].

Initially, neither chiefs nor village headmen nor VIDCO members were involved in the process of allocation, although before the introduction of the project they had been the authorities entrusted with settling land issues. However, later, when organisational problems loomed (see below), project management decided to involve the District Council, Ward Councillors and VIDCOs. This led to some changes in the allocation criteria. District Council demanded that in order to qualify for land in the project area farmers would have to be registered in Guruve District (of which Dande forms part). This was to prevent recent migrants from obtaining land at the expense of those who considered themselves autochthons. The Council also decided that migrants who had arrived after 1985 would not qualify. Cogently, certain provisions for women were demanded. Project management gave in to these claims, with the important proviso that women could only obtain land - albeit not more than two and a half acres - if they were widowed and had minor dependants. However, neither Bill Derman (personal communication) nor I have found villages where actually two and a half acre plots have been demarcated for widows.

The process of moving farmers to their new fields proved to be a tremendous task. In some cases whole villages had to be moved to fulfil the goal of the project plan: to move away from 'non-arable' land. Problems rained thick and fast. No transport was available to move farmers to their new villages. The project budget did not provide people with financial compensation for houses or other immovable property that had to be left behind. There had been plans to provide selected farmers with loans for constructing new houses, but these were never materialised. Nevertheless, some assistance was provided. On each new

---

[32] Plans to create separate classes of farmers and workers appear in many development plans formulated by the post-Independence government. Several studies, however, show that this is impossible to accomplish. According to some because it is an economic necessity for households to derive income from both farming and wage labour (see e.g. Potts & Mutabirwa 1990); others maintain that is part and parcel of the life-styles of households in the Communal Areas (see Andersson 2001).

[33] Several Resettlement Officers as well as the Project Manager obtained twelve-acre plots and residential stands in the project area, and they certainly had sources of income other than from farming. Pertinently, none of them were 'autochthonous'.

twelve-acre plot, one acre was stumped and ploughed by project personnel, and seed and fertiliser packages for one acre were distributed.

When already existing villages were being re-organised, the procedure was as follows. Once fields and residential stands were demarcated, VIDCO secretaries had to compile lists of those applying for plots, employing the official criteria. These were handed over to the Ward Councillors, who then discussed the lists with the Resettlement Officers responsible for the actual allocation of plots and stands. Those who were not able to obtain land in their original village were told to apply in one of the new villages, or the less densely settled areas - usually north of the old game fence.

When existing villages were re-organised, the newly demarcated fields were often already partly under cultivation. In such cases, the twelve-acre plots were allocated to the person who was cultivating the most acres within the boundaries of the new plot, provided this person met the criteria for resettlement.

Originally, the project was scheduled for completion in 1992. However, owing to technical and organisational problems, but perhaps even more importantly, to increasing resistance among the local population, the project lagged far behind schedule. In 1992 project funding was extended for another three years. In 1995 project staff were withdrawn from Dande and DERUDE ended its activities.

Results of the Mid-Zambezi Project

Most of the infrastructural development has been completed, with the (important) exception of the construction of water points. Access to health care and education facilities has improved significantly. The upgrading and construction of roads has rendered the area less inaccessible. Local residents have generally welcomed the infractructural developments provided by the Mid-Zambezi Project.

The financial scene is less propitious. Access to credit has not improved as much as predicted. The Agricultural Finance Corporation did not establish a branch at Mahuwe. By the end of 1993, only 435 individuals and fifteen groups had benefited from AFC loans, according to an AFC representative reporting to the Mid-Zambezi Project Co-ordination Committee; details on who exactly were the beneficiaries were not provided by the representative. There have also been cuts in staff extension. The number of Agritex Extension Officers was increased to seven, not to ten as was foreseen in the project appraisal document.

Although the idea of reserving the northern project zone for wildlife was abandoned, project staff retained the restriction on cattle keeping north of the game fence - which, it must be noted, was not reconstructed as had been planned. For a long period the veterinary officers tried to enforce a ban on cattle keeping in the northern project area, but discovered that this was impossible. First the restriction was lifted for farmers who had come from the southern zone, already possessed cattle, had not managed to obtain land in the southern zone and had been told to move northwards. This change in regulations was never officially announced, but was applied informally by project staff members. At a later stage, farmers north of the game fence were told that they could keep oxen for ploughing, but no cattle for breeding purposes. Nowadays, however, many farmers in the northern part of the project area do breed cattle.

One of the reasons why it was difficult for project staff to enforce the ban on cattle keeping in the north was that the planned tractorisation scheme was never materialised. Though the Lower Guruve Development Association (see previous chapter) operated tractors in the area, the failure of the Mid-Zambezi Project tractor scheme was successfully used as an argument against the ban on cattle. When the demarcation and allocation exercise took up much more time than expected, project management postponed working on the tractorisation project. By the time they finally decided to buy the tractors, the money budgeted for the project was no longer sufficient as it had lost its value because of devaluation and inflation.

The Project Manager and the Senior Executive Officer of Guruve District told me that ·an African Development Bank mission, who evaluated the Mid-Zambezi Project prior to the three-year extension, only criticized the failing of the tractorisation scheme; otherwise its members were quite positive about the outcomes and advised favourably on the extension of the project.

Controlling the number of cattle kept by each household has not only been a problem in the area north of the game fence, but in the whole of the project area. The Veterinary Officer based at Chitsungo in 1994 estimated that in the whole of Dande the number of cattle was about 24,000; that is, between five and six animals per household. This number coincides with the results from the small survey I conducted in Bazooka and Rutendo VIDCO (an average of eight cattle for migrant households and four for autochthonous households was reported). Derman (1995: 19) claims this means that the rate of increase in cattle population has been higher than the rate of increase in human population. Whether the tractorisation programme would have militated against an increase in the cattle population north of the old game fence remains doubtful. Sibanda (1986) conducted a study of a tractorisation scheme in Mzarabani and found that the participants used their profits to purchase livestock and then left the scheme.

The paddocks proposed for the communal grazing areas required fencing, and therefore wood for poles as well as wire. Agritex advised each of the villages in Matsiwo A Ward to create paddocks that would need fences with a length varying from thirty to forty km (Agritex Planning Branch 1993: 24). No assistance was provided to local farmers to fence the paddocks and so very few have been established.

The main component of the Mid-Zambezi Project, the resettlement/villagisation exercise, was never fully completed. When project management applied for an extension of the project, one entire Ward as well as several villages in certain other Wards had not yet been resettled. When project staff left the area in 1995, the plots in Matsiwo A Ward had still not been allocated. In the Ward where plots were allocated very few people who did not obtain land under the project had actually left the project area.

Effects of the Mid-Zambezi Project on Local Communities

The project has created immense insecurity over land. As already mentioned, project planners had seriously underestimated the number of households already residing in the project area. Instead of bringing new families to Dande, the Mid-Zambezi Project now threatened to evict a large number of those families that had already been present when the project was introduced. The Agritex Planning Branch mentioned that 27 per cent of the population of Matsiwo A Ward would not be able to obtain a plot in their Ward (1993: 19). Whether these people would be able to obtain a plot somewhere else in Dande was uncertain. Derman (1993) estimated that despite the designation of more plots and residential stands in the northern part of the project area, about a third of the present population, that is, about 3800 households, would have been made officially landless if the project had ever been completed. Where these new landless people would have had to go to was totally unclear. The imminent landlessness resulted in a scramble for twelve-acre plots and increasing conflicts over land within the project area.

The designation of 'arables', residential stands and grazing areas was not based on existing settlement patterns at all. Local farmers determine the quality of the soils, among other things, on the basis of vegetation, thus in a similar way to the Agritex experts - though, of course, without aerial photographs or remote sensing. Pertinently, in choosing where to settle and cultivate, they also take into account other factors, for example the availability of water and the presence of wildlife.

Most villages in Dande were established along the banks of the many rivers, which flow from the Escarpment into the Zambezi River. The rivers provide water for drinking and the fertile riverbanks are very valuable resources, crucial to survival in an area where rainfall is highly irregular and unpredictable (see Chapter Three). Through the Mid-Zambezi Project, the government tried to enforce the ban on riverine cultivation. Farmers were told to abandon their *mudimba* and in several cases whole villages were moved away from the rivers. The major reason for enforcing the ban on streambank cultivation by confining agriculture to the upland fields was concern about erosion and siltation. However, Scoones and Cousins (1991) demonstrate that the technical evidence on which the continuation of the ban is based contains many inaccuracies and that the practice is far less damaging than is often assumed (see also Dambo Research Unit, Loughborough University 1987). When research demonstrated the profitability of maize production on wetlands, this resulted - as I already mentioned - in legalisation that allowed wetland cultivation in the European areas in the 1960s (see Murombedzi 1991). Farmers in the Communal Areas, on the other hand, remain bound to the old legislation.

Strangely enough, the Mid-Zambezi Project itself tampered with the riverine areas by designating them communal grazing areas for goats and cattle. Many villagers complained that grazing was much more damaging to the streambanks than cultivation.

By moving them away from the rivers, people were not only deprived of their most valuable resource for agriculture, but also of their main source of potable water. The Mid-Zambezi Project was supposed to solve this problem by drilling boreholes and installing hand pumps in the villages in the project area. Yet, this part of the project tarried seriously behind schedule and far fewer pumps have been installed than had been planned - not to mention the fact that the boreholes that had been drilled often ran out of water and pumps broke down frequently. Villagers received very little training or support to assist them with the maintenance of the pumps. Project staff was not able to deal with the many breakdowns, and there were conflicts between project staff and the District Development Fund (DDF) over who was responsible for maintenance and repair once the pumps were installed.

With the separation of residential areas from agricultural areas, the project planners limited the diversification in land-use that is so important to the livelihood strategies of farmers in Dande. Most farmers had 'homefields' surrounding their homesteads, where they mainly grew food crops - maize, millet and sorghum. These were often intercropped with vegetables such as beans and pumpkins, which provided households with vegetables in the period before they could prepare wintergardens in the riverbeds. Most of the 'outfields' were used for cash crops - mainly cotton - and maize. Chibudu et al. (2001) have described the cultivation of both homefields and outfields which is practised in other Communal Areas of Zimbabwe as well, and remark that it is in the homefields that many farmers invest most in terms of enhancing soil fertility - especially by making good use of manure and household waste. In Dande, where there are large wildlife populations, the homefields have the advantage of being easier to guard against marauding wildlife destroying crops. In the new (or re-organised) centralised villages there was no room for 'home-fields'. Many people in Dande furthermore complained that at the new residential stands - 'living in lines', as they are referred to locally - without the home-fields surrounding the homesteads, the population is thrown too closely together, resulting in more conflicts with neighbours.

The project documents advise that the riverine fields be replaced by small gardens within the boundaries of the residential stands or around the boreholes, which could be hand-irrigated with water from the boreholes. Given the lack of functioning boreholes, this has not turned out to be feasible. Mahuwe, situated close to the escarpment, is one of the very few exceptions. Here, piped water is available for hand-irrigation.

Agricultural upheavals are not the only problems induced by the programme. The Mid-Zambezi Project has created tensions between those who consider themselves autochthonous and recent migrants. 'Autochthons' felt that the process by which fields were demarcated and allocated, worked in favour of the more recent settlers. As the number of migrants expanded, it became increasingly difficult for them to gain access to riverine fields other than by borrowing or renting (see Chapter Three). The fields allocated to the more recent settlers were therefore generally situated farther away from the riverbanks, though migrants were allowed to plant gardens in the riverbeds when the rivers dried up in winter. When existing villages were reorganised, migrants stood a better chance of obtaining fields since they were often already farming in the upland areas demarcated by Agritex. 'Autochthons' had most of their fields near the rivers and hardly ever came across demarcation pegs in their fields. The regulation that the DC imposed on the project management that only those who with 'district citizenship' could qualify for the allocation of a plot, was supposed to correct this situation which disadvantaged 'autochthons'. What had not been anticipated was that most migrants, especially those from Communal Areas on the Plateau, had changed their registration certificate and obtained district citizenship in time to qualify for a twelve-acre plot. Only some of the poorest migrants, often elderly, who had formerly been farm labourers, did not have the Guruve District number 71 on their IDs. As time went by it became increasingly difficult for them to change their IDs as the fees payable to the DC for a new registration certificate increased dramatically[34]. Furthermore, quite a number of 'autochthons' did not have number 71 on their registration certificates, since many never bothered applying for a certificate until they started working at a Commercial Farm or in town. Many obtained their ID at their workplace, and had the number of the district where they used to work registered on their certificate. I even met a village headman who did not have Guruve District number 71 on his registration certificate and thus could not obtain a twelve-acre plot.

Once Agritex had demarcated twelve-acre plots in a certain area, this was often followed by a scramble for land within the new boundaries, even before the new plots were officially allocated. 'Autochthons' suddenly claimed large parts of the newly demarcated fields, stating that the chief or headman had long ago allocated that land to them for future use. They transferred all available labour to the new plots, clearing as many acres as possible in order to stand a better chance of obtaining the land from the Resettlement Officers. In Mburuma the scramble took place in 1993/4. After the 1992 drought most 'originals' had concentrated their efforts on the production of food crops in their riverine fields and had decided to abandon some of their upland fields. In 1993/4 they had a hard time reclaiming their upland fields again.

---

[34] This was not a deliberate strategy used by the DC against the migrants; the amount of the fees was determined at national level.

Below I present a map of Mburuma sketched by my research assistant, showing the cultivated upland fields and the plots demarcated by Agritex, which appear as rectangles (the riverine fields do not appear on this map). Most of the area on the right hand side, below the Masomo-Musengezi road, had already been cleared and was under production before the rectangular plots were demarcated. An 'S' on the map means that the area had not been growing produce previously, but had been cleared of trees and stumps only recently. What is clear from the map is that many different families were cultivating within the boundaries of the demarcated plots, which were subdivided into small patches, much smaller than the fields that appear on the left hand side below the road, which did not contain demarcation pegs. Some households were cultivating in more than one demarcated plot to enhance their chances. North of the road a number of plots appear in an area that was still bush before the

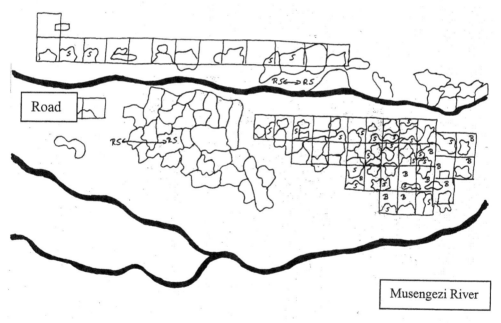

B = Bush
S = Recently stumped/cleared
RS = Residential Stands

Map 5.   New plots (rectangular), old fields and recently cleared areas in Mburuma village, 1993.

demarcation exercise. Claiming land there was more difficult, as it required cutting down trees and removing stumps. Yet, a number of families opted to do so in order to claim the plot. Some people had been cultivating upland fields on the other side of the road, but these fields were located on the right side of the map. The map also shows that there is only a partial overlap between the areas cultivated before the introduction of the project and the area deemed suitable for agriculture by the project planners. Farmers would have to abandon their riverine fields - which are not shown on the map but lie along the Musengezi River - and clear part of the forest across the road.

Conflicts arose over the definition of 'migrants' and 'autochthons'. For instance, before the project was implemented Mozambicans originating from areas just across the border in the valley, speaking the same chi-Shona dialect, were considered autochthons. However, following the introduction of the Mid-Zambezi Project, they were increasingly regarded as foreigners. Violent clashes between migrants and long-term residents have been relatively rare; the killing of one migrant in a fight over a twelve-acre plot in Karai VIDCO was a sad exception. But tensions were noticeable and accusations of witchcraft widespread. In Mburuma the brother of the village headman of the neighbouring village, normally considered an 'autochthon', was farming within the boundaries of plot number 1. At beer parties other villagers would shout at him, telling him to go back to his own village and obtain a plot there. He stayed on until he discovered a goatskin that had been soiled with hyena dung in his field, a clear sign to him that someone was trying to bewitch him (see Chapter Eight for a more detailed description of this case).

When I interviewed migrants in Dande in 1988, just after the introduction of the project, the majority had a rather positive opinion about it, thinking it would provide them with more secure rights to land than they felt they had. As one migrant remarked:

> It is better if the government allocates the land. Some of the Chiefs used to refuse migrants wanting to live in their place. Villagisation is not a new thing to me, we had that in a Bikita long time ago.

Another migrant agreed, but also saw the limitations of the project:

> The Ministry of Lands should allocate the land. If the Chiefs do it you have to pay a bribe to the sabhuku to get a good field. There is also tribalism, it would be a problem for migrants to get a good field here. But, if I could manage more than the ten acres I was allocated by the sabhuku, I could go to him to ask for more land, now I cannot, you cannot get more than the twelve acres allocated by the Ministry.

Cogently, as the project seriously disturbed their relations with their hosts, many migrants changed their minds and when I returned in 1992 it was hard to find migrants who still - openly - supported the Mid-Zambezi Project.

Environmental impacts

The Mid-Zambezi Project has not succeeded in meeting its environmental targets. First of all, the goal of reserving the northern project zone for game utilisation was abandoned. According to Derman (1995: 26), the Mid-Zambezi Project management bowed to government pressure in choosing the resettlement option. The political priority for the project was to be able to say that 7600 households were being resettled, which would demonstrate the government's ongoing commitment to solving the problem of land shortages.

The tractorisation programme, which was to help keep cattle out of the northern project zone, was never materialised. Whether this is a bad thing for the ecology of the northern zone nevertheless remains debatable. Tractors require stumped fields, which are consequently rendered treeless (see also Derman 1995).

The premise that by rationalising land-use the Mid-Zambezi Project would be able to stop uncontrolled movement of migrants into the area turned out to be false. Despite growing tensions between migrants and 'autochthonous' residents over land in the project zone, quite a number of village headmen still allowed new settlers into their villages. In the villages where I conducted research, I frequently witnessed the arrival of new settlers. Pertinently, it must be admitted that not all new settlers who have moved to Dande since the introduction of the Mid-Zambezi Project were 'strangers' to the area. News about the project resulted in an early return of large numbers of wage labourers, whose roots were in Dande; eager to claim land for future use, before all the land would have been redistributed.

Government itself also contributed to an increase in the number of new settlers following the introduction of the Mid-Zambezi Project. While one part of the Department of Rural Development was involved in attempting to halt migration through the project, another part of the Department still considered the Zambezi Valley as an empty area ideal for settling displaced people. In 1992 and 1993 DERUDE settled a number of evicted squatters from Porter's Farm and Mazoe in Dande. As late as 1994 more than fifty retrenched miners from Mutorashanga were encouraged to settle in Dande with their families.

In collaboration with the Veterinary Services Department, the Mid-Zambezi Project has carefully sought to regulate the numbers of livestock in the project area. Despite their best efforts, new and old valley residents alike have ignored the policy of restricting livestock ownership to two oxen, except for those families owning cattle prior to 1987. Even the clear admonition that there was to be no livestock north of the old game fence is not being observed, as mentioned above. The Veterinary Services Department does not have enough manpower to control the regulations effectively. Statements by the local MP - the late Border Gezi - denouncing the regulations at public rallies did not help either.

Meanwhile, a debate is raging about the degree of damage to the environment caused by cattle. Scoones (1996) argues that many of the scientific data on which both estimates of carrying capacities and the advice to practice rotational grazing are based, are questionable (see next chapter). Soil erosion continues to be one of the main concerns in relation to the environment in Zimbabwe. Scoones (ibid.) and Chibudu et al. (2001) argue that in many Communal Areas in Zimbabwe cattle play an important role in improving soil fertility by providing manure. An important practice enhancing soil fertility, according to these authors, is the grazing of cattle on fields after harvest. Cattle feed on crop residues and leave behind plenty of manure. This practice is rendered more difficult by paddock grazing, as this requires farmers to harvest crop residues and take these to paddocks, where afterwards they have to collect manure and spread this on their fields. In Dande most cattle owners also prefer to take their animals to the fields after harvest to graze on crop residues instead of establishing paddocks. They do build small cattle pens to fence the animals in at night, often close to the homesteads. Some cattle owners move their cattle pens every few years to another location in their homefields, using the very fertile soil that remains after the removal of the pen for intensive cultivation of food crops.

The Mid-Zambezi Project has resulted in massive deforestation (see also Derman 1995). Entire villages have been moved, which meant that new fields had to be cleared while old fields had to be abandoned. It was the same story when people had to change the location of their fields in the re-organised villages, as the map presented above shows. This, combined with the scramble for land in the project zone, has led to more damage to the environment than the project was designed to prevent (see Derman 1995). Villagers have been encouraged to fence their new residential stands and establish fenced paddocks for cattle. Where people have taken heed of these calls, this has led to further deforestation for the provision of poles to support the fences.

Quite a number of farmers have been moved by the Mid-Zambezi Project into areas hitherto occupied by wildlife. In the western part of the project zone people have been resettled in such a way that the dry-season route for elephants to the water of the Manyame River has been blocked. All this has increased competition between humans and wildlife. Personnel from the Department of National Parks and Wildlife Management responsible for dealing with so-called Problem Animals say that following the introduction of the Mid-Zambezi Project they have received many more requests to kill wild animals destroying crops.

The environmental damage as well as the widespread ignoring of project guidelines are the results of the lack of attention paid to pre-project land-use practices and tenurial arrangements (see also Derman 1995: 57). The majority of Dande residents considered the project a violation of their way of life and a threat to their livelihoods. As residents were not consulted, the only options they had were to resist implementation and to ignore project guidelines rather than negotiating for project improvements.

Reactions to the Mid-Zambezi Project

Resistance to the Mid-Zambezi Project started already early on in the imple-mentation phase of the project. When Agritex demarcated the first fields and residential stands late 1987, early 1988, the eyes of the valley residents were opened to what the project would bring about. In one area close to Mzarabani, angry villagers uprooted the metal pegs used for demarcation. They marched to Mzarabani where they dumped the pegs in front of the DA's office[35]. Unfortu-nately, the DA had somehow received news about the protest march and had called in the army. The protesters were received by the DA, who was surrounded by heavily armed men. While these pointed their guns at the protesters, the DA asked if there was anyone who wanted to come forward and express his or her objection to the Mid-Zambezi Project. Not surprisingly, nobody dared to do so and the protesters left without having had a chance to air their grievances, let alone have them addressed.

From then on resistance to the Mid-Zambezi Project took on different forms. Not all of these were concerted efforts and some actions caused conflicts between different sections within the communities concerned. Some of the reactions could also be interpreted as coping strategies rather than deliberate attempts to frustrate the implementation of the project. The most common reaction was a widespread disregard of project guidelines and regulations. In villages where resettlement have officially been completed, that is, where all arable plots and residential stands have been distributed and allocated, it is not uncommon to find many people living there who have not been allocated land there. In some cases, people who were rendered landless by the project obtained permission from village headmen to settle in the grazing areas or other areas outside the boundaries of the areas demarcated for agricultural production. In other cases they borrowed or rented land from people who had not (yet) cleared all of their twelve acres[36]. Farming 'outside the pegs' became an important coping mechanism as well as an expression of protestation in Dande. Several village headmen I interviewed claimed that the lands outside those areas demarcated under the Mid-Zambezi Project were still under their jurisdiction, and that they could still allocate these to people who had not received a twelve-acre plot.

People who had access to riverine fields prior to the implementation of the project often still cultivate their *mudimba*. This, however, increasingly causes

---

[35] Mzarabani is part of Centenary District, and the DA had set up an office there.

[36] This is the same kind of resistance that was used against the 1951 Native Land Husbandry Act (NLHA). Studying conflicts over land in Buhera, Andersson (2002: 88) came across the heritage of the NLHA. This included people farming in parts that had been designated as grazing areas under the NLHA, with permission from the village headman.

conflicts with farmers who own cattle but no *mudimba*, and want to graze their livestock in those riverine areas now designated as communal grazing areas.

In compiling lists for the Resettlement Officers of people requesting twelve-acre plots, the VIDCO secretaries did not always apply the official selection criteria. For instance, many divorced women were registered as widows so they could at least obtain a 2.5-acre plot. Furthermore, some VIDCO secretaries and Ward Councillors were known to discourage certain people from registering by giving them false information concerning the selection criteria. Many migrants of Mozambican origin were told not to bother registering for a plot because even if they had Zimbabwean citizenship and were officially registered in Guruve District, they would not qualify on the basis of their foreign origin.

Sometimes the different ways of frustrating the implementation of the Mid-Zambezi Project revealed internal inconsistencies and caused clashes within the communities. For instance, many village headmen were still allowing new settlers in their villages. At the same time this increased conflicts over the definitions of 'autochthons' and 'migrants' and who would have rights to land in the villages. Buying more cattle than the project allowed for increased already existing conflicts over grazing areas, especially as the grazing areas were often used as 'over-flow' areas for those who did not obtain plots. As already mentioned, the continuation of riverine cultivation in areas that had been designated as grazing areas also caused conflicts with cattle owners who insisted on using these areas as such. How these internal conflicts were acted out will be described in Chapter Eight.

Though the resentment against the Mid-Zambezi Project was fairly widespread, it was not always unanimous. As I will describe in Chapter Six, at a certain stage project management decided to put pressure on villagers to accept the project by threatening them that all infrastructural development activities - including the construction of schools, clinics and boreholes - would be put on hold until people abided by project regulations. Some people actually believed they would risk losing out on 'development' and decided that having no schools and clinics would be worse than accepting the project. They struggled to convince others to come round to their point of view.

Project management had seriously underestimated the problems involved in convincing people to comply with project regulations. When it became clear that co-operation from local residents was necessary but not forthcoming, a change of strategy was decided upon. The idea was to mobilise the support of the traditional authorities, hoping their subjects would obey them. This opened the way for the mediums of the *Mhondoro* cult, who became the spokespersons for the opponents of the Mid-Zambezi Project. In Chapter Six and Seven I will describe the mediums' role in the resistance to the Mid-Zambezi Project in greater detail.

In 1995, as already mentioned above, project staff was withdrawn from Dande. By that time the land-reform exercise was still not completed, nor were some of the infrastructural developments in place. Responsibility for the latter was transferred to the District Development Fund. Responsibility for the land-reform exercise, especially the proposed eviction of those who failed to obtain land under the Mid-Zambezi Project, was transferred to the Rural District Council. The RDC was not looking forward to dealing with this sensitive issue. In fact, the (R)DC[37] had been quite divided about the Mid-Zambezi Project from its beginning, and its reactions to the project showed many inconsistencies, which I shall come to shortly. It was very unlikely, however, that it would succeed in what the project staff failed to accomplish. In fact, the last time I returned to Dande, in 2000, the RDC was still debating the issue, but did not seem to be doing anything about it. So far, none of the landless, who are now officially labelled 'squatters', have been evicted. In the meantime, the political situation in Zimbabwe has changed drastically, and evictions seem less likely, unless perhaps 'squatters' are suspected of being members of the opposition party.

In the next chapter I will try to explain why project staff underestimated the problems involved in implementing the Mid-Zambezi Project, and describe the way they interacted with the people in the project area.

---

[37] At the time of the withdrawal of project staff, the District Council had completed the process of amalgamation with the nearby Rural Council, and had become the Rural District Council. I occasionally add an R in brackets to indicate that both the old District Council and the new Rural District Council were involved.

5

Up there, down here: Struggles between project staff and local residents

Introduction

When studying a project like the Mid-Zambezi Project, which has had such negative consequences for the population it was supposed to benefit, it is easy to resort to writing in a very negative way about project staff members who, on behalf of the government, tried to enforce the project on the population of Dande. Yet, as I will show below, most project staff members actually believed they were doing the right thing and were helping local farmers to 'develop'. Many thought it was only a matter of educating local farmers concerning 'proper' land-use practices. Once educated, they would see for themselves that accepting the Mid-Zambezi Project was in their best interest. In this chapter I will explore where these ideas came from, and why they were so persistent.

The Mid-Zambezi Project was based on a manner of analysing and simplifying local circumstances that Scott (1998) has described as 'seeing like a state', that is, the inevitable - and to some extent also necessary - reduction of local complexities by state agencies to create some governmentability. However, one should avoid applying a similar kind of simplistic analysis to state agencies themselves. It is not easy to discover what exactly were the motives for the implementation of the Mid-Zambezi Project, and it should be stressed that several organisations - both governmental and international - played a role in the introduction of the project. Cogently, the same cautions that have been issued by anthropologists against treating 'communities' as homogeneous bodies (see for example Barrow & Murphree 2001) apply to the organisations involved in the project (cf. Bate 1997; Martin 1998).

More and more literature is devoted not only to the negative consequences of certain land-use policies, but also to attempts to understand how and why these policies emerged in the first place (see for example Leach & Mearns 1996; Keeley & Scoones 1999). In Southern Africa this trend is fuelled by the striking similarities between colonial and post-colonial land-use policies. The Communal Areas internal land reforms, of which the Mid-Zambezi Project was a pilot project, are almost carbon copies of those introduced in colonial times through the Native Land Husbandry Act of 1951 (see also Chapter Three). Why this persistence?

In this chapter I will try to answer this question on the basis of a review of existing literature. Rather than describing the history of land-use policies implemented in Zimbabwe, as I did in Chapter Two, here I want to focus on the development of the ideas behind these policies and look into possible reasons for their continuance after Independence. In order to do so I will start by looking at the history of the organisations involved in the implementation of the Mid-Zambezi Project.

Encouraged by a recent trend in environmental history to study the role of agricultural and veterinarian extension agencies in the construction of particular environmental discourses, more and more literature is becoming available that describes the history of the agricultural extension service in Rhodesia/Zimbabwe. This literature deals with the political context in which the predecessor of Agritex - one of the organisations involved in the implementation of the Mid-Zambezi Project - was created, and the construction of the 'land degradation narrative'. This narrative provided the rationale for the implementation of the Native Land Husbandry Act of 1951 and continued to underpin the post-Independence land-use reforms in the Communal Areas.

Bate (1997: 1155-6) argues that to understand everyday practices in organisations and the meaning which the members of the organisation attribute to these, it is important to study the historical context of these organisations. The way project personnel in Dande operated cannot be understood without reference to the histories of the organisations that were involved in the project. Nor can it be understood without the wider political context in which these organisations were established, or the political contexts in which they operate today.

Much of the literature on Agritex and its history focuses on the dominant discourse within the organisation as if this was unquestioningly shared and supported by all staff members of Agritex. The rub is that organisational anthropologists have shown us that it is rather naive to assume that this is the case. The lessons learnt from anthropology 'in general', namely that culture is contested and fragmented (see for example Clifford 1986), should be applied to the study of organisations as well (see Bate 1997; Martin 1998). My own research shows that these lessons are very relevant when it comes to the Agritex officers and DERUDE employees who together made up the project staff. Not only were there differences between different people within the organisation; staff members also told different stories at different times.

The histories of the organisations involved as well as the 'land degradation narrative' that underpinned agricultural extension will undoubtedly have influenced the way staff members working on the Mid-Zambezi Project interpreted their work, as well as how they interacted with the population of Dande. Conversely, the interactions with a population that did not always appreciate their work, in turn have affected project staff members. In this chapter I want to explore those effects by both looking more closely at the ideas and attitudes of project staff members and at their interactions with their 'clients'.

First the scene will be set with a brief history of agricultural extension in Rhodesia. This history is linked closely to the development of the 'land degradation narrative'. I will describe how initial appreciation of local, African, agricultural techniques evaporated when it became clear that the Reserves, or Tribal Trust Lands, could no longer support their growing populations. The 'land·degradation narrative' explained the problems in the Reserves by arguing that the soils had degraded because of bad farming methods employed by African farmers. In this chapter I will show the continuation of the dominance of this narrative in post-Independent natural resource management policy in Zimbabwe. This is important for an understanding of the context in which the staff of the Mid-Zambezi Rural Development Project operated, and the problems they faced with regard to the implementation.

A brief history of agricultural extension in Rhodesia/Zimbabwe

In the early days of the settler-state, European attitudes towards African farming practices were quite positive. In those days the European economy was focused mainly on mining. African farmers were quick to respond to the new demands for agricultural produce made by the miners and their labourers (see Ranger 1985). The taxes that were imposed on them were met through the sale of crops and cattle as well as through wage labour[38]. Acreage under cultivation was

---

[38] Ranger (1985) argues that most Africans preferred to meet taxes through the sale of agricultural produce, rather than by selling their labour. Andersson (2001) disagrees with this point of view. He describes how colonial administrators thought that taxes were the only inducement for the African population to engage wage labour. Yet, Andersson maintains that the relation between tax and readiness to engage in wage labour is not as direct as these administrators thought. He found cases in Buhera of people moving to South Africa in search of jobs before the colonisation - and thus tax imposition - of Rhodesia. In the early days of the settler-state many different migration trajectories already existed with some farmers looking for jobs mainly during slack periods in the agricultural season and other moving away from the rural areas for longer

increased, and by 1903 the sale of agricultural produce constituted 70 per cent of African farmers' cash earnings. The success and viability of African farming techniques did not pass unnoticed, and those white settlers who did venture into agriculture often adopted these techniques (see Kramer 1997).

Many African farmers were combining intensive and extensive farming practices. Wetland cultivation was combined with the limited shifting cultivation of grains on the uplands. Intensive gardening was pursued, often involving complex mounding systems to regulate water flows and enhance fertility. The upland fields were cultivated for up to four years, then they were left fallow for up to fifteen years before they were planted again. Land was prepared using hoes, the soil was not deeply ploughed so that the topsoil was not dislodged (see Kramer, ibid.: 160; Chibudu et al. 2001: 126).

Agricultural production for the market did entail changes in farming practices. Chibudu et al. (ibid.: 126-33) describe these changes for two sites: Chivi (southwest Zimbabwe) and Mangwende (about 60 km northeast of Harare). The introduction of the plough and a rise in cattle numbers - building up draught power - led to an expansion in the extensive cultivation of dryland areas. In Chapter Three we saw that the same kind of change occurred in Dande with the introduction of cotton. Cultivation of the dryland areas was, according to Chibudu et al., an opportunistic affair with large areas planted, but only low yields expected. Ploughing was rudimentary and, at least in the first years, no fertilisation was required. In 1910, The Native Commissioner of Chivi praised the adoption of the plough: '(...) the teachers and some of their relatives, on the mission farm "Chibi", use ploughs and cultivate in European style, and in this way set a good example and teach the natives in the vicinity (cited in Chibudu et al. 2001: 127)'. The NC for Mrewa was less optimistic; in 1923, he wrote in his report: 'with few exceptions the ploughing was done very carelessly. The land is not properly harrowed or drained with the result that a large part of it gets waterlogged and is useless. The native system of ridging their gardens showed to advantage in the heavy wet season we had last year (cited in Chibudu et al. 2001: 129)'.

During the first decade of the twentieth century there was hardly any competition from white farmers, and no pressure on the land. Although the Native Reserves had been established, many Africans remained in unclaimed parts of what had become 'European Areas', close to the markets where they could sell their produce. In those early years no efforts were made to evict them and force them into the Reserves.

This changed when it was discovered that the large gold deposits believed to be available in Rhodesia had already been exploited by the local populations, and very little gold was left. With the mining sector on the verge of a collapse,

---

periods of time (ibid.: 21-4). According to Andersson, '(...) it was not merely an issue of either/or, but a combination of labour migration and agricultural production (...)'.

land became the new source of wealth (see Palmer 1977). From 1908 onwards the White Agricultural sector began to expand and more and more African farmers were expelled and sent to the Reserves. By 1922, 64 per cent of the African population was living on the Reserves (Kramer 1997: 162).

With the expansion of the nascent White agricultural sector, attitudes towards African farmers and their techniques changed dramatically. Whereas early in the twentieth century Native Commissioners produced enthusiastic reports about the capacity of African farmers to adapt to the changing demand by growing more and diverse crops, their success was now seen as a threat to the rising numbers of White farmers. Pertinently, it was feared that it reduced their willingness to work as labourers in the mines or at White-owned farms (Ranger 1985; Kramer 1997).

The more African farmers moved into the Reserves, the more agricultural production declined. Many Reserves were situated far from markets, and the increased costs involved in marketing crops meant that production for the markets was uneconomical. Productivity declined further as congestion in the Reserves increased (Palmer 1977; Kramer 1997). The European economic sector depended on cheap labour from the Reserves, and wages could only be kept very low if families could provide for at least part of their subsistence through agriculture in the Reserves. Too much decline in productivity in the Reserves was therefore not desirable (Palmer 1977; Drinkwater 1989).

Despite increased pressure on the land in the Reserves, the government was not prepared to allocate more land to the African population. Their agricultural techniques, which hitherto had been praised as: '(...) avoid[ing] the main problems that plague Southern Rhodesia: soil erosion and declining fertility of the soil (W. Roder cited in Kramer 1997: 160)', were now considered to lie at the root of the problem of declining productivity in the Reserves:

> An adjustment in the agricultural and pastoral systems hitherto practised by the Natives is essential if the land assigned for their use is to prove adequate to their needs (...) already there are signs of congestion and overstocking in certain areas where the Natives have been left to follow their own time honoured agricultural and pastoral methods. (Native Commissioner quoted in Kramer ibid.: 162).

In 1920 a separate Native Development Department was established, with H.S. Keigwin as its Director. Keigwin recommended that Native Agricultural Instructors be trained who would go to the Reserves to demonstrate 'modern' cultivation techniques (Kramer, op.cit.: 165). He also advised the establishment of industrial training schools where Africans could be educated in order to become self-sufficient in their own areas. Keigwin's plans were adopted and in the early 1920s two industrial training schools were opened, one at Domboshawa in Mashonaland, and one at Tjolotjo in Matabeleland. Initially the focus of these schools was on industrial training, but in 1924 a Native Demonstrator programme was launched in the two schools. Various Native Commissioners selected twenty-one men for training. Two years later E.D. Alvord was appointed Agriculturalist for the Instruction of Natives.

Alvord was an American missionary who had been stationed at Mount Silinda, in the dry region of Matabeleland. He had instructed pupils at the mission school in 'improved agricultural methods'. When he arrived at the mission in 1920 he discovered that the maize crop had practically failed, and that the soils in the region were arid and barren. He noticed that despite the fact that plenty of cattle were kept in the area, nobody used cattle manure to alleviate the soil fertility problems. He then selected six acres of overworked school land and established demonstration plots. He fertilised these with cattle manure, planted two with maize, and planted the remaining four with legumes applying systematic crop rotation. On these practices he based his system of 'Agricultural Work for Adult Natives', which he later integrated in the curriculum of the Native Agricultural Instructor training programme (Kramer, ibid.: 169).

Alvord became responsible for the agricultural curricula at Domboshawa and Tjolotjo. He introduced a five-year course in practical agriculture, following the methods he employed at Mount Silinda. He also inaugurated similar courses at several mission schools. Students were to study soil conservation methods, gardening, animal husbandry, fish farming, water conservation, crop cultivation, general farming and farm mechanics (Kramer, ibid.: 172).

Though opposed to their agricultural techniques, Alvord was sympathetic to the African populations of the Reserves. He undertook extension services in a genuine effort to improve the livelihoods of African farmers. This attitude was not particularly appreciated by the government, which wanted to increase the carrying capacity of the reserves to have more land available for White farmers. It did not want to create competent, competitive African farmers. In the 1926 yearbook of the Colony the following synopsis was written to define the purpose of the demonstrators:

> The aim of farming Demonstrators on Native Reserves is not to stimulate the production of cash crops, but to teach the Native farmer how to get good returns from his labour, and at the same time build up and maintain the soil fertility for himself and his children. It must be remembered that land in Native Reserves is communal and limited. No individual can be permitted to go extensively into the production of money crops, wear out the land and crowd out other individuals who have an equal right to a share of the land. (Quoted in Kramer, op.cit: 171/2).

Not everybody, however, was convinced that Alvord's programme would work, or indeed was even necessary. In the 1920s not all Reserves were so crowded that productivity decreased. In 1926, the Native Commissioner for Makoni District, in the east of the country - the area on which Ranger focused when he wrote his book on the 'peasant option' and the competition between African and White farmers (Ranger 1985) - wrote: 'So long as European farmers continue to fail to produce good crops while the Native regularly reaps ample harvests, the Native can hardly be expected to change much (quoted in Kramer 1997: 170)'.

Yet, the tone was set. The problem facing African farmers in the Reserves was not the fact that they had less and less land available. What was a political problem was re-defined as an environmental problem - soil erosion and loss of soil fertility due to poor agricultural techniques - requiring a technical solution - teaching gAfrican farmers proper farming techniques (see also MacGregor 1995).

Alvord not only wanted to improve farming techniques, he also turned his attention to land-use practices. African farmers did not spatially separate their different agricultural activities such as cultivation and grazing. Alvord was convinced that spatial separation of activities would contribute to solving the problem of soil erosion, and advocated 'proper land-use planning'. Beinart (1984) and McGregor (1995) link these ideas to the Christian doctrine of man as master of nature, and the need to 'domesticate' and 'civilise' the landscape. Many of the commentaries on African farming practices were based on norma-tive interpretations of what the farming landscape should look like. According to Scoones (1996: 47; see also Scott 1998), these normative interpretations stemmed from a European aesthetic ideal of a tidy and ordered landscape, as well from scientific ideas about optimal farming methods imported from the temperate zones of Europe and North America. The latter emphasised concepts like carrying capacity, stable grass species composition, and mixed farming. All these concepts were based on notions of stability and equilibrium, and, Scoones (ibid.) claims they were alien to the highly dynamic, opportunistic approaches to farming found in dryland Zimbabwe.

Alvord proposed to reorganise the landscape through the centralisation of habitation. Ranger (1985: 32-3) describes how increased production for the market led to changes in settlement patterns. People moved away from the fortified settlements that had failed to protect them from the White invaders, establishing dispersed farms away from the scrutiny of village headmen. Alvord argued that to achieve better control over land-use and production techniques, as well as for administrative purposes, settlement and land-use patterns needed to be 'rationalised', and (re-)centralised. Grazing areas needed to be separated from arable fields, and villages organised 'in lines'.

Kramer (1998) describes how the first attempts at centralisation failed to win the support of the government. By the 1930s, however, the idea gained currency. In 1939 a commission to enquire into the preservation of the natural resources of the colony, led by McIllwaine, concluded: 'For the regeneration of the reserves there are two essentials: organisation and control (Southern Rhode-sia 1939: 57, cited in Scoones 1996: 44)'.

The 1930 Land Apportionment Act formalised the racial distribution of land and left only 49 per cent of all arable land to African farmers. Between 1930 and the early 1950s the last African farmers were evicted from land classified as European. The situation in many of the Tribal Trust Lands deteriorated even further. Yet, again the solution for the declining productivity in the African areas was sought in improving agricultural techniques and land-use practices, and in 1951 the Native Husbandry Act was passed (Ranger 1985; Drinkwater 1991). Through this Act and with the assistance of the Native Agricultural Demonstrators, the government tried to implement the centralisation plans that had been proposed by Alvord in the 1920s. The idea was to confer individual tenure rights on specific parcels of grazing or arable land presuming that individual tenure would lead to more efficient land-use. The right to allocate land in the Tribal Trust Lands was taken away from chiefs and village headmen. Grazing areas were to be separated from arable land, and villages were to be centralised.

The implementation of the Act also involved compulsory de-stocking of cattle. Scoones (1996) and Beinart (1996) describe the historical background of Rhodesian livestock policies. These policies were geared towards modernising and improving beef production and management. Work on pasture improvement was initiated in the early 1930s (Scoones ibid.: 39). Researchers focused on fertilising natural pastures to increase yields, the introduction of pasture grasses and rotational grazing. Scoones says this work borrowed directly from research carried out in Britain and South Africa, where most Rhodesian research officers were trained. Pedigree bulls were imported into Rhodesia with the aim of improving African cattle breeds. A Native Commissioner, cited in Scoones (ibid.: 40) summed up the policy: 'It is hoped that the natives will realise shortly that it will be to their advantage to raise few graded cattle in preference to keeping a large herd of almost valueless scrub cattle'.

Research scientists achieved remarkable increases in beef production under ranch conditions. However, this success could not be replicated in the Reserves. According to Scoones, this failure was not surprising given the fact that African livestock owners were not particularly interested in beef production. In their eyes, the value of cattle was mainly in the intermediate products the animals delivered like milk, manure and draught power. Europeans interpreted the African tendency to hold on to their cattle and sell only a small proportion of their animals not in terms of the functions cattle had in African agriculture, but in terms of 'culture' and 'tradition' (Scoones op. cit.: 42). Cattle were said to be important for prestige and status, and the solution was once again to 'educate the natives' and propel them into modernity. Scientists were expected to come up with carrying capacity figures for all Reserves so that 'appropriate' stocking levels could be maintained. These figures were derived from the research trials initiated in the 1930s, based on an assumed beef production objective which was wholly irrelevant to the African farming setting (Scoones ibid.: 43).

In most Tribal Trust Lands the resistance to the Act was strong, objections were raised to the demarcation exercises as well as to the compulsory de-stocking of cattle[39]. Resistance became so widespread - and coincided with the growing membership of the first African nationalist movements - that the Act was abolished in 1963 (Drinkwater 1991).

The land degradation narrative in post-Independence Zimbabwe

After Independence, the Zimbabwean government at first stressed the political nature of the problems in the Tribal Trust Lands - which were renamed Communal Areas - namely the unequal distribution of land between European and African farming sectors. The new government promised to redistribute the land between those sectors. As was described in Chapter Two, after a promising start, not much land was redistributed between the mid-1980s and the elections in 2000.

In the mid-1980s, after a series of droughts, the problems in the Communal Areas were increasingly being redefined, again following the logic of the colonial government: if only the farmers in those areas would use their land more efficiently, much less land would need to be redistributed (see Drinkwater 1991). Plans to re-organise land-use in the Communal Areas were officially introduced in the first Five Year Development Plan of 1986, but in fact had already been prepared when the Communal Land Amendment Act passed in 1985 (Thomas 1992: 15). These amendments facilitated the intention of the government to introduce the demarcation of arable and grazing lands and that of areas for rural housing construction. The reforms in the Communal Areas were to be implemented by the Department of Rural Development, which was part of the Ministry of Rural and Urban Development, and the agricultural demonstrators who were now working in the new national agricultural extension office Agritex. As Alexander (1995: 118) remarks, the continuity in policy within the Ministries was not surprising given the fact that there had been very few changes in personnel within most of them. As described in Chapter Two, the President made little use of the presidential directive, which allowed the appointment of Africans to any section of the public service if this was deemed necessary in order to redress past imbalances.

Keeley and Scoones (2000) have studied the persistence of the 'land degradation narratives' (cf. Roe 1991) in Zimbabwe, in both the colonial and post-colonial periods, which inexorably influenced the land reform programmes. In their paper they try to analyse why policy processes in Zimbabwe (but also in other Southern African countries, see Keeley & Scoones 1999) have consistently reinforced a highly technocratic approach to natural resource management. They argue that the inflexible land-use planning regimes emerge from 'a hybrid realm of science and bureaucracy (2000: 1)' and are the result of the way

---

[39] Similar policies in East Africa also engendered resistance to colonial governments (see Scott 1998: 225-6).

in which knowledge about soil erosion is created. This entails processes of black boxing of uncertainties, that is, questionable premises are concealed from further investigation or simply ignored. The 'results' are then spread through relatively closed networks of scientists, scientific institutions and certain parts of the state and this leaves virtually no space for actors with alternative knowledge or opinions to have their say. Since the days of Alvord, whose work focused so much on soil erosion, a range of scientific research has documented apparently alarming trends in soil erosion and soil fertility decline in Zimbabwe as well as elsewhere in Africa (cf. Leach & Mearns 1996). This technical knowledge reinforced and shaped a process of policy making for colonial programmes, and this has been pursued in post-independence programmes and development aid (ibid.: 3, see also Beinart 1989; Drinkwater 1991).

Since the early colonial era, concrete programmes for natural resource management in Zimbabwe have consistently reflected particular discursive framings of environmental problems; these were based on the assumptions that traditional farming practices and land-use practices degraded the land. Keeley and Scoones (2000) interviewed over seventy people in Zimbabwe and the UK, including politicians, scientists, government and NGO officials, and donor representatives. Many of these expressed trepidation about a growing crisis requiring urgent action. A senior scientist in Zimbabwe commented: 'There is serious soil fertility depletion in the smallholder sector (...) soil fertility is associated with a lack of food security (...) if you come to Zimbabwe in 20 years we will just be like Ethiopia (quoted in Keeley & Scoones 2001: 5)'. A more junior Agritex official told Keeley and Scoones that pressure on marginal lands was the major issue he faced in his work (ibid.: 5). An NGO director said: 'Particularly for soils the cry of Alvord is what we are hearing today - we still think the solutions are the same'.

The main solution is indeed still, as Keeley and Scoones call it, the 'technocratic command-and-control approach' (op. cit.: 6). Adhering almost religiously to the findings of formal science, recommendations are disseminated and regulations are made and enforced. The state plays a key role in this: decisions are made through interaction with people in the research community and the implementation is done through the different ministries and departments. Agritex plays a key role in pushing recommendations.

The content of the recommendations has not changed much either. The 'mixed farming' model that was developed by Alvord and improved by leading soil scientists at the University of Rhodesia is still being promoted. As a matter of fact, the mapping and planning frameworks that have guided land-use and settlement designs still closely resemble the frameworks proposed by Alvord and promoted by the Native Land Husbandry Act of 1951. In some cases there has been more than just resemblance: the exact same land-use reform plans were implemented using the maps and aerial photographs that were made in the 1950s (Drinkwater 1989; Scoones 1996: 46). The scientific recommendations in the post-colonial period are still based on the same core assumptions that date from the colonial period. As one senior national NGO official commented to Keeley and Scoones (2000: 7): 'We do not know better because the way we do science has not changed. Going out and measuring slope changes. Soil estimation methods. All these come from the turn of the century - there is no fresh way of doing science'.

Keeley and Scoones state that discussions with those producing scientific data with which the continuation of the same old colonial programmes is justified, suggest reasons to view the data with care, implying the need to be careful with conclusions drawn from them (ibid.: 8). One soil scientist who had been involved in plot-based soil loss research commented: 'The numbers came out of a hat (...) the figure of 50 tons per hectare came from the same source as US soil loss tolerance. It was just a wild guess from a conversation we had one evening on how to extrapolate nutrient losses. Our footnotes say so'. However, awareness of uncertainty has a habit of disappearing when science interacts with policy. The publication in which this figure was cited was quoted over and over again, by scientists and policymakers alike, without incorporating the original cautionary footnote. Another scientist cited by Keeley and Scoones (ibid.: 9) recalled that the FAO was pushing his research team to make extrapolations, even though the researchers themselves felt that they could not.

Ineluctably, politicians and bureaucratic staff have their own agendas and pick up on, and ignore, different types of science and scientific information. This prompts scientists to strategise to promote their findings. One way is by presenting crisis narratives (see also Leach & Mearns 1996; Adams & Hulme 2001). As one scientist cited in Keeley and Scoones (2000: 10) remarks: 'One of the key things researchers can do is to present the situation as really bad (...) if policy is going to be influenced by researchers then there has to be an alarmist message (...) we need broad level scenarios rather than ecosystem complexity'.

The view that farmers in the Communal Areas need to be told how to manage natural resources and instructed on how to farm can be traced back to colonial times. The strategies used and the relative emphases between different approaches has varied over time, often with substantial conflicts over certain issues emerging within the scientific community and government bureaucracy (see Alexander 1993), but there has been a remarkable persistence in the ideas concerning local farmers' capacities. There are several explanations for the persistence of this general attitude. In the colonial period the land apportionment played a role; Drinkwater (1989: 288) argues that 'land apportionment not only had to be maintained, it had to be justified'. Munro (1998: 84) provides another rationale for state activity in the Reserves, namely the uncertain status of colonial authority in those areas. Robins (1994) argues that the preference for straight lines of grazing areas, settlement areas and arable land stems from the idea that these facilitated control and surveillance of rural populations. Keeley and Scoones (2000) as well as Scott (1998) offer yet another possibility: perhaps technicians profoundly believed in the superiority of 'modern'

European farming practices. These different explanations obviously do not exclude one another.

The same explanations could apply to the rationale for the post-Independence activities of Agritex and other ministerial departments active in the Communal Areas (see Drinkwater 1991). Moyo (1995) maintains that the government wanted to protect the Large-scale Commercial Farming Areas. Keeley and Scoones (2000: 14) argue that to establish the new post-Independence state as a legitimate source of authority in rural areas meant identifying problems - such as environmental crises - which required state intervention or state underwriting. The new government wanted to do something for the rural populations and also needed to be witnessed while doing something (cf. Derman 1995: 14). However, the interventions that followed were to bring remote rural areas, with long traditions of suspicion towards the state, more firmly within reach (see also Munro 1995; Hammar 1998). This ostensibly 'neutral' project, promoting well-demarcated, orderly, efficient, scientific farming, could be justified entirely in technical terms in a climate in which administrators were convinced that traditional shifting cultivation and transhumant pastoralism eroded soils, were inefficient and led to a 'tragedy of the commons' (cf. Hardin 1968) through overgrazing. In the Conceptual Framework for the Communal Lands Development Plan the rationale for the land reforms was formulated as follows:

> (...) the need to restructure and reorganise existing dispersed and isolated peasant settlement, to make for cost effective provision of social and physical infrastructure and services and to release additional land for agricultural development...(...) [it] is for all intents and purposes an agrarian reform strategy [that] will result in more clearly defined land-use patterns, more intensive us of land, thus resulting in higher productivity. (Government of Zimbabwe 1986: 53-4)

All this does not mean there have been no challenges to the dominant discourse. Keeley and Scoones (2000) argue that policy does not move neatly from stages of agenda setting and decision making to implementation - see for example the initial refusal of Alvord's centralisation plans. Policies are contested, reshaped or initiated from a range of places or points between macro and micro levels (cf. Shore and Wright 1997). It is this complexity and dynamism that may allow spaces for the assertion of alternative storylines and practices, which, in turn, can gradually result in shifts in the knowledge and practices associated with previously dominant discourses (Keeley & Scoones 2000: 4). Moments of 'policy space' (cf. Grindle and Thomas 1991) emerge, allowing room to alternative perspectives to challenge the power of more totalising discourses, influential social interests and particular patterns of state formation.

Keeley and Scoones (2000) describe how in one area of Zimbabwe, Masvingo, debates between local populations, NGOs and local Agritex extension officers led the last to change their ideas about the damaging effects of streambank cultivation. The local extension officers were then able to get permission from headquarters for a pilot project. However, this did not lead to changes in legislation concerning streambank cultivation. In another publication, Scoones (1996) describes the inverse process. Some senior Agritex officers became convinced that the policies concerning livestock management and carrying capacity figures needed to change. Yet, they found it difficult to convince the Agritex officers working in the field to adopt more flexible approaches. At the same time as the senior Agritex officers were advocating a new approach, the training colleges and the in-service training unit continued to use course materials that resembled what was being taught in the 1930s, convincing Agritex extension officers of the idea that farmers in the Communal Areas were inadequate farmers and natural resource managers.

Murwira, Hagmann and Chuma (2001) describe changes in Agritex occurring in the late 1990s involving successful attempts to use the experiences described by Scoones in Masvingo to 'mainstream' a more participatory approach in Agritex. It is unclear, however, whether the new approach will be sustained. Agritex is now mainly focusing on demarcating land for 'Fast-track resettlement' - that is, pegging plots on invaded farms.

In the next section I want to look at how project staff involved in the Mid-Zambezi Project, one of the pilot projects for the post-Independence Communal Areas land reforms, interpreted their work. This is important since, as Keeley (2001) tells us, policy includes practice. It does not only refer to legislation, programmes and official communication, it also deals with how those implementing policy at local levels interpret, select, prioritise and implement policy directions.

Project management and Agritex in Dande

When I first arrived in Dande in 1988 the Mid-Zambezi Project had been running for less than a year. In one Ward, Matsiwo B Ward, most designated plots had been pegged and the Resettlement Officers and Agritex extension officers were selecting people who would receive a new plot. I was staying close to the old Rhodesian Forces camp that had been transformed into the Mid-Zambezi Project headquarters. The wooden army barracks were used as offices and storage space. Whenever the Project Manager was in Dande, he stayed in a caravan parked close to the barracks. Other project staff members were housed in tents. This working and living arrangement seemed to emphasise the fact that almost all staff members were outsiders. The project document stressed that given the fact that project staff was going to consist of locals, relations with the people in the project area were expected to be good (ADF 1986: 37). Apparently, the consultants who wrote the report probably meant 'Zimbabwean' when they used the term 'local'. This does not mean that project staff members or Agritex Extension Officers did not share some commonalties with the Dande residents. They had received specialised training, mostly at the training centre at Domboshawa. Yet, most of them had a background in communal farming. Almost all of them still had ties with a Communal Area on the Plateau of Zimbabwe, and often returned home to assist their families with the work on the fields. Nevertheless, as I will describe below, their training as well as the fact that they were not from Dande did set them apart from the people they were working among, even though some of the project 'outsiders' did become 'locals', and ended up settling in Dande at a later stage.

Both the government and donors assumed that virtually any development activity would be welcome. The Appraisal Document of the Mid-Zambezi Project states that '(…) the Mid-Zambezi Valley is recognized to have been a neglected area requiring development (ADF 1986: 43)'. It also stated that no problems were to be expected with the land reform, or resettlement component as it was called in the document, 'since the concepts of resettlement are well-known to the people (ADF 1986: 37)'. When I arrived in 1988 many project staff members were still enthusiastic about the project, convinced they were doing something good for Dande, finally bringing development to those who in the past were always last in ·line to receive any positive attention from the government. They enthusiastically adopted the title of Chambers' famous book 'Rural Development: Putting the Last First' as a slogan for the project. This slogan had been printed on T-shirts and in 1988 many project staff members could still be seen wearing these T-shirts. Most had not actually read Chamber's book, and hence did not know that the book is advocating a participatory approach to rural development, which the Mid-Zambezi Project was clearly not designed to do. Since the people in Dande were not consulted about the project, they did not feel 'put first' at all.

Even at this early stage some project personnel started to have doubts about the feasibility of the Mid-Zambezi Project. In 1988, the Resettlement Officer, for instance, who was responsible for allocating the fields and stands in Matsiwo B Ward already foresaw that the project would never be completed in time:

> The [Mid-Zambezi Project] is the biggest project undertaken by the government, it is a rural re-organisation project, a Model A resettlement scheme but in a Communal Area. The main constraint with resettlement projects is that they are not properly planned, there is no organisation.

> The project should be finished by 1992. But the officers have to stay until all the people can fully utilise their twelve-acre plots. I am convinced it will take a lot longer than 1992.

Despite misgivings, there were few doubts that the project was needed. The 'land degradation narrative' was frequently brought up by staff members when I asked them about the rationale behind the project. The idea that farmers in

Dande were not good at farming was quite pervasive. When I asked the Project Manager why the Mid-Zambezi Project had been introduced he said:

> You ask me why we are here? To bring development of course, to stop soil erosion. Many people are farming where they should not. The people here have been left to their own devices for a long time. Now we will educate them, where they can farm and where they cannot. That is why we are pegging the plots.

The Resettlement Officer who was quoted above said:

> A lot of people here are farming where they should not. This causes erosion. That is why the project is here, to address these problems.

The staff members with whom I spoke considered the land reforms, the pegging and the allocation of the plots the main aspects of the Mid-Zambezi Project. The other aspects, improvement of services and infrastructure, were often only mentioned as an afterthought. As for the local farmers, they, too, mainly identified the Mid-Zambezi Project with pegging and pegs. The Mid-Zambezi Project was often called '*mapegs*' - the prefix 'ma-' is the one normally used in combination with words borrowed from the English language. One of the farmers I interviewed said the following when I asked what he thought the Mid-Zambezi Project was about: 'Mugabe said he wants people to live like in an English town, a suburb, not in the old-fashioned way scattered all over'. For many people President Mugabe had become the personification of the state, of the government, and it seemed that this man saw the Mid-Zambezi Project as part of an overall government plan - which in fact it was. Pertinently, he expressed a link with the European origin of the idea of living along neat lines that was stressed by some of the authors quoted above. The continuation of pre- and post-Independence policies was not lost on the people subjected to the Mid-Zambezi Project; one of the teachers living in Mburuma kept referring to project staff as 'those people from the Native Land Husbandry Act'. A woman in Mahuwe village, who apparently associated me with the Mid-Zambezi Project, put it to me in the following way:

> You people think you can shift us to wherever it pleases you. First Smith [Ian Smith, the last Prime Minister of Rhodesia] told us to move and live along lines. Now you people come and tell us to do the same. This is not what we fought the war for; this is what we fought against.

All staff members I spoke with spontaneously offered the phrase 'people are farming where they should not' as an explanation of why the Mid-Zambezi Project was introduced. The question of why local farmers had selected the areas where they were farming was not asked. The 'originals', as project staff referred to them in English, were considered uneducated and stubborn. Even the

Resettlement Officer who was most sympathetic to the plight of the local farmers in the interviews I had with him commented:

> I have been here only one season, the rainfall was unusually high so the yields were also very high, but that is not standard. There is a serious problem with development here. People do not know how to organise themselves. The Lutheran co-ops[40] are successful because they develop co-ops in stages, with education, not only input and machinery. You cannot run when you are a baby, first you start to crawl, and then you learn to walk

One Veterinary officer commented on the difficulties he experienced in teaching local farmers 'the right way': 'What makes extension work so difficult is that you want to educate people. They know that what they are doing is not good, but they refuse to apply the knowledge we give them'. The Agritex officer for Masomo offered a similar remark: 'The problem here is that most people are illiterate. In my home area you give people a leaflet. Here you always have to be present. People here refuse to follow advice'.

The Resettlement Officer who mentioned the Lutheran co-ops, however, seemed to realise what the main problem with the Mid-Zambezi Project was: 'But still people feel powerless, it is imposed on them'.

When I returned to Dande in 1992 the Mid-Zambezi Project lagged seriously behind schedule. The project had just obtained extra funding to enable it to be continued for another three years. Major problems were experienced in Matsiwo A Ward, and that is where I chose to settle for a two-year period.

The Project Manager had a difficult time. The Provincial Governor and the Ministry were putting tremendous pressure on him to finalise the implementation, but this turned out to be very difficult. The people in Matsiwo A refused to take up their plots, and even in Matsiwo B, where implementation was nearly complete, people were complaining about the lack of plots. The Project Manager summarised the progress made with the Mid-Zambezi Project during my absence:

> Matsiwo B has been pegged. Most people have taken up their plots. There is still illegal farming [*many people who had not been able to get a plot were farming outside the village boundaries or in the grazing areas, M.S.*], people extend their plots and farm beyond the boundaries. Perhaps there is a problem with the extended families, they do not have enough land.
>
> In Matsiwo A we have a lot of problems, especially with the spirit mediums.

---

[40] The Lutheran World Federation had started several development projects in Dande, including a tractor co-operative.

In Chiriwo Ward, Gonono [*in the northern part of the project area, far away from services and facilities*], we have demarcated 380 plots, (...) but the ploughs are lying idle, people refuse to go there. That is where the forty-six squatters from Mazoe will go. One truck came in late last night, another will come today.

The Project Manager acknowledged that the fact that not enough plots were available was the main problem experienced with the Mid-Zambezi Project. He brought up the problem without me having mentioned it, and sometimes seemed sympathetic and understanding, then again reverted to taking a firm stand. It was clear that the problem was bothering him and he seemed reluctant to deal with it, preferring to hand it over to the Rural District Council:

In Matsiwo B there were too many people with small plots, that was no problem, but with the twelve-acre plots there were too many people. There are problems with grown-up children who want land after the pegging, they cannot be accommodated in their old area. We cannot peg again. People will have to move but they want to stay in their old area. People will resist. They resist changes, development. But this is now a problem of the Council, we only advise. Also if people want more land, they have to do so through the council.

Indeed, the problem of the shortage of plots featured regularly on the agenda of the Rural District Council (RDC) meetings. The Project Manager was often invited to the meetings to respond to the requests from Ward Councillors for the pegging of more plots in their Wards. These invitations angered the new Resettlement Officer, who had replaced the officer who foresaw the delays:

The [Mid-Zambezi Project] cannot be expanded like a rubber band. We go by the advice of Agritex. But the problem will lead to illegal cultivation. The correct number of people and cattle have to be in place, otherwise the project makes no sense, then it will cause degradation. But the Councillors and the people do not think so, the Councillors are sympathetic to the people.

The Project Manager seemed to realise that the creation of standardised land holdings might have contributed to the shortage of plots. He admitted that the project design made no provisions for future generations:

I admit that the project does not cater for those who have or will grow up after the allocation. We have reported that to DERUDE. This is not only a problem with the Mid-Zambezi Project, also with other resettlement schemes. Hopefully something will be done about that.

Unfortunately, DERUDE did not respond. Other project staff members, however, refused to admit that the project had created land shortage, blaming instead the continued in-migration into Dande. In-migration was a recurrent theme in the conversations I had with project staff. Resettlement Officers blamed headmen for continuing to allow people to settle in Dande:

People are still moving into the valley. They are allowed to come by the headman. The ROs [Resettlement Officers] asked for a stop. Before 1985 a lot of illegal people were let in. The VIDCOs said they would sort the problem out but they hadn't done so when we arrived. All settlers who have arrived after 1985 will have to return, I estimate that about 30 per cent of the immigrants came after 1985.

The same Resettlement Officer, however, admitted that perhaps government contributed to the continuous influx of people:

This is a problem, which is also caused by the government which keeps telling people that this area is empty. People do not know the right procedure.

Squatters occupying abandoned Commercial Farms on the Plateau had been loaded on trucks and dropped off in Dande; the same happened to a group of retrenched mine labourers from Mutorashanga.

Although migrants were believed to be causing problems for the project, most staff members considered them better farmers than the autochthons. A remark made by the Project Manager was quite representative of what I often heard from project staff:

They bring cattle with them, that is an advantage. They can cultivate the lands demarcated for agriculture by Agritex. The originals of the area often cultivate by hand, they cannot manage the new plots.

When I objected by making the point that the survey I had conducted (see Chapter Three) showed that in many cases the 'originals' were more productive, he nevertheless insisted:

Well ... yes.... some progress has been made, some have learnt from the immigrants. But most of the people here are illiterate, how can you expect them to know?

Both Dzingirai (1995) and Nyambara (2001) conclude that autochthonous Zambezi Valley dwellers suffer from a strong prejudicial bias, and have been considered backward people, as well as bad farmers. Both authors show in their articles that government officials in Gokwe - farther west of Dande, situated under Lake Kariba - were convinced that the migrants in the valley were more progressive farmers who introduced cash crop farming in the area. In Dande, many of those who consider themselves autochthons are also convinced that this is true, and the following statement made by my research assistant was echoed by many others who considered themselves autochthons:

The people down here were only used to cultivate sorghum, for their own consumption and to brew beer. Then the people from up there came down here, and that is when it changed. The people from up there were good farmers, they brought ploughs and started growing cash crops. Now the people from down here also try to grow cotton and maize, but they are not so good at it.

I thought it was particularly surprising that my research assistant should be making this remark, because allegedly his father was among the first who had started cultivating cotton in Dande. One day when I was visiting my assistant's homestead I saw his father sitting under a tree with an elderly man I had not seen before. The father introduced me to his old friend, Mr. Mutero. Mr. Mutero told me he was the one of the first Agricultural Demonstrators to work in the area. He said that he had introduced cotton to Mahuwe in 1967. This was after the establishment of the two TILCOR (Tribal Development Corporation)[41] estates at Mzarabani and Mushumbi Pools. Cotton was grown on those estates, and the Agricultural Demonstrators were urged to try to persuade local farmers to cultivate the crop. Mr. Mutero told me that it took some time before people responded:

> You see, at first people distrusted me, they thought I was CID [Central Intelligence Dept.]. Agricultural Demonstrators were not well known here in those days. But Mr. M. here was one of the first people who started growing cotton, right here in Mahuwe. That must have been [in] 1967.

Despite the fact that many 'autochthons' believed that the bias of project staff in favour of migrants was justified, they often complained to me about the attitude of project staff:

> They are always shifting us around, telling us we are farming where we should not. But do they know this area? No they do not. Look at the plots they have pegged, some have big rocks in them, others get waterlogged when it rains. These people from up there (Mugari wechikomo), they do not know this area. The sabhuku does.

The distinction between 'people from up there' and the 'people down here' (*Mugari wepasi* or *Mugari wemuno)* was quite important, it seemed. Wherever you are in Dande, you can always see the Escarpment. 'Up there' was where the power was, where people had more money, better farming skills. But 'up there' was also where wealth from Dande, that is, the money earned from the wildlife 'down here', the hunting concessions, went to. The term 'people from up there' (*Mugari wechikomo*, literally those who stay on the hill) could refer to various groups of people, depending on the context in which it was used. It might indicate recent migrants, as the citation about the better farming skills showed, or it could mean the government and party officials, or the RDC Councillors

---

[41] According to Derman (1995: 13), the Tribal Development Corporation (TILCOR) was established in the late 1960s as a belated response to African grievances in relation to the implementation of the NLHA, and in an effort to enhance rural development. During the war the TILCOR estates were closed. After Independence they were re-opened under the auspices of the Agricultural and Rural Development Authority (ARDA).

from Upper Guruve. Project staff, with the exception of the temporary hired hands who assisted in construction works, were all 'from up there'.

The distinction between 'down here' and 'up there' became politically acute in 1993/1994. After the Council elections and the amalgamation, for the first time a Ward Councillor from Lower Guruve was elected Chairman of the RDC. This boosted the morale of Lower Guruve Ward Councillors and in early 1994 a majority of them decided to establish the Lower Guruve Councillors Coordination Committee. This move was not appreciated by the government officials serving on the RDC, and neither by the Central Intelligence Officers attending RDC meetings. Soon after the establishment of the Committee, the Chief Executive Officer (CEO) addressed the 'problem' at an RDC meeting. According to one of the Councillors from Lower Guruve the CEO said that the formation of the Committee had 'sent waves of shock in many quarters'. The CEO apparently said the establishment of the Committee had been taken to be a secessionist act and an act of political dissent. The Ward Councillors defended themselves by saying that the Committee was established only to co-ordinate action towards donor organisations and was not meant to be a gesture against Upper Guruve or the government. They decided however to disband the committee[42].

According to many valley residents, waterlogged plots were not the only consequence of the project staff's unfamiliarity with Dande; this unfamiliarity was also believed to have caused the land shortage created by the project. As the person cited above argued:

> The sabhuku also knows his people. Some people are strong, they can cultivate many acres, so they will be allocated many acres by the sabhuku. Other people can just cultivate one or two acres. It is not good to give people twelve acres and then tell them that if they cannot manage they will lose their fields. With our traditional system everybody can have a field, some small ones, some bigger ones.

Whether the Mid-Zambezi Project contributed to or even created land shortage in Dande was an issue that divided project staff and valley residents, but as was shown above, project staff was not unanimous in their opinions and some staff members recognised the problems associated with the introduction of the Mid-Zambezi Project.

Another contested issue was that of riverine cultivation. Here project staff members seemed to agree with each other, whereas the Agritex personnel were more divided on the subject, as will be shown below.

The Project Manager and the Resettlement Officers I spoke with all condemned the practice. They all claimed it was causing erosion and siltation.

---

[42] The motion to do so was put forward by the new Ward Councillor for Ward 5 who was pro-Mid-Zambezi Project (see Chapter Six).

When they talked of people 'who were farming where they should not', they often meant people who were farming *mudimba*. When I asked them why they were so against riverine cultivation when the ban on the practice had been lifted for Commercial Farmers, they would either say that they were following the advice provided by Agritex, or would refer to the lack of education among the 'originals' of Dande. Reference was also made to the Natural Resource Management Board officer at Guruve who was claiming that the rivers in Dande were drying up because of riverine cultivation. My objections that following a series of droughts the Commercial Farmers on the Plateau had significantly increased the number of dams in the rivers that flow into the valley, and that, since farmers in Communal Areas did not have water rights, Commercial Farmers were not obliged to let water go through to the valley, did not seem to impress anyone[43].

The Veterinary Officer was also convinced that streambank cultivation and gardening in the riverbeds would cause serious damage. He volunteered this information when I was asking him where the best grazing areas were in his opinion:

> The best grazing areas are in the north. The areas close to the rivers are now designated as grazing areas. We have a lot of problems with people who have their gardens in the river in wintertime, that causes a lot of erosion. The people know that, but they do not want to listen. [*M.S.: But do cattle not cause damage to the riverine areas?*] No, not if you control them well. [*M.S.: But can you control them?*] Yes, people are not allowed more than two oxen, they know that, we have taught them.

Elsewhere it has been concluded that the Mid-Zambezi Project has not at all been successful in controlling the number of cattle. Why this particular Veterinary Officer was so adamant about being able to control cattle keeping when some of his colleagues freely admitted that control was almost impossible, I do not know.

The actual land-use planning exercise was conducted by the Agritex Planning Branch at the Provincial level. I have not been able to interview any of the staff members involved, but I did have access to the plan drawn up for Matsiwo A in 1993. This plan did not include the village of Mburuma, Fungai VIDCO, since the land-use planning for that VIDCO had been done when the village was still under Matsiwo B, and it was the only VIDCO in that area that

---

[43] One of the Commercial Farmers who had joined the RDC after the amalgamation of Rural and District Councils had been effectively implemented, confirmed my observation about the dams. He would later make an attempt to persuade farmers in Dande to form corporations so they would be able to apply for water rights. The exclusion of Communal Farmers from of water rights later led to an adaptation of the Water Rights Act. Derman and Ferguson (2000) have written extensively on the issue of water rights for Communal Farmers in Zimbabwe.

had been pegged before the Agritex Planning Branch proposal for Matsiwo A was published.

The report starts with a description of the current situation. Population figures are presented, based on data provided by VIDCO secretaries, but no mention is made of the fact that these clearly indicate that the population numbers mentioned in the overall project proposal - which are repeated in this document - could not have been accurate. The Agritex document mentions the influx of migrants that according to the document started only after Independence and involved 'thousands of people'. A striking passage calls to mind the debate about land-use planning to satisfy a need for order by planners: 'Settlement has not been planned, migrants have settled haphazardly. Fortunately enough for Matsiwo A, due to water shortages people have tended to settle in clusters along or close to the two perennial rivers, giving some degree of orderliness although there are always exceptions (Agritex Planning Branch 1993: 7)'. The stereotype of communal farmers who lay out their farms without paying attention to anything is repeated, whereas in Chapter Three of this book clear evidence is given that migrants did not settle haphazardly at all.

Other such stereotypical ideas about communal farmers, and particularly those in Dande, frequently recur in the document. Under 'crop management' the authors state that 'seedbed preparation by most of the farmers is by hand hoes because they do not have oxen to pull the plough (ibid.: 11)'. Yet, under the caption 'Livestock production' (ibid.: 12), a table shows that in only one of the villages in the Ward less than fifty head of cattle are kept. In Chapter Three cattle hiring and sharing for ploughing is described. The authors state that even cattle owners do not use manure to fertilise their fields (ibid.: 11). Cogently they state that they are surprised that farmers leave crop residues in the fields to be grazed by cattle (ibid.: 13), and yet, Scoones (1986) claims this is a commonly applied method of both feeding cattle and manuring fields at the same time. The authors claim, however, that farmers do not remove crop residues because they think it is too much work (Agritex Planning Branch 1993: 12).

Streambank cultivation is mentioned as well. In the document it is stated that, in the wake of agricultural activities near the riverbanks and on the riverbeds, siltation has been inevitable (ibid.: 7), but how siltation has been determined is not explained. The cutting down of trees is said to be done indiscriminately and replacement is not given a second thought. According to the authors trees are cut down for firewood and construction poles. McGregor has conducted a very detailed study of the use of the use of wood in Shurugwi and concluded that most households gather dead wood to use as firewood, and instead of cutting down trees for construction poles prefer lopping trees (McGregor 1991). Though I have not studied the use of wood systematically, I have observed both practices in Dande as well.

After the presentation of the agricultural production and a description of the infrastructure - which according to the report leaves much to be desired - the authors of the Agritex report move on to their vision for Matsiwo A Ward. Land

Capability analyses are presented for each village, and the number of acres of arable and non-arable land are calculated. Non-arable land is defined as areas that are closely dissected by streams, areas of extensive gravel outcrops and the verges of rivers and streams '(...) which are not recommended for cultivation for conservation purposes'. Derman (1995: 43) mentions that farmers in Matsiwo A Ward had extracted promises that riverine areas be included in the arable areas, but the definition of 'non-arable' land offered shows that those promises have not been kept. The Land Capability analyses apparently are used only to determine arable and non-arable land, since the recommendation concerning allocation of land and cropping patterns are standard for all villages and patterns which are in line with those endorsed for the other wards in Dande. In their review of local agricultural production the authors conclude that the plot holdings in Matsiwo A range in size from 0.5 hectares for small families with no draught power to 1.5-3 hectares for large families or those with cattle. Nevertheless, they opt for the familiar 4.5 hectares (about twelve acres) per household - although if Agritex cropping patterns are followed only 2.5 hectares will be under cultivation each season. Apart from the 4.5 hectares of arable land, each household will receive 0.5 hectares of residential stand, and 0.1 hectares of vegetable garden. The authors admit that if this allocation pattern is followed almost 300 households will not be able to receive a plot in those areas that they have classified as arable. 'The excess households will have to be settled elsewhere outside the ward or some of the land reserved for wildlife [could] be used for resettlement (Agritex Planning Branch 1993: 19)'. No mention is made of the fact that other wards suffer from the same problem, and that, apart from the wildlife area, there may be no other areas where 'excess households' can be settled.

A cropping pattern quite similar to the one proposed for the whole of the project area in the appraisal document (ADF 1986) is proposed for Matsiwo A Ward, and the document contains an appendix with the recommended crop rotations. Another appendix shows the exact amounts of inorganic fertiliser to be used, all standardised.

The literature cited at the end of the document on land classification includes the classic work by Young on Tropical Soils. The crop rotation schemes appear to be based on a 1976 Farm Management Handbook. The only 'concession' to the alternative policy literature mentioned by Keeley and Scoones (2000) is the report on Conservation Tillage. A policy of 'minimum tillage' is proposed, though in another part of the document deep ploughing every four years is advised (Agritex Planning Branch 1993: 22, 23)

Livestock, according to the authors, is to be restricted to 1.5 Livestock Units per household. These are to graze in paddocks, using rotational grazing schemes that Scoones (1996) has described as inefficient. The establishment and maintenance of the paddocks requires heavy work; fences need to be built - for Matsiwo A the authors propose fences ranging from 30 to 40 km, which require an enormous number of poles that need to be cut to hold up these fences and consequently foster 'indiscriminate' wood cutting. Cattle need to be watered with water either from boreholes within the fences or water carted in from outside. Apparently the establishment of the paddocks requires not only wood for the fences: 'No allocation of land for woodlots has been done because it is assumed that with controlled cutting of the indigenous tress from the grazing areas, the resources should last for years'. (Agritex Planning Branch 1993: 20).

All in all, the report shows the familiar biases towards communal farmers as well as the familiar standardised solutions to solve the problems in the Communal Areas. But what did the local Agritex extension officers think of the Mid-Zambezi Project and the valley residents?

The Agritex extension officers in the field were to some extent involved in the Mid-Zambezi Project. Some of them were employed as a result of the project, but they were nevertheless operating more or less independently from the project staff. The same applied to the Veterinary Officers. The actual demarcation of the plots mapped out by the Agritex Provincial Planning Branch was conducted by teams that were sent down from the Provincial offices, but local extension officers sometimes assisted them. The task of the local extension officers was to educate local farmers on 'proper' farming methods. They had to advise those who had moved to their new plots on the cultivation and rotation scheme that had been developed for the plots, and help enforce the ban on streambank cultivation by educating farmers on the supposed negative consequences of the practice and, if necessary, report offenders to the Natural Resource Management Board Officer in Guruve. Some of the opinions of Agritex officers have already been mentioned. Here I want to provide more details about their interactions with and opinions about local farmers.

Though hardly anybody had taken up the allocated plots in Matsiwo A, the Agritex officer in that area was already instructing people on the proper ways to cultivate their twelve-acre plots. He used the occasion of the distribution of a drought relief package, which included maize for consumption as well as fertiliser and seeds. I went to the distribution exercise. Worby (1998: 561) has described the Agritex field days and distribution exercises as '(...) minor theatres of bureaucratic power in which the authority of the state and the forms of modernity it embodies and demands is both performed, acknowledged, (...) and contested'. Worby argues that the seating arrangements at such meetings, as well as the way the farmers are addressed by Agritex officers, serve to assert the power of the state in the local arena. The field days are often organised at the homestead of a farmer who has been selected as an example by the local Agritex officer for his 'modern' farming methods and 'modern lifestyle' - that is, a 'modern' rectangular, preferably brick house, farming and household utensils that have been bought at the store, and the presence of European style furniture. According to Worby, the acknowledgement part of the theatre is constituted by the pride of the selected farmer and the way he displays his 'modern' possessions, but also by other farmers' acceptance of the procedures of the field days and the way they respond to the remarks by the Agritex officer.

Worby says that the references made to 'tradition' constitute contestations of
state power; in the cases he describes they take the form of the 'traditional'
dances often performed by schoolchildren on the field days. Why this is so, he
does not explain in great detail, but this theme will be explored in more detail
below as well as in Chapters Six and Seven of this book.

Worby's descriptions do fit the distribution exercise I witnessed in Masomo.
Below I have reconstructed the meeting on the basis of the notes I took. The
exercise did not take place on the farm of a selected 'modern' farmer, but at
another place symbolising 'modernity', the newly constructed primary school. It
was not an ordinary distribution exercise; normally these are held at the Cotton
and Grain Marketing Boards Depots at Mahuwe and Mzarabani. The seeds and
fertiliser were part of a drought relief project and the officer had managed to
persuade the drivers to deliver the seeds at the same time as the drought relief
food - which is normally distributed in the villages - at the school.

> The Agritex officer is seated on a chair under a shelter, which is erected close to the
> newly built primary school. The village headmen, and also the VIDCO chairmen
> and the teachers, are seated on wooden benches. The villagers coming to collect
> their seeds and fertiliser are all seated on the floor.

> The meeting started with one of the village headmen who clapped hands - a gesture
> of respect - to the ancestral spirit of the area, the *Mhondoro*, and asked the spirit for
> a fruitful meeting. The *Mhondoro* are referred to as the *varidzi ve nyika*, the owners
> of the land. All present, including the Agritex officer, followed suit in clapping
> hands for the spirit. The acknowledging aspect - but also a small contestational
> aspect - of the 'theatre' could be detected in the welcoming address by one of the
> VIDCO chairmen that followed the honouring of the spirit. He started with the usual
> slogans, which were repeated by all present: Forward with ZANU! Forward with
> development! Down with erosion! The VIDCO chairman thanked the Agritex
> officer for providing the community with seeds and fertiliser. He thanked him for
> bringing development to the area with his sound agricultural advice. He also said he
> was hoping that next time Agritex would provide tractors for transport, because the
> people who were not living at Masomo would have to pay a substantial sum of
> money for the transportation of their bags to commercial transport operators. The
> Agritex officer took the floor and thanked the villagers for coming. He asked them if
> they had heard about the Mid-Zambezi Project. He said the project would bring
> development to the area. It had brought the school they were gathered in now. At
> this the men uttered thanks and the women ululated. The Agritex officer then told
> people that they should move 'to the pegs'. If they cultivated the twelve acres
> properly, they would be able to harvest more than they did now. He told the people
> present that they would not get the seeds unless they were to take the fertiliser as
> well. At this there was some protest from the audience, as this meant that people
> would have to pay extra for the transportation of the fertiliser bags. But the Agritex
> extension officer maintained that were they to use the fertiliser they would be able to
> harvest about seventy bags per acre. Upon this the audience grew quiet again. The
> Agritex officer then continued to tell people to follow the cultivation plans for the
> twelve-acre plots. On their new plots they should cultivate five acres of cotton, two

acres of maize, one and a half acres of sorghum, one and a half acres of millet, and leave two acres fallow. They should adopt crop rotation. [This pattern differs a little from the pattern proposed by the Agritex Planning Branch (1993) but it conforms to the pattern proposed in the ADF (1986) appraisal report.] He told the people present that those not fit to utilise their plots would have to share a plot with their relatives. This led to lots of murmuring among the audience, and the Agritex officer had to shout to announce that the actual distribution was starting soon. The meeting ended with one of the VIDCO Chairmen shouting the party slogans, which were repeated by the audience.

The seating arrangement showed the higher status accorded to the representatives of the state who were present at the meeting: the Agritex officer, the VIDCO Chairmen. In Dande - and elsewhere in Zimbabwe - being seated on a higher level, on a stool, chair or bench, implies a higher status. Not only were the VIDCO Chairmen and Agritex officer given higher seats, this honour was also accorded to the teachers, perhaps because they were also state representatives - they are employed by the government - or because they were the bringers of 'modernity'. The slogans shouted at the beginning and end of the meeting asserted the identification of the state with the ruling party ZANU(PF).

Worby (1998) maintains that the references to 'tradition' should be interpreted as contestations of state power. He does not explain clearly why this is so, but in relation to the Mid-Zambezi Project it could be argued that the inhabitants have used references to 'tradition', more specifically, the *Mhondoro*, the owners of the land, to contest the government's ownership of the land (see Chapter Six and Seven). The *Mhondoro* were thanked before the party slogans were cited. The contestations were not limited to references to the *Mhondoro* only, people also showed their disagreement - as well as their acquiescence - but as a group, never as individuals. It is not easy for local farmers to contradict Agritex officers. 'Autochthonous' farmers especially often consider themselves less productive, less educated farmers. When I started the survey on agricultural production, I was often confronted with a certain awe of the Agritex officers. The Agritex officer who had organised the meeting at Masomo and was responsible for Mburuma had told farmers to practise crop rotation, and to separate the different crops neatly and to avoid intercropping. During the survey I would ask farmers if they grew vegetables in between the maize. About a third of the farmers told me they did not because the Agritex officer had advised against it. It did not mean, however, that they actually practised what he preached; in all of these cases I could see that pumpkins, cowpeas and other vegetables were mixed with the maize plants.

The extension officer was not always sure about his own advice either. After the meeting I asked him what his duties are:

I organise short courses, for example, how to castrate animals, how to plant tobacco, how to apply manure. The problem here is that most people are illiterate. In my home area [Mhondoro, on the Plateau], you give people a leaflet. Here you always have to be present. People here refuse to follow advice. (...) People also refuse to use fertiliser, but there is no need to use it now. People can continue another four to five years without fertiliser. Then they can also use the old crops, legumes, and cow dung and then plough deep. That is what I try to teach people, because I know they do not have money for fertiliser. Fertiliser can also be dangerous because the rains here are very unreliable. And fertiliser can be very damaging in a drought. (...) No, we do not take soil samples, it costs Z$10.- to have a sample analysed, and the people have to pay that themselves. Besides, most people do not have money to follow the advice about fertilising.

So the official line was that people had to use fertiliser, but in private the officer admitted that maybe fertiliser is not very suitable to an area like Dande, which experiences frequent spells of drought. The solution he provided to farmers who did not want to use inorganic fertiliser, namely to use legumes, seemed to come straight from Alvord's textbook, and actually some higher-ranking Agritex officials are now proposing a return to the use of legumes and manure instead of inorganic fertiliser (Keeley & Scoones 2000). Yet, the Agritex Planning Branch proposal for Matsiwo A still advocated the use of inorganic fertiliser.

I came across such inconsistencies in officials' stories fairly frequently. When I interviewed the District Agritex officer, and asked him about his opinion of the Mid-Zambezi Project, he began by defending it:

The people in Dande are not good farmers. They should be forced to use the land efficiently. There are too many people coming into Dande, and if we don't teach them the proper use of the land, we will have serious environmental problems. The rivers are drying up already.

When I asked him about one of the goals of the project, to enforce the ban on riverine cultivation, he proved hesitant:

I think in the valley it is okay, the valley bottom is quite flat, the rivers do not run so fast. But I am afraid I cannot say that at the level of the Province. But do not worry, I think scientists will soon develop a model for streambank cultivation, then we can admit freely there is no problem. In Chitsungo the Agritex extension officer is allowing people to use the streambanks to cultivate snuff tobacco, bhande. The tobacco is bought by a firm in Harare, and the officer is encouraging people because it is a good way to make money. The tobacco is harvested in June, when the rivers are dry, so there is little chance of siltation.

Unfortunately, neither local people's knowledge concerning riverine cultivation nor the officer's own experiences with it were deemed valid enough evidence to lift the ban, they had to wait for a scientist to prove what people in Dande have known for a long time.

The contradictions between the different personnel involved in the implementation of the Mid-Zambezi Project, or even between the different statements by one and the same person, were perhaps not so surprising given the environment in which the staff members were working. They witnessed people continuing their own practices, felt their resistance. And though they were not from the same area, they often came from similar background, all having a *musha* in some Communal Area.

The implementation of the Mid-Zambezi Project was a difficult task. The Project Manager had to oversee the different activities in a project area that covered an enormous geographical area where roads were few and often in bad condition - despite improvements because of the project itself. He had to co-ordinate work with other ministerial departments for the execution of certain tasks - for example road construction. But the most difficult part of his and his staff's job was dealing with a large population that was not convinced of the goals of the project. Convincing people to move to their new plots when they did not want to and when no provisions had been made for transport, proved to be much more of a problem than the FAO consultants who had written the project document had foreseen. Then there were also the local authorities to deal with.

In Chapter Four I have already mentioned that after pressure exerted by the (R)DC some of the regulations governing the criteria for allocation had to be changed. The Project Manager was regularly summoned to the (R)DC meetings to discuss problems arising from the implementation of the project. There he was confronted with a Senior Executive Officer (SEO) - who became the Chief Executive Officer after the amalgamation of the Rural and District Councils - who in principle was sympathetic to the project, convinced by the 'land degradation narrative' underlying it, but who on some issues supported the Ward Councillors serving on the (R)DC. In successive interviews with the SEO/CEO, his attitude seemed to grow progressively negative towards the project, though he still seemed to support the general ethos behind the Mid-Zambezi Project. He may have been aware that my colleague researcher at CASS and I did not support the project, as we had asked him to allow us to develop an alternative land-use plan working in conjunction with the population in the area beyond Mzarabani, where the 'Mid-Zambezi Project Phase II' (see previous chapter and below) was planned. This awareness may have influenced the way he discussed the project with us. In one of the first interviews I had with the SEO upon my return in 1992, he was still convinced that the implementation of the Mid-Zambezi Project was absolutely necessary:

I think it is [for] the best, people have to be re-organised. We are afraid of degradation. There is a lot of bush [being] cleared, we have got to manage it. Not all the soil is good. People from outside may not know the soil.

About a year later, when the project was extended for another three years, his views were more negative:

The Mid-Zambezi Project has received money to continue for three more years. I do not think it is enough, there are so many problems. The biggest problem is that they use a top-down approach. The people are not involved, they have not been asked for their advice. If you say your project is for the people, then you will have to ask them first if they want it.

There are many conflicts over land, there are more and more people moving into Dande, from Masvingo and other areas. (...) Then there are also problems with water. In fact, you should find water before demarcating the residential stands. The Mid-Zambezi Project causes a lot of conflicts.

More land-use plans were being developed for the Zambezi Valley - land-use planning was the 'in' thing in the donor community - including the Mid-Zambezi Valley Land Use Programme, which was often referred to as 'Mid-Zambezi Project Phase II'. I had heard that some of the Ward Councillors had proposed an evaluation of the Mid-Zambezi Project before 'Phase II' was embarked upon. When I asked the SEO about this he said:

Yes, we have proposed an evaluation. But nothing has been done. We do not know whether the donor community will do the evaluation or the government, after all, this is a government project. But then the government would be evaluating the government. [*M.S.: What about an independent outsider?*] There is no money for that, and then the reports will end up in some drawer, we never see those reports. [*M.S.: What if the council was to demand an evaluation?*] Yes, but we do not have the money. Besides, this project is implemented under the authority of the Province, of Mashonaland Central. Any complaints should be reported to the Province.

[*M.S.: but what about the preparation of Phase II?*] Maybe there are no funds for an evaluation. The consultants who wrote the report for Phase II were not interested in Phase I.

Yet, in 1995, after the project staff had withdrawn from Dande, the former SEO, who by then had become the Chief Executive Officer, still thought land-use planning was the solution for Dande:

Mr. M. [Project Manager] has been asked to retire[44]. DERUDE has been dismantled and integrated into DDF. The project will continue. I have asked for the development of new land-use planning, because a lot people still do not have a twelve-acre plot or a residential stand. Those who have been allocated plots and stands have not yet taken these up. The Councillors should urge them to do so.

---

[44] The Project Manager was one of those staff members from 'up there' who 'went local'. He had acquired a twelve-acre-plot in Dande where he settled permanently after his retirement, accompanied by his new wife, who was from Dande.

He recognised the fact that many residents had been left officially landless, and thought these should be accommodated, but not without a 'proper land-use plan'.

Relations between the (R)DC and project staff were not running smoothly. The SEO and the Councillors regularly complained that they were not involved in decision-making about the project and that the Project Manager often did not show up when he was invited to attend Council meetings. The Project Manager, in his turn, complained that he was often invited at the last moment, and that the Councillors did nothing but complain about the lack of plots and did not do enough to encourage people to move to their new plots.

Some attempts were made to improve relations and provide better information. In 1993, shortly after the amalgamation of the Rural and District Councils and the ensuing re-drawing of Ward boundaries, a number of new Ward Councillors appeared in the RDC. The Project Manager organised a course on Resettlement Management for a selection of the new Councillors at the government training school in Domboshawa - the same school where Alvord introduced his curriculum for agriculture demonstrators in the 1920s, and where the Project Manager and Resettlement Officers had been trained. Judging from the report drawn up by one of the Resettlement Officers from Dande, the course offered was the standard programme on resettlement schemes on former Commercial Farms. No adaptations were made to account for the fact that this time the students were Councillors and not Resettlement Officers, or for the fact that the Mid-Zambezi Project was in fact a land reform and villagisation project forced upon extant communities with existing local authorities, and was not dealing with communities that were resettled on former Commercial Farms and had to be built up from scratch. Even the criteria for selecting plot-holders were not adapted and the report still mentions the Agritex Farmer's Certificate that would be needed, which in fact was not required in Dande. Strangely enough, the new Ward Councillor for the old Matsiwo A Ward, now Ward 5, the Ward that proved to be most difficult to resettle, was not invited for the course, despite the fact that he was one of the few pro-Mid-Zambezi Project Councillors (see next chapter).

A Mid-Zambezi Project Co-ordinating Committee had been set up in 1993. The committee consisted of the Ward Councillors whose Wards were in the process of being re-organised, the Resettlement Officers, Agritex extension officers, Veterinary officers, representatives of the government officials serving on the RDC and other government representatives including police officers. According to the participants I interviewed, the main problems discussed were: the lack of boreholes that the Councillors claimed prevented people from moving to the new residential stands; the shortage of plots; plots that the Councillors said were pegged in areas unsuitable for cultivation - this time the term 'unsuitable' was not used to indicate the riverine areas but areas still rich in wildlife; areas in which there were many depressions that would become waterlogged or were littered with rocky patches, and so forth. The problems with Matsiwo A/Ward 5 also regularly featured on the agenda. Shortly after the election of new Ward Councillors in 1993 the Committee met regularly but, as very little follow-up was given to the meetings, they became more and more irregular.

The Resettlement Officers also had to deal with local authorities in their day-to-day activities. Initially they were the ones responsible for registering and selecting applicants for a twelve-acre plot, and plot allocating, but this turned out to be unfeasible without some help from local authorities. The (R)DC exerted pressure on the Project Manager to involve the Ward Councillors. In the end the following procedure was decided upon. In each VIDCO, residents wanting to qualify for a plot would have to register with the VIDCO secretary. Those registering would have to provide details about the composition of their households, sources of income, and the number on the registration certificate of the head of the household. The VIDCO secretaries would then hand these lists to the Ward Councillors. The Ward Councillors were supposed to discuss the selection and allocation with the Resettlement Officers. The Ward Councillors would then report back to the VIDCOs.

Almost invariably the lists handed over to the Resettlement Officers contained more applicants than there were plots. Ward Councillors and VIDCO secretaries alike registered applicants who did not officially qualify for a plot. They registered divorced women as widows, left out information on sources of income, or advised households to put another person forward as head of the household if this person did have the right district number on his registration certificate. In some cases they also excluded people from registering. A number of VIDCO secretaries discouraged the registration of former farm labourers originally from Mozambique or Malawi, even if they had the Zimbabwean citizenship. There was an enormous pressure on Ward Councillors to register people for a plot. Every day they would have people coming to their homesteads to register for a plot, refusing to leave until their details had been recorded. Even in areas where all the plots had been allocated, people still asked to be registered, especially young couples that had married after the allocation had taken place. As a result the Ward Councillors continued to pressure the SEO of the (R)DC to ask the Project Manager for the pegging of more plots.

In Neshangwe and Chitsungo Wards where conflicts over plots were rife, the Provincial Administrator and Provincial Governor were called in by the Ward Councillors to address the population about the Mid-Zambezi Project. The Administrator and Governor then appointed a group to carry out a verification exercise into plot allocation in order to check on the rumours that 'aliens' were receiving plots at the expense of 'autochthonous' farmers. This exercise, which took place from December 1991 until May 1993, was carried out the (R)DC Chairman, the (R)DC Works and Planning Committee Chairman, Chief Chitsungo, Provincial ZANU(PF) party leaders, the Resettlement Officers, Agritex Officers and the local Police. Plot holders had to bring their national registration certificates to the task force, who would compare the details with the registration books of the Resettlement Officers and the VIDCO Chairmen. Though the exercise had been set up in response to complaints from local farmers, the result was that it exposed the bending of the rules in which the VIDCO Chairmen and Councillors had been engaged on their behalf, designed to correct rules that locally were considered unfair.

Yet, like project staff, the Councillors themselves were not consistent in their reactions to the Mid-Zambezi Project either. Though they complained many times in Council meetings about the imminent landlessness of such a large part of their constituency, gradually they adopted the language of the project. They probably could not ask for the project to be halted, but could do no more than request adaptations in line with the terms used by the projects. In short, they asked for the pegging of more plots. At times they were subjected to pressure from the government officials on the (R)DC - the SEO and District Administrator. Importantly, it must be noted that Council meetings were often attended by CIO (Central Intelligence Office) Officers who were likely to interpret critique on the Mid-Zambezi Project as critique on the government[45]. Councillors themselves wavered in their opinions on riverine cultivation. Many practise it themselves, but condemned the practice in Council meetings. One Ward Councillor who had often explained to me the ins-and-outs of *mudimba* cultivation and why it was not harmful for the environment, became a member of the Natural Resources Committee of the (R)DC. He was invited to take a flight over the District with the Natural Resource Management Board Officer. This Officer pointed to the dry riverbeds and the many riverine fields, maintaining there was a connection between the two phenomena. When I saw the Councillor shortly after the flight, he said he now was convinced that riverine cultivation was a bad practice. I asked him if they also had flown over all the new dams on the Commercial Farms in the District. 'Do you think that is the cause of the drying up of the rivers here? I don't know, the NRMB Officer says it is because of the mudimba. Why would he lie? Besides, he is an expert, he has learnt for this'. The (R)DC Natural Resource Committee of which the Ward Councillor was a member proposed some new by-laws in relation to the MZRD:

> That any person found allocating land in grazing areas or an area not demarcated for settlement, shall be guilty of an offence and shall be charged a fine to be determined by the Zimbabwe Republic Police.

> That any person found to have settled in a grazing area or an area not earmarked for settlement, shall be guilty of an offence and shall be liable to pay a fine as recommended by the Zimbabwe Republic Police.

---

[45] The presence of CIO officers during Council meetings is not just based on 'hearsay'. A Council member once showed me the official minutes of some Council meeting, and the CIO presence was mentioned openly.

This could be interpreted as a first step towards the development of a policy to the evict 'squatters' - as project staff had begun to call those that not had been allocated a twelve-acre plot - which the Project Managers was urging the (R)DC to do.

The Resettlement Officers had been trained to work in areas where new communities had to be formed on former Commercial Farms, in other words to work in areas where no local authorities were functioning until they arrived. In Dande they were confronted with existing local government structures, both the structures set up by the government and 'traditional' structures. Relations with the (R)DC and individual Councillors were not without problems. Before the extension of the Mid-Zambezi Project 'traditional' authorities were not involved in the project. Many Resettlement Officers, though, held them accountable for the problem of continued in-migration. After the extension of the project a change in strategy was decided upon. Especially in Matsiwo A/Ward 5 the implementation of the project had proved to be extremely difficult and the Project Manager decided to involve the chief. His idea was that if the chief and his headmen could be persuaded to accept the Mid-Zambezi Project, their subjects would follow. As will be shown in the next chapters, this assumption turned out to be highly problematic. Even before the new strategy was tried out, some of the Resettlement Officers expressed doubts about the influence 'traditional' leaders held over their subjects. As one Resettlement Officer remarked in 1988:

> People are still moving into the valley. They are allowed to come by the headman. The ROs [Resettlement Officers] asked for a stop. Before 1985 a lot of illegal people were let in. The VIDCOs said they would sort the problem out but they hadn't done so when we arrived. There is a power struggle going on between the headmen, who used to allocate land, and the Councillors.

Another Resettlement Officer said:

> People go to the person who will do what they want. Sometimes they will ask the chief, if he does not listen, they go to the Councillor.

These opinions expressed by his subordinates should have made the Project Manager think twice about embarking upon his new strategy. However, he went ahead, unwittingly enhancing the possibilities for the opponents of project to resist it.

Concluding remarks

In this chapter I have described the development of the 'land degradation narrative' in the context of colonial, discriminating policies concerning access to land for African farmers. As the White agricultural sector expanded more and more African farmers were moved to the Reserves. When agricultural production in the Reserves declined the solution was sought in educating African farmers to 'properly' use the land and adopt 'modern' farming techniques, rather than in giving them access to more land.

Soon after Independence the new government's land policy moved away from redistributing land to promoting land reforms within the Communal Areas, the former Reserves. Hence, the political problem of differential access to land was redefined as an environmental problem caused by traditional farming methods, requiring technical solutions and the education of local farmers. In this chapter I have presented several explanations for the continued importance of pre-Independence explanations and solutions to the problems of the Communal Areas. Some authors have stressed the need for the new post-Independence government to bring remote rural areas under its control (Robins 1994; Munro 1998). Moyo (1995) argues that despite its Marxist orientation the government wanted to protect large-scale commercial farming. Others have pointed at the interactions between governmental departments, scientific institutions and NGOs (Keeley & Scoones 2000). They have described how many colonial policies were based on research conducted in the temperate zones of Europe, the United States and South Africa. Furthermore, this research was on production aims and a compartmentalisation of farming activities that did not fit with agricultural strategies employed by most African farmers. The Agritex extension officers are expected to implement the resulting recommendations. Keeley and Scoones (ibid.), however, warn against viewing policy development and practice as a neat, linear process and call attention to attempts to challenge totalising discourses.

In the second part of the chapter I have described the land reform policy in practice. I have looked at the attitudes of Mid-Zambezi Project staff as well as of the farmers who were subjected to the internal land reforms towards the project. Project personnel had to work with the approach that followed from the 'land degradation narrative'. Many of them seemed to believe firmly in this narrative, arguing that the Mid-Zambezi Project was needed since many farmers were 'farming where they should not'. Yet, confronted with challenges from their 'clients', who resisted their attempts to make them conform to the regulations of the projects, some changed their minds, contradicting themselves every now and then. This is an indication of the relevance of the cautionary remarks made by Keeley and Scoones (2000) as well as by Bate (1997) and Martin (1998) against assuming that dominant organisational narratives are unquestioningly accepted by all members of the organisation. Some staff members seemed to understand that the lack of prior consultation was problematic. Others admitted that the project created a problem of landlessness, though they also accused the village headmen of contributing to that problem by continuing to accept migrants into their villages. A number of Agritex officers doubted the validity of the ban on riverine cultivation. Still, many were convinced that the farmers in Dande were not very successful and needed to change.

Internal contradictions could be detected not only in the opinions of project staff members, but also among those subjected to the Mid-Zambezi Project, including Ward Councillors. Some aspects of the 'land degradation narrative' seemed to have been accepted by local farmers, particularly the idea that autochthonous people were not such competent cultivators. Ward Councillors - as well as government officials sitting on the (R)DC - seemed to fluctuate between accepting the ideas underlying the project and resisting its consequences. During Council meetings they seemed to adopt the language of the project, but one should not forget the pressure they were under to do so.

Despite these internal doubts, a powerful counter-narrative was developed by a large part of the population of Dande, and spirit mediums were involved in the staging of it. This will be the subject of the next two chapters.

6

Mhondoro mediums and the Mid-Zambezi Rural Development Project

Introduction

When the funding for the three-year extension of the Mid-Zambezi Project was granted in 1992, the Project Manager decided on a new approach to persuade the population of Matsiwo A Ward to give up its resistance against the project[46]. He decided to involve the hitherto ignored 'traditional' authorities, and enlist their help to convince their subjects to accept the Mid-Zambezi Project. The first step he took was to ask Chief Matsiwo for his permission to implement the project in the Ward that was part of his chiefdom. The chief, who at first refused to become involved on the grounds that he had never been asked to give permission for the re-organisation of the other Ward in his chiefdom, Matsiwo B, referred the Project Manager to the mediums of the royal ancestral spirits, the Mhondoro. As far as he was concerned, these were the real owners of the land. This change in strategy thus helped open up the 'front' stage to the mediums, who were the main actors in the staging of the counter-narrative to the 'land degradation narrative' underlying the Mid-Zambezi Project. This counter-narrative challenged government control over land. It stressed ancient ties with the land through the ancestors, legitimising the role of chiefs and headmen in

---

[46] After the amalgamation of the Rural and District Councils in 1993, the boundaries of the Wards were redrawn. Mburuma, where the population had also resisted the project and where I was staying, then became part of Matsiwo A Ward. Matsiwo A Ward was renamed Ward 5, but in this book I will continue to refer to the area as Matsiwo A.

the allocation of land. Such narratives of ancestral belonging are not unique to Dande; elsewhere in Zimbabwe, similar narratives are used to justify claims to land (Hammar 1998: 22). They are a common theme in literature on ethnicity and nationalism (see Anderson 1985; Harries 1989; Marks 1989). The relation between religion and claims to land has been discussed in 'Guardians of the Land', edited by Schoffeleers (1978) and 'Regional Cults', edited by Werbner (1977).

The counter-narrative revealed a fairly consistent story underpinning claims of local authority over land; the way it was acted out, however, did not. The drama that unfolded not only teaches us about the way in which the people of Dande resisted the Mid-Zambezi Project, it is similarly an exposition about the functioning of the Mhondoro cult.

It is clear from the existing body of literature on the Mhondoro cult in Zimbabwe that this cult has been involved in all the major upheavals that have occurred since the end of the nineteenth century. A good deal of attention has been given to the role of the cult in both armed struggles against the white settlers' regime (e.g. Ranger 1985; Lan 1985, see also Chapter Two). This suggests that the cult, far from being inwardly directed, does respond to socio-political challenges. However, after observing the involvement of the Mhondoro mediums in the struggle against the Mid-Zambezi Project, I found something lacking in most studies. Many authors attribute an active role to the mediums of the cult: they are depicted as initiating and directing resistance. The behaviour of adherents is often neglected. Did they unquestioningly and unanimously follow the mediums? Lately, some authors have raised doubts about the leading role of the Mhondoro mediums and the implicated passive role of the adepts of the cult (e.g. Beach 1986; Bourdillon 1987b). I would like to argue that we might clarify our thoughts on the role of the Mhondoro cult by distinguishing the mediums, their inner circle of ritual assistants, and the wider audience which actively responds to a medium's pronouncements.

My observations suggest that the Mhondoro cult serves as an important platform for discussions concerning socio-economic relations and political developments. The community of followers of the cult constitutes a heterogeneous group, at times holding widely different economic interests and political affinities. Each interest group may be seeking support from the Mhondoro cult. Not only do spirit mediums strive to have their messages accepted as real expressions of the Mhondoro spirits; the followers of the cult also wish to see their interests reflected in the mediums' pronouncements. The mediums' statements are subject to discussion and negotiation. This results in a process of alternate questioning and preserving of the mediums' reputation.

This chapter describes the role of mediums of Mhondoro spirits in shaping and staging the counter-narrative of local authority over land, looking at how their pronouncements were shaped by reactions from the audience. I will analyse the different themes in the narrative and at the same time hope to contribute to a more balanced view concerning the role of the Mhondoro cult, taking into account the influence of an active following. In the case described in this chapter, the interaction between mediums and their adherents is quite visible. One of the mediums involved openly consulted his following on their opinion of the Mid-Zambezi Project. The medium became a spokesman for those opposing the project in their confrontation with the project management. At a later stage, when the opponents of the project feared that the medium was withdrawing from the debate, they appeared to resort to indirect means like the circulation of rumours to force the medium to continue his overt resistance. Rumours focused on the reputation of the medium, casting aspersions on his authenticity. Another medium saw her reputation damaged, seemingly beyond repair, when she could not provide her followers with a personal and clear statement about the project. The case material presented also shows how the State attempted to appropriate the cult in the process.

But before I move on to describe the involvement of the Mhondoro mediums in the resistance against the Mid-Zambezi Project, I will first present a more general description of the Mhondoro cult and the actors involved.

The Mhondoro Cult in Dande

March 1993, Mburuma village. The crops in the field have started to wither after a dry spell of about three weeks. If it will not rain soon, the harvest will fail. In the village a ceremony is organised in honour of a deceased relative. Many people attend the ceremony. I ask those present whether they think it will rain again soon.

> Elder: We have a problem with rain. Long back ago we had this ritual. The medium of the Mhondoro of this area would make snuff tobacco, chitekwe. This he would take to Nehanda, who would take it to Musuma. Then Musuma would know that this chitekwe is for rain and then usually it would rain.

> Another elder: He thinks that the cause of the drought is that some Mhondoro are disappointed, especially Nehanda and Musuma. After the death of their former mediums they did no longer posses anyone. The other reason may be the Mid-Zambezi Project, maybe they are disappointed about the project.

> Young man: There are some people who pretend to be Mhondoro mediums. They ask for money so they can make rain. But if you give money, they fail to make rain. Then you go to a real Mhondoro medium, but he will tell you to go to the spirit medium of your area. In the old days you could see many mediums performing miracles. There was one who could hang upside down from a tree for days, others could see into the future. These days, you do not see any medium performing miracles.

> M.S.: Does the power of the spirit depend on the power of the medium?

Second elder: Yes.

First elder: No.

Another young man: Other Mhondoro are angry because some Mhondoro mediums were given money by the government. For example, Chidyamauyu was given a house and money which the medium banked for himself. Chiwawa did not get anything. Maybe the Mhondoro are angry about that.

First elder: In the old days, (...) we did not have these problems, we always had enough rain. The problems started soon after Independence. Maybe these days the people do not show enough respect to the Mhondoro anymore.

Third elder: Maybe the Mhondoro cannot make rain after all. A white farmer told me that it is a natural process.

First young man: But some white farmers also donate money and black cloth to Mhondoro mediums to make rain.

The conversation above is illustrative of many of the discussions I overheard or participated in when I was in Dande. For me, these discussions were sometimes very confusing.

I had come to Dande to study the conflicts over land resulting from the introduction of the Mid-Zambezi Project. While doing fieldwork, I was constantly confronted with the cult of the Mhondoro. People referred me to the Mhondoro, telling me that they were the 'real owners of the land' (varidzi vepasi). Although from the start, I had planned to devote some attention to the role of the Mhondoro cult, I soon found myself drawn into this cult deeper and deeper. When I visited David Lan, the author of 'Guns and Rain' (1985), he told me a similar story. Initially, he had not set out either to study the Mhondoro cult, but the tales of his interlocutors had led him to this topic so often that it in the end the cult became the focus of his book. Paradoxically, as much as I was pulled towards this cult, I was also often left with doubts about the importance of the cult. The Mhondoro were one of the main topics that came up in daily conversation. Many discussions of new developments and problems invoked reflections about what the Mhondoro would think of it all. At the same time, there were constant complaints about 'those mediums who are not what they used to be'. People who informed me about the 'rules of the Mhondoro' were sometimes seen to be violating these rules themselves. Many times I had the impression that the influence of the cult was waning, only to reject that idea again later when the cult became involved in some important issues.

The more I looked into the cult, the more complex the picture became. Though the Mhondoro spirits remained the focal point of many discussions, the organisation of the Mhondoro cult as well as the relations between Mhondoro mediums and the adherents of the cult were subject to many changes and fluctuations. What I saw was an arena in which many individuals and groups, all with different economic interests, political affinities and religious convictions, were active. They discussed new developments and socio-political issues, argued, competed and co-operated. Different actors played different roles at different times.

How can I begin to explain the chaos I encountered? Let me commence by presenting some of the 'cultic agreements', though these are also partly subjected to negotiation. Despite this flexibility, there are some basic points of understanding through which the cult mediums and supplicants can communicate with one another.

Owners of the land

A central feature of the religious beliefs of the people in Dande, indeed of most chi-Shona-speaking people, is the belief in the importance of the dead for the living. As Daneel (1987:191) states: '(...) religious mentality thrives upon the concern for continuing meaningful ties between the dead and the living (...)'. All women and men are expected to look after their families as best as they can. After their death, this concern for their relatives does not cease. The dead are believed to transform into ancestral spirits, or midzimu (singl. mudzimu, see Bourdillon 1987; Lan 1985). Upon the death of a person, it is believed that the spirit leaves the body and takes the form of mweya, breath or air. Although they have no material form, they are believed to have sensory experiences and emotions. They are still concerned about the welfare of their relatives, and will try and protect them from illness and misfortune. Midzimu will only harm a descendant if they wish to make clear that they want to possess this descendant. Through their human medium they will warn their relations of dangers threatening to harm them or they will complain that they are being forgotten and ask for beer to be brewed for them.

A special category of more powerful spirits is that of the Mhondoro (plural and singular). Mhondoro are the spirits of royal ancestors, the great rulers of the past. When a chief dies, it is believed that his spirit moves to the bush where it enters the body of a lion (see Lan 1985), hence the name Mhondoro, which means lion[47].

The Mhondoro are believed to continue to look after the territories they once ruled when they were still alive. In Dande, these areas have relatively clear-cut - but not necessarily fixed - boundaries which are known to most inhabitants. Garbett introduced the term 'spirit provinces' to refer to these areas (1969;

---

[47] Mhondoro are known among the majority of chi-Shona-speaking people (see Fry 1976, Bourdillon 1982), but I will deal specifically with beliefs concerning Mhondoro as they can be found in Dande.

1977). The size of a spirit province varies. As I already described in Chapter Three, some spirit provinces encompass only a few villages, while others may extend into different chiefdoms. Every tract of land in Dande belongs to one of the Mhondoro. The land and all other natural resources in a spirit province ultimately belong to the Mhondoro of that province[48].

Most Mhondoro dealt with in this book have little significance outside Dande. There are, however, a few exceptions. The Mhondoro Nehanda, Kaguvi and Chaminuka have acquired quite a reputation nation-wide. Beach has tried to trace the rise in significance of these, what he calls, super-Mhondoro who stand '(...) in rank between the ordinary dynastic mhondoro and the high-god [Mwari]' (1980: 314). Beach claims that the first of the super-Mhondoro, called Nehanda, became prominent around the end of the eighteenth century. The Mhondoro Chaminuka and Kaguvi only became famous by the end of the nineteenth century. It is not quite clear why the figure of Nehanda acquired such importance at the end of the eighteenth century, but most of her present-day reverence has its roots in the period of the first chimurenga (1896-7) when Chaminuka and Kaguvi also acquired fame.

Each Mhondoro has a place in a genealogy and is part of a sort of conceptual hierarchy (Garbett 1969; 1977). In Dande it is possible to discern two main lines or lineages of Mhondoro: the lineage which is headed by Bangomwe representing the 'autochthonous' ancestors, and a lineage representing fifteenth century invaders of Dande headed by Mutota (see Chapter Two).

In contradiction to most authors who have dealt with Mhondoro, I refer to the whole set of beliefs and practices concerning Mhondoro as the Mhondoro cult, instead of referring to separate cults centred on a specific Mhondoro (e.g. the cult of Mutota, the cult of Bangomwe). The description of small separate religious cults is part of the 'tradition' within religious anthropology, which presents 'traditional religion' in Africa as very localised and 'small' (see Fardon 1990). Garbett (1977) has attempted to group several cults together under two different banners; he distinguishes autochthonous cults from so-called invader cults. Autochthonous cults focus on the Mhondoro Bangomwe and his offspring. The invader cults centre on Mutota and his offspring, who are believed to represent the fifteenth century Karanga invaders of Dande. I believe that in some instances this distinction between autochthonous and invader Mhondoro is important for some of the adherents. Yet, the people I talked to treated the Mhondoro cult as one cult. All Mhondoro fall into the same category of spirits. The fact that each Mhondoro has his or her own territory does not

---

[48] Ultimate dominion over all the country is in the hands of *Mwari*, the high god (see Bourdillon 1987: 69-70). In the Matobos, where one finds shrines dedicated to *Mwari*, it is *Mwari* who is approached to provide rain and soil fertility. However, to most people in Dande the high god is too remote from the concerns of men to be closely associated with the day-to-day management of the land (ibid.: 70).

mean that they are independent, that there are no connections with other Mhondoro. In fact, the reverse is true, all Mhondoro in Dande are believed to be either related to Bangomwe or to Mutota. Complicated affinal relations are constructed even between the autochthonous and invader Mhondoro. The relations between the Mhondoro, however, are not immutable (see Garbett 1992; see also Lan 1985: 84-91). The links between the two 'lineages' of Mhondoro as well as the place of specific Mhondoro within these 'lineages' are perceived and depicted differently depending on the political situation at a given time, and the ranking of the Mhondoro's mediums by adherents of the cult, as I will show below.

Adherents are not tied solely to the specific Mhondoro in whose territory they live and farm. Certain rituals are indeed dedicated to the Mhondoro of the spirit province in which they live. However, when problems have to be dealt with and the Mhondoro of the spirit province does not posses a medium (or the medium is not trusted), adherents will approach a medium in another spirit province for advice. Mediums of different Mhondoro often communicate with one another, especially when major problems have to be dealt with. Pertinently, the mediums are related to each other and connected through flows of tribute in association with rain making ceremonies (see also Garbett 1977).

Collective problems and possibilities for social commentaries

The Mhondoro cult is mainly concerned with rain and fertility. Each year, two rituals are conducted for the Mhondoro. These are huruva (or mbudzirume or kamutimuti) and tsopero (or doro retsepero)[49]. The huruva ritual is conducted before the onset of the rainy season. Its purpose is to beg the Mhondoro for rain and for protection of the crops. After an abundant harvest, the ritual of tsopero will be held to thank the Mhondoro. Each village, or cluster of villages, has its own shrine (dendemaro) dedicated to the Mhondoro of the spirit province, at which the rituals are conducted. The Mhondoro mediums need not be present at all the rituals that are organised in their province. These will be conducted by the mutape, the assistant of the medium, who in most cases is also the village headman (see below). Each village, or cluster of villages, which has a shrine will have a ritual assistant resident there, even if the Mhondoro of the spirit province has no medium.

In general a Mhondoro medium is concerned with the collective problems of the community living in his or her spirit province, whereas a n'anga, or healer, is solely concerned with the problems of an individual and his or her immediate

---

[49] Mbudzirume comes from mwedzi mwembudzi, the month of the goats, the month during which the ritual will be conducted. Huruva means dust. The ritual is conducted in order to calm the winds, let the dust settle and the rains fall.

family. Mhondoro mediums are consulted by village elders in times of drought, when locusts or other plagues threaten crops, and in case of epidemic diseases threatening large groups of people. In practice, however, the distinction between n'anga and Mhondoro mediums is not as rigid as it would seem at first sight. People claiming descent from the Mhondoro may also consult the Mhondoro's medium when suffering from individual or family problems. Some Mhondoro mediums may acquire such a good reputation that they also attract individuals and families living outside of their spirit province who consult them for more personal afflictions.

Despite the broad scope of their powers, collective community problems are the major concern of the Mhondoro mediums. The Mhondoro spirits are supposed to provide rain and soil fertility. However, they are believed to only do so when the inhabitants of their territories follow their rules. Schoffeleers (1978) refers to this as 'management of nature through the management of society'. Many of the Mhondoro's 'rules' concern the moral values of the community; incest, murder and theft are believed to provoke droughts. Other rules concern the observance of 'traditional' resting days (chisi), respect for sacred places, and a·long list of other such structures. When village elders consult a Mhondoro medium for an explanation of a drought, they are usually told that individuals committing offences against the Mhondoro's rules are responsible. Today, in most cases, no actual perpetrators are identified.

The explanation of climatological abnormalities also offers possibilities for Mhondoro mediums to deliver social commentaries. Natural disasters can be, and often are, attributed to social and political problems. The introduction of new cash crops, which may upset existing differentiation patterns, or abuse of authority by local leadership can be identified by Mhondoro mediums as potential causes of natural disasters. Nor do Mhondoro mediums confine their judgement to local situations. For example, the nation-wide drought of 1992 was attributed by most Mhondoro mediums in Dande to the Zimbabwean government failing to fulfil the promises made during the struggle for Independence. This expansion of scope may partly have been facilitated by the 1991/2 drought afflicting the whole country and therefore requiring a 'nation-wide explanation'. Cogently, even before this major drought, Mhondoro mediums in Dande had been issuing critical remarks about the Zimbabwean government.

Apart from offering 'political explanations' for natural disasters, Mhondoro mediums can become involved in socio-political issues in a number of other ways. As the Mhondoro are the 'real owners of the land', they have to be consulted on all major developments introduced in their territories. The introduction of new cash crops, immigration of large numbers of people and the foundation of a new village are just a few examples of cases that have to be presented to Mhondoro mediums for approval. Furthermore, when a chief dies, his successor needs to be appointed by the medium of the senior Mhondoro of the chiefdom.

Becoming a Mhondoro medium

Mhondoro are believed to be able to communicate with the living through human mediums. However, not all Mhondoro will have a medium at any given time (see Lan 1985: 50). After the death of a medium of a specific Mhondoro, it may take several years, even decades, before a new medium of that Mhondoro comes forward.

Mhondoro mediumship is not inherited, nor is it considered to be a voluntary career option: the Mhondoro are believed to select the mediums. The first sign of possession manifests itself as an illness that cannot be cured. Sometimes the illness is of a physical nature; the new medium of Badzabveke for instance told me that he had suffered from severe intestinal problems. He visited the mission hospital at Chitsungo several times, but the doctor there could not help him. In other cases, the possession first manifests itself as a spate of bad luck. The new medium of Nobedza, for example, said he lost job after job. Both men suspected they were being bewitched and visited a n'anga (healer). It was the n'anga who discovered that the men were not the victims of witchcraft, but possessed by spirits who tried to draw attention to their presence through illness and bad luck[50]. Many mediums stress their initial resistance to becoming a medium, and their suffering as result of the spirit's choice, emphasising that they did not choose to become a medium. For instance, the new medium of Badzabveke told me how the Mhondoro was fighting inside him with another, lesser, spirit, which had been diagnosed earlier as the cause of his health problems. As a result of this battle the medium said he had been overcome by a spell of dizziness and had fallen into the cooking fire. I met him while I was visiting the local mission hospital where he was treated for his burns. He said he disliked his possession, but 'there is nothing you can do once the Mhondoro chooses you'.

Once the n'anga had determined the identity of the Mhondoro possessing the mediums and their areas of origin, the patients were sent to Mhondoro mediums in the vicinity of the area over which the patients' Mhondoro held authority. These mediums helped the men come to terms with their possession and prepared them for their new role. In other words, they assisted in the process of transforming the sufferer into a medium, a healer. This transformation, which Janzen (1992, cf. Eliade 1959) refers to as the 'wounded healer complex', is a feature that the Mhondoro cult shares with many other spirit medium cults in the region.

The established mediums as well as the assistants of the aspiring medium need to be convinced that the patient is actually possessed by a Mhondoro, before they will help prepare the patient for the final testing procedure. Not every aspirant medium manages to obtain support. When I was living in

---

[50] Lan (1985: 49-56) offers a detailed description of this process.

Mburuma, a man appeared who claimed to be possessed by a Mhondoro. He had visited a mutape in a nearby village that he wanted to become his ritual assistant, but this mutape had refused to help him, accusing him of being a fraud. Some of the villagers in Mburuma told me that this was the third time the medium had been chased away by the mutape.

Candidate mediums that do manage to obtain support from established mediums and vatape are allowed to settle in the spirit province belonging to the Mhondoro possessing them, and wear the conventional mediums' dress. There they will start the long process of preparing for their test. The first years are said to be the most critical; at any point in time the Mhondoro may decide to abandon the patient. The preparation period can last for years. During this period, it is believed that the Mhondoro may leave the patient for short periods of time to allow him or her to lead a normal life (see also Lan 1985: 52). Over time, the patient may establish a reputation for some special powers (e.g. prognostication or healing). When the patient is finally confident of his or her powers, the final testing procedure can commence. Unfortunately, I have never been able to attend an actual test, but Lan (1985: 52-6) offers a detailed description, which was repeated to me in virtually the same terms by the mutape of the late medium of Chivhere. At a large public ritual, the patient must become possessed and recite the genealogy of the Mhondoro as well as details of their history. The patient also has to trace the walking sticks, ritual axes and other items that once belonged to either the Mhondoro while he or she was still alive, or to the previous medium of the Mhondoro. In the case of the Mhondoro of Chivhere, the candidate also has to reveal the place where the late medium had hidden a pot filled with coins. It is possible that the patient will not pass the test at once, but will require several rituals. Once the final test is passed, the patient is accepted as a true medium of a Mhondoro. This does not, however, mean that a medium once established will always retain this position, as will be shown later.

Most people I have spoken to adhere to the theory that the mediums are outsiders and therefore all knowledge they display of the history of their Mhondoro, the staffs and the hidden things must come from the spirit. Mediums are not supposed to belong to the same clan as the Mhondoro, which would also be the clan of the chief of the area. Consequently, mediums, as persons, are classified as vatorwa, strangers (see also Lan 1985). However, I found that nearly all mediums I interviewed were born or grew up in Dande. I also discovered that quite a number (seven out of the fifteen mediums I spoke to) actually do belong to the same clan as the Mhondoro possessing them[51].

---

[51] Bourdillon (1987) is quite skeptical about the idea that mediums are outsiders called to their profession through illness. He maintains that in many cases the mediumship is passed on from one family member to another, and that most mediums have been trained from an earlier age. I have neither been able to confirm nor reject Bourdillon's ideas on this.

A final important remark that needs to be made is that both the adherents and the mediums themselves separate the medium as a person from the spirit possessing him or her. The word used for medium is 'homwe', which means 'small pocket' or 'small bag', which means that he or she is considered nothing but a 'container' of the spirit. Mediums cannot be held responsible for the pronouncements that spirits make using their voices. When I started interviewing Mhondoro mediums about the Mid-Zambezi Project, I found many of them reluctant to speak to me when they were not possessed. Often they seemed relieved when I asked for a consultation with the Mhondoro spirit. The medium of Karembera, for instance, seemed to avoid me when I tried to speak to him. Several times my research assistant and I went to the village where he lived to ask to see him. Each time his neighbours told us that he should be around, but we never managed to contact him. The third time we told the neighbours that we wanted to speak to the spirit, not to the medium. When we had almost reached my car, which was parked at some distance from the medium's homestead, a boy came running after us, informing us that the medium was home and wished to see us. We made an appointment with him and his mutape for a possession séance. During this séance he criticised the Mid-Zambezi Project unreservedly.

The actors involved in the Mhondoro cult

The chiefs are the leading members of the lineages that claim descent from a Mhondoro spirit (see also Bourdillon 1987: 103; Lan 1985: 19). The land within the chiefdom is 'owned' by the lineage of the chiefs, through their link with the Mhondoro. Large chiefdoms can be divided into wards, often ruled by a branch of the chiefly family.

As I have already described in Chapter Three, the boundaries of chiefdoms and those of spirit provinces hardly ever coincide. Chiefdoms may contain several spirit provinces under different Mhondoro. They may also contain just a part of a certain spirit province, while the other part is located in another chiefdom. The medium of the most senior Mhondoro in the chiefdom is responsible for selecting and installing the successor to the chieftaincy upon the death of a chief (though the present government has retained some influence in this procedure as well).

Members of the chiefly lineages may consult the medium of a Mhondoro from whom they claim descent, even if this medium lives outside their chiefdom. They may do so when problems of a more individual or family character arise. When problems arise that affect their subjects as well, for example droughts, the chief can consult the mediums of the spirit provinces that are located within his chiefdom.

Each spirit medium has several assistants, called vatape (singular: mutape). The vatape look after the shrine and conduct the annual rituals. When a spirit medium is possessed, one of the vatape will serve as a mediator. Questions cannot always be posed directly to the possessed medium, but may have to be referred to the mutape who will then pass the question on to the medium. The mutape interprets or explains the answers given by the possessed medium. During the possession séance, the mutape also looks after the medium, which is no longer conscious of what is happening around him or her. After the séance, the mutape informs the medium of the pronouncements of the Mhondoro.

Most, though not all, vatape are also the headmen of the villages within the spirit province (or at least closely related to the village headmen). Village headmen may belong to the chiefly clan, but this is not a prerequisite for headmanship. Usually the chief grants headmanship to the family that is believed to have founded a village. Sometimes these families migrated into the chiefdom from distant places; others broke away from another headman in the same chiefdom. Village headmen can be considered appointees of the chief. But this is not a purely top-down relationship; headmen also depend upon their subjects, as these may threaten to break away to form a new village. In most areas in Zimbabwe the possibility to establish new villages is rather limited because of population pressure and land shortage in many Communal Areas. Dande was an exception as, prior to the implementation of the Mid-Zambezi Project, breaking away was still a viable option. Headmanship is adelphically inherited, as is mutape-ship. Occasionally, a headman may pass the mutape-ship on to his brother, when he is convinced he will not be able to bear this extra burden.

The vatape also play an important role in determining the authenticity of any claims to the mediumship of 'their' Mhondoro. Aspiring mediums will have to convince the vatape to work with them. Without the assistance of the vatape they cannot function or gain acceptance from the adherents. Many vatape told me that they have detailed knowledge of the characteristics of mediums usually chosen by 'their' Mhondoro and the particular way in which the Mhondoro behaves when he possesses a medium. This knowledge is handed down from generation to generation. The vatape's judgement of aspiring mediums is therefore taken seriously, and they are present during the final testing of an aspirant medium.

The vatape are not the only assistants of the mediums. Some mediums are also helped by matunzwi, people who run errands. Many mediums also have a 'spirit wife' (mukaranga) who will help cleaning the shrine, wash the medium's clothes and who does the cooking for him before or after possession séances. The number and the degree of specialisation of assistants differ from medium to medium.

Participation in the Mhondoro cult is based on two principles: linearity and territoriality. Those who are considered lineal descendants of a Mhondoro, may consult a medium representing their ancestor regardless of where they are living. But the majority of the potential following of the Mhondoro cult is formed by those who are simply living on and, more importantly, cultivating land in a particular spirit province (see Garbett 1977: 70-1). I use the term 'potential' here, since not all cultivators within a spirit province will actually participate in the activities associated with the Mhondoro cult. Some may join one of the mainstream mission churches or so-called Independent churches and refuse to pay their respects to the Mhondoro, although quite a few church members combine their Christian faith and their adherence to the Mhondoro cult. Several Independent churches are active in Dande, among them the Apostolic Faith Church, the Apostolic Church of Johane Marange and ZAOGA. Of the mainline churches, only the Roman Catholic Church is still active in the valley. The Methodist mission stations were abandoned and destroyed during the struggle for Independence, and have never been rebuilt.

The principle of territoriality almost 'ensures' that the potential adherents of the Mhondoro cult constitute a heterogeneous group. Spirit provinces harbour many different people occupying different places within the power equation. First of all, there are those who are related to the chiefs and headmen, and then there are those who are not. Those who do not belong to the chief 's clan are referred to as vatorwa, strangers (see also Lan 1985: 19). Though the chief 's lineage usually forms the largest single lineage, together the members of the different 'stranger-lineages' outnumber the chiefly lineage. The rapid increase in migration to Dande after Independence led to the introduction of even more 'strangers' into the area.

Other distinctions that can be made among the potential supplicants of the Mhondoro cult, and that have received quite a bit of attention in literature, are based on age and gender. Pertinently, potential adherents occupy different places within the pattern of socio-economic stratification. Some are subsistence farmers, others successfully grow cash crops, and many increase their income from farming by doing wage labour or other off-farm activities. Some farmers have cattle, while others have not. Furthermore, there is also a local elite of shop-owners, teachers, nurses and the like.

Lastly, there is also a group of people who are part of the new local administration structure, which was put into place after Independence in 1980 (see Chapter Two). Relations between those participating in this new structure on the one hand and chiefs and headmen on the other vary from village to village and Ward to Ward.

The Mhondoro cult and the Mid-Zambezi Project

Below I will describe the role of two Mhondoro mediums in the struggle against the Mid-Zambezi Project. The mediums concerned are the medium of Chidyamauyu and the new, aspirant medium of Nehanda. The medium of Chidyamauyu resides in and looks after the spirit province, which largely coincides with Matsiwo A Ward. This area actually 'belongs' to Nehanda. After the death of the last medium of Nehanda in 1973, the medium of Nehanda's grandson, Chidyamauyu, assumed responsibility for the area while awaiting the appearance of a new medium for Nehanda[52]. In 1990, the people in Dande first heard of a woman in Karoi District claiming to be possessed by Nehanda. Her mutape, who had inherited this function from his late brother, told me that his brother had visited the woman several times shortly before his death in 1993. During these visits he was accompanied by the medium of Chidyamauyu. They asked her various questions to which it is believed only the real medium of Nehanda can provide the answers, and concluded that her claims of possession had to be taken seriously. They agreed with her that she should remain in Karoi district for some time in order to gather strength - physical and ritual - to travel to Dande on foot[53] and perform the final test. Ever since, each year, at the end of the dry season, there would be rumours that the medium would come to the valley.

In the year 1992, when I had just arrived for my second stint of fieldwork in Dande, Chief Matsiwo had been asked to give permission for the implementation of the resettlement exercise in Matsiwo A Ward. As described above, the chief referred the issue to the medium of Chidyamauyu on the grounds that the Mhondoro are the real owners of the land and only they could give permission.

The Project Manager persuaded the chief to visit the medium of Chidyamauyu on behalf of the Department of Rural Development (DERUDE), the department responsible for implementing the Mid-Zambezi Project. The manager provided the chief with a piece of black cloth, the usual fee for consulting a spirit medium on such an important issue. When the chief visited the medium of Chidyamauyu, the latter told him that he could not accept the piece of cloth. He could not be sure that it actually came from DERUDE. The chief was ordered to inform the Project Manager that he should come to visit the spirit medium personally and bring another piece of cloth. Cogently, the medium stated that his Mhondoro refused to give permission for the implementation of the project. Project activities were to halt at the Sapa Stream, which forms the boundary of the spirit province of Nehanda, and is situated a few kilometres south of the Ward boundary.

After some delay, the Project Manager, accompanied by the chief, decided to pay a personal visit to the spirit medium and donated the required piece of cloth. At the meeting with the spirit medium, the Project Manager was given the same verdict as the chief.

The chief found himself in a difficult position. On the one hand, he received a salary from the government, which wished to implement the Mid-Zambezi Project. On the other hand, he was very much aware that by that time most of

---

[52] The medium of Chidyamauyu accompanied and took care of Mazviona Kawanza-ruwa, the late medium of Nehanda, during the struggle for Independence.

[53] A distance of roughly 250 km. Especially on their first journey to their spirit province, spirit mediums are not allowed to travel by bus or to use other forms of modern transport.

his subjects opposed to the project[54]. Like most chiefs he was invited to attend the (Rural) District Council meetings 'ex officio'. There, he experienced the confusion generated by the mixed messages described in the preceding chapter. The government officials serving on the Council defended the general assumption underlying the project that proper land-use planning was needed. The Councillors in their turn were reporting on the problems experienced during the implementation. When I asked the chief why he had referred the Project Manager to the spirit medium, he told me that the Mhondoro are the real owners of the land, and it was therefore up to them to give permission or not. Though I do not doubt this statement, my feeling was that he was washing his hands of the matter when he tried to pass the responsibility of judging the project over to the medium of Chidyamauyu, partly because he himself, not unjustifiably, found it difficult to condemn the project openly. He told me that he also needed the medium's advice since he did not know all the sacred areas in his chiefdom, and these should never be pegged. According to the sabhuku of the village where I stayed this was nonsense; everybody knew the sacred areas since cultivation is forbidden in these places.

When the chief involved the medium of Chidyamauyu, the latter was very popular. Numerous stories were recounted of his behaviour during the struggle for Independence. He had joined the guerrilla fighters operating in the area and had become caretaker of the medium of Nehanda. There is a strong chance that people thought that his role during the war and his close association with the medium of such an important Mhondoro made him a powerful actor in a confrontation with the government. Interestingly, in the hierarchy of Mhondoro based on the genealogy of the two main 'Mhondoro families' in Dande, Chidyamauyu occupies a rather junior position. In fact, he does not even have his own spirit province. After the death of the medium of Nehanda, he claimed responsibility for her spirit province, and his vatape as well as many adherents agreed with this decision. His opposition to the Mid-Zambezi Project may also have played a role in his popularity. Often, when I asked people why the medium of Chidyamauyu was so important they referred to his pronouncements concerning the Mid-Zambezi Project. Chidyamauyu's junior position was now taken as an advantage. As the mutape of another Mhondoro medium said: 'Chidyamauyu is very important, as he is the grandchild of all the Mhondoro of Dande, he has access to all of them.' Some people even claimed that it was the Mhondoro Chidyamauyu who had divided Dande into different territories and 'allocated' these to the different Mhondoro. The headman of Mburuma adopted 'project-speak' to explain this situation to me: 'Chidyamauyu has pegged the area for the other Mhondoro. He forgot to peg a place for himself. But he can

---

[54] Opposition to the Mid-Zambezi Project has not always been unanimous, as I will describe in Chapter Eight; many recent migrants initially supported it. Furthermore, I will describe below how interventions by the ruling party later resulted in some internal rifts over the project.

stay in all the other areas since he is everybody's grandchild'. In growing numbers, people living outside Nehanda's (and thus Chidyamauyu's) territory, went to consult the medium of Chidyamauyu instead of the medium of their own spirit province. When a dry spell occurred in January 1993, in the middle of the rain season, the mutape of the village of Mburuma, where I stayed, went to consult the medium of Chidyamauyu instead of the medium of Chivhere, in whose spirit province the village was situated.

In October 1992, Bill Derman, a visiting professor from an American university, asked his research assistants to interview people in Matsiwo A Ward about their ideas on how the land in the Ward should be used. His idea was to develop, in co-operation with local farmers, an alternative land-use plan, which could be presented to the staff of the Mid-Zambezi Project.

Most people who were contacted by the research assistants refused to give any information. They accused the assistants of being 'spies' for the project management, whose goal was to find out if there was any resistance to the project. The research assistants were told to visit the medium of Chidyamauyu, in order to ask permission for their research. In November, I was invited to join Bill Derman ·and his assistants on their visit to the medium. It took us some time to locate the medium, since he was not at his own homestead. In the end we found him at the homestead of a n'anga where he was recovering from the flu. We were invited to lunch and spent a long time discussing our plans with the medium and the n'anga. We tried to convince them that we were not associated with the Mid-Zambezi Project, that on the contrary, we wanted to help the people of Matsiwo A to prevent the negative consequences people in other Wards had suffered from because of the project. Finally the medium recognised me: "Ah, you are that girl who walked all over Dande before she even learnt how to speak proper chi-Shona, some years ago. You were taken to us by that professor from the university." The professor he was referring to was probably Professor Murphree, at that time Director of the Centre for Applied Social Sciences. I confirmed that indeed I had done research in Dande before, and that I hoped that my chi-Shona had improved since then. The medium then came up with a proposal that we had not expected. He would arrange a meeting with all VIDCO Chairmen and village headmen of the Ward during which we could explain our plans. If all were to agree to co-operate with the exercise, the medium promised he would ask the spirit of Chidyamauyu to give his opinion on what would constitute a proper land-use plan. Perhaps we should have taken the fact that both the visiting researcher and I came down with food poisoning after the lunch - for me the first and last time in all the time I spent in Dande - as an omen that the meeting would not proceed the way we would have liked it to.

The meeting took place about a week later. I could not attend it because I had not yet obtained permission from the Council to start my second period of fieldwork in Dande. Bill Derman kindly provided me with the transcript of the meeting and his assistants gave me a description of how it proceeded·

The village headmen were present, as well as many other people, mostly village elders. It was very early in the morning and the medium was possessed. After the research assistants explained their plans, the medium referred the problem to those present: 'It is the duty of the people to give opinions about how they want their land used. I am a spirit. I have nothing to do with present-day life. Let us ... hear what the people (...) have to say'. After some deliberation, one of the village headmen said that he and his colleagues refused to co-operate with the creation of an alternative land-use plan, because they still suspected that Bill Derman and his assistants were working for the Mid-Zambezi Project and they '(...) [did] not want the difficulties that had been experienced by other villages'. Then the possessed medium gave his opinion on the plans:

> Village headmen and people, is there anything that you have grasped from these people? As I can see from these three men, they bring no trouble into your villages. If you co-operate with them, no trouble will befall you. But if they are roots that supply water to the trunk to allow the leaves of the tree to grow, if they want to pave the way for the introduction of the Mid Zambezi Project, that is where we will disagree. I see the future of your villages will be bright if you co-operate with these people. Village headmen, you need to observe carefully and learn if you can benefit from them or if it is [they] themselves who benefit. What I do not want is you, village headmen, to bemoan later, saying Chidyamauyu did not warn us. But as I foresee, the future has no tears. If you do not work with them, what happened in Hwata will also happen here, you will be forced to move against your wishes. These three men will come later and say 'did we not tell you to work with us?' Listen carefully everybody; I will not be happy to see my children from Mukombe (...) and Mamhuri moved to Chidodo, Karusanzi or Gonono.

Though he had been quite decisive about the Mid-Zambezi Project in his discussions with the Project Manager, in this case the medium seemed less eager to make a definite pronouncement. He first asked those present for their opinion. His own opinion about the alternative land-use plan was more positive - though as a precaution he added that if they 'were to supply water to the tree' of the Mid-Zambezi Project he would disagree - and he tried to persuade the audience to co-operate. However, he did not force his opinion upon his followers and in his pronouncement paid attention to their worries. In the end he concluded: 'My final answer is: we did not say yes or no to working with you. Give us more time to discuss the subject of land-use planing, alone. We will tell you later'.

By March 1993, no decision had been reached about co-operating with the creation of an alternative land-use plan. By this time, the Project Manager of the Mid-Zambezi Project decided to pursue the matter of resettling the people in Matsiwo A Ward again.

After mediation by the chief, a meeting was organised with the medium of Chidyamauyu and the village headmen. The meeting was held at Tsokoto, one of the most sacred places in Dande, which is believed to be the place where the bones of the last medium of Nehanda were taken for burial after she died in Mozambique. The meeting took place early in the morning, just before dawn. It was still dark when we were taken to the shrine, the dendemaro, which consisted of a thatched roof on poles, no walls, more a shelter than a hut. We were told to take off our shoes and watches, and sit on the ground in front of the shrine. Inside the dendemaro the medium was lying on a mat, surrounded by his paraphernalia: a calabash with snuff tobacco, a kudu horn and several baskets. He was dressed in black cloth and wore necklaces made from black and white beads. He was already in a state of possession when we arrived. Two vatape were sitting next to the mat, ready to assist the medium. About fifty villagers were attending the meeting, seated on the ground, clustered around the dendemaro. The chief, the Project Manager and the Resettlement Officer were sitting closest to the dendemaro. The women were sitting farthest away, separate from the men. The meeting started with everybody clapping hands to the Mhondoro. The possessed medium then asked the vatape why the chief had called Chidyamauyu. The chief answered that he might be the leader of the people, but that the Mhondoro is the owner of the land. His answer was repeated to the possessed medium by one of the vatape. The Project Manager and the Resettlement Officer then asked whether they could get permission to start the demarcation exercise. The possessed medium answered by proposing a separate meeting of the village headmen to discuss the matter. The chief agreed. The village headmen withdrew from the meeting and discussed the matter among themselves elsewhere in the village. The rest of the audience stayed close to the dendemaro, waiting and discussing the issue amongst themselves. Most of the comments on the Mid-Zambezi Project I picked up were quite negative, as a general atmosphere of opposition towards the project prevailed. When the village headmen returned about half an hour later, they told the Project Manager and the Resettlement Officer that they did not want the resettlement project to be introduced in their area. Most people in the audience greeted this with enthusiasm and the women ululated. An older man in the audience remarked that in the previous week elephants and buffaloes had been spotted close to his village and that this was a sure sign that Nehanda disliked the project. Then the possessed medium said:

You people from DERUDE are just tempting the mediums and the Mhondoro, but you do not satisfy our needs. The first time DERUDE came to Dande, the Mhondoro were not consulted. Now that you are facing problems you consult the Mhondoro. I already told you that the Sapa Stream is where you should stop pegging. And still you come to ask me permission to continue. I cannot accept that. Mugabe and Nehanda did not agree to this pegging project. In the areas that have been pegged sacred areas of the Mhondoro have been allocated to people. I am not happy about that and the other Mhondoro are not happy about it either. DERUDE is using power so they can peg without my permission. I am refusing and if you want to put my medium in prison, that is fine, I dislike the pegging. DERUDE will have to pay a fine for the areas it has already pegged without my permission. You will have to wait for Nehanda and ask her permission. The Mhondoro of Zimbabwe caused last year's drought because Mugabe is not listening to them.

Upon this statement from the possessed medium, the chief publicly remarked that he, too, opposed the project. The Project Manager turned to the audience and asked the people to say yes or no to the project, but it was the medium that answered:

> Tell your seniors that Chidyamauyu has refused and that they should wait for Nehanda to come to Dande. Matsiwo [the chief], report to me any trouble you have with DERUDE.

The chief then told the Project Manager that he could not accept the project if the Mhondoro was against it.

Here again we see the spirit medium openly consulting the audience before he issues a statement. The people he specifically asked for their opinion were the village headmen; among them were the vatape of Chidyamauyu and Nehanda. He then provided supernatural legitimisation for their objections. Note that he was careful to make a distinction between the medium and the spirit possessing the medium. When the possessed medium said: "You can arrest my medium if you want", it may seem that he did not care about the consequences of the rejection of the project, but this remark can also be interpreted as emphasising that it was the spirit speaking, and not the medium. Furthermore, the medium of Chidyamauyu seemed to shift some of the responsibility to the new aspirant medium of Nehanda. As indicated earlier, this aspirant medium was living outside of Dande, in Hurungwe District.

The possessed medium blamed the drought on the implementation of the Mid-Zambezi Project in other Wards in Dande. The rainy season of 1991/2 had been particularly bad. The medium of Chidyamauyu was not the only Mhondoro medium in Dande who blamed the drought on the Mid-Zambezi Project. All over Dande, village headmen who consulted the mediums on the causes of the drought were given similar explanations. Of all fifteen mediums I interviewed, only one did not mention the project when asked about the reasons for the drought.

After the unsuccessful meeting with the medium of Chidyamauyu, the Project Manager and the Resettlement Officer organised three other meetings in different villages of the Ward, at which the chief was present as well. Perhaps these were the 'awareness meetings' mentioned in the land-use proposal for Matsiwo A (Agritex Planing Branch 1993, see previous chapter). Many people attended. The Project Manager tried to obtain support for the project by focusing almost entirely on the services and infrastructural development the project would bring. The audience was told that only if they were to accept the project, schools and clinics would be built, and roads would be improved so that buses could start servicing the area. In the project proposal no new clinics had been planned for Matsiwo A Ward. The Agritex land-use plan (ibid.: 27) proposed the upgrading of the clinic at Msengezi Mission, one of the bigger villages in the Ward, which used to have a Roman Catholic Mission Station, but this was not foreseen in the overall plan for the Mid-Zambezi Project, and consequently there was no budget for the upgrading. One clinic that was built with funding from the project - at Masomo - had just started operating when the Project Manager organised the 'awareness meetings'. The only new school planned for Matsiwo A had already been constructed. The rub was that DERUDE had not officially declared the school completed, so that no teachers could be employed. It is not unthinkable that DERUDE used the approval of the school as a means to apply pressure. The Project Manager blithely informed people that the project would provide them with boreholes. He did not mention that the schedule of drilling for water points had been very much delayed in other areas in Dande and that there were serious problems with maintaining and repairing boreholes that were already constructed. He stressed the importance of the availability of clean water, especially in the light of the cholera epidemic that had hit some villages in the Ward. At one meeting, the audience openly objected to the project. However, when the chief then said that he thought people should accept the project because of the development it would bring, a few people began to doubt whether they should continue their resistance against the project. At the other two meetings some young men asked the elders to accept the project, citing as a reason that it would bring development to their area. One of them told the Project Manager that the only reason why the audience at the meeting with Chidyamauyu had rejected the project was because they were afraid of the medium.

The statements made by the chief during the 'awareness meetings' contradicted what he had said during the meeting with the medium of Chidyamauyu. There, faced with all village headmen and the spirit medium opposing the project, the chief had objected to the project, in the presence of the Project Manager. Village headmen at that time no longer received government salaries and seemed freer to object to the project. Authorities at district level were pressuring the chief into supporting the project. At the meetings organised independently by the Project Manager, the chief actually did publicly express his support. Yet, in a private interview I had with him the following month, he stated that he opposed the project as it was causing a host of conflicts:

> The people dislike the project but they are forced by the government. The Mhondoro do not want these pegs. (...) In Chitsungo one person was killed because of [a fight over] the boundaries of the pegs. Long ago we did not have such things.

'Long ago': the opponents of the Mid-Zambezi Project often conjured up the past. The vision of the past presented was that of an era in which chiefs and village headmen, supported by the mediums, had control over the land which they allocated fairly amongst their subjects, an era when there was plenty of land for everybody. In Chapter Three, I have already argued that before the implementation of the project, the allocation of land was a messier, more complicated story than often suggested in literature on communal tenure. But then this representation of the past was part of the counter-narrative forwarded by the opponents of the project. The struggle for Independence, they said, was fought because people wanted to return 'to the old ways'. This idealised version of the past was also put forward by the experts on that past: the mediums of the ancient chiefs. The war featured just as often in their pronouncements.

When I became aware of the importance attributed to the medium of Chidyamauyu's verdict on the project, I decided to interview more Mhondoro mediums. I managed to speak to fifteen mediums in the project area - that is, all but two of them actually living and working in that area. This part of my research required plenty of travelling on badly maintained roads, since I had to look for the mediums in their own spirit province. Some of the mediums I visited were living a fair distance from Mburuma, the village where I was living. Although I was surprised to discover that even in villages situated more than a hundred kilometres away from Mburuma people knew of my existence - witnessed by the fact that children would shout my name whenever they saw me - many people did not know exactly what I was doing in the area and whether I was connected to the project or not. Because of my white skin I was often associated with 'development', and the Mid-Zambezi Project was presented as 'development', so it was logical that I would be associated with it. People who did not know me very well were often reluctant to discuss the project with me, and so were the mediums; unless, as already mentioned, I made it very clear that it was the spirit I wanted to speak to, and not the medium as a person. The fear of speaking one's mind with a stranger who might be connected to the project was quite understandable, given the violent reactions to the early protest marches, and the fact that the Central Intelligence Office (CIO) had many officers in Dande, the more senior ones openly and officially attending the meetings of the (Rural) District Council.

An indication of how sensitive the issue was can perhaps be drawn from the interview I had with the medium of Kadembo. This medium was a young man in his early twenties. He had only recently been accepted as the new medium when I first visited him. When I arrived at his village I was taken to see him by the headman, who was also his mutape. We were invited to sit on the veranda of the headman's hut and I explained why I had come. The medium became very nervous when I mentioned the Mid-Zambezi Project. When I said that I would like to speak to the spirit, not to him, this did not seem to help much. The medium said he was still not sure if I could talk to the spirit about the issue. Suddenly he started making noises as if he was about to throw up, he then started coughing and growling, and rolling his eyes. He turned away from me and started writhing, coughing and growling for about five minutes. Then he turned towards me again, and spoke with a very low voice. The spirit

announced himself and said that I could speak to him. My research assistant
was astonished and said that he had never seen a Mhondoro medium actually
become possessed in front of his supplicants[55]. Maybe this young medium was
so afraid of talking about the Mid-Zambezi Project that he did not even dare to
give permission for a meeting with the Mhondoro without being possessed. The
spirit possessing him had no such scruples and was quite outspoken against the
project:

> When we fought the vanhu vasina mabvi [people without knees, that is, white
> people[56]] we were expecting to live the way we used to live in the past. (...) I do not
> like the pegs, I do not want to see the iron pegs. Tell Zvimba [Zvimba is the home
> area of President Mugabe] that he should tell his people to uproot the pegs.

With the other mediums the procedure was different. We would ask the mutape
and the medium if we could speak with the spirit. Then the mutape would go to
the shrine, the dendemaro, to inform the spirit that someone was seeking advice
from the spirit and ask the spirit to possess the medium. We would then spend
the night in the village, usually at the homestead of the mutape who often has
guest huts for those who want to consult the Mhondoro. Early in the morning,
while it was still dark, the mutape would wake us up and take us to the
dendemaro where we would have to take off our shoes and watches before
entering. The medium would be waiting for us, already in a possessed state. My
research assistant and I were never the only ones attending the séance.
Sometimes there were other people who had also asked to consult the spirit, but
even if this was not the case there were always villagers present who wanted to
hear what the spirit had to say to us.

Of the fifteen mediums - or spirits I should say - I interviewed, all but one
condemned the Mid-Zambezi Project and blamed the drought on it. The
medium who did not condemn the project outright was the medium of
Chiwawa, who had been living in Upper Guruve since the Independence, after
he had been released from prison where he spent almost seven years for
assisting the freedom fighters. He had therefore been confronted with the
consequences of the project to a lesser degree. Perhaps he was also more afraid
than the other mediums to criticise the government, since the last time he had
done so it had cost him dearly. Or perhaps he still supported the present
government for which he had spent all these years in jail. He wanted to return to

---

[55] I had often witnessed people becoming possessed by family or 'shave' spirits during
beer parties. However, Mhondoro mediums would usually surrender themselves to their
spirits in private. People who wish to consult the Mhondoro will only be taken to the
medium when he or she is already in a state of possession.
[56] Some people claim that whites were called 'men without knees' because they wore
long trousers; others claim that it was because they would never kneel to show respect
to the nobles.

the valley, and in 1994, the Ward Councillor of the area to which he wanted to return, asked the Project Manager to peg a plot for the medium.

In the possessed mediums' pronouncements two themes came up: representations of the past as an era of local control over land and the war for Independence which was supposedly fought for 'a return to the old ways', that is, local control over land. When I asked the possessed medium of Bangomwe, one of the most senior Mhondoro in Dande - head of the 'autochthonous' Mhondoro lineage - what the spirit of Bangomwe thought of the Mid-Zambezi Project, he answered:

We see it as war. Long back people were shifting from where their homes were because of ants eating their huts or they were able to change their fields because they were no longer good. So (...) when these people were fighting during the war, they said they want to live their traditional way. (...) the Mhondoro looked after the boys well because in the bush there were lions, snakes, elephants, buffaloes and rhinos, but none of them was injured because the Mhondoro were always looking after them. After the war we were expecting to live in our own traditional way. Then, after the war, they came saying they want to peg plots. Why do you want to demarcate plots when before you told us that after the war we are going to live like we did in the old days? We were happy when we won the war expecting to live as we had done in the old days but so far we have not seen the living of the old days being practised. They started demarcating the plots and if the Mhondoro ask why they were doing the demarcating, they would say we are going to arrest your homwe [medium] because he is troublesome. Then the Mhondoro told them that there are some areas to which people should not be shifted (...) They said that people should shift and live along the road, but none of the Mhondoro is happy about this. There are no rains these days and if people ask the Mhondoro, the Mhondoro tell them to go to Mugabe. And if people go to Mugabe they are told to go to the Mhondoro. How are you going to feed these children? And the war is not yet over. All the spirits are saying the war is not yet over and when it is over we will start seeing people practising the life of the old days.

In August 1993, I asked the possessed medium of Chidyamauyu the same question, and he too referred to the war:

I have fought for this country for eight years. When I went to Mozambique I [was] with this medium. I represent all Mhondoro of Dande to the government. If you come here with an idea of destroying this area, pegging this area, that is what I do not want to hear. Even if it is Mugabe telling me that, I will tell him to stop it. If we are talking about pegging, it is a very disturbing issue. The government just used its powers there. It did not ask us or send people like you to ask us our suggestions about it. When they started their war they asked us, the Mhondoro and the chiefs. The chiefs gave them their children to go to war. Even today some of these children have not returned home. Even the medium of Nehanda died there at war. (...) The government ha[s] forgotten us the Mhondoro and the chiefs, the owners of the land. Look now, the soil is now speaking.

The remark that 'the soil is now speaking' refers to the 1991/2 drought. The Mhondoro mediums of Dande were not the only ones blaming this drought on government policies. In 1995, a special issue of the Journal of Religion in Africa was devoted to religious responses in Zimbabwe to this drought; and the way in which the complaints by spirit mediums and Independent Church leaders were formulated, sounded very familiar (see Ranger 1995; Mawere & Wilson 1995; Mafu 1995). The problems addressed in the Journal were related to the introduction of the Economic Structural Adjustment Programme in 1989, the consequences of which unequivocally emerged in the early 1990s: massive retrenchments; increases of schoolfees; access to health care becoming more expensive; and so forth. The corruption scandals that began to emerge in the late 1980s and the lack of progress in solving the land issue also featured in the complaints. Spirit mediums and church leaders alike stated that the government had betrayed the ideals of the struggle for Independence to which they - the mediums and church leaders - felt they had contributed enormously. Many complained that the ancestral spirits had not been properly informed that the war had been won, and that little had been done to cleanse the country of the bloodshed that had taken place, or to appease the spirits of those who had lost their lives during the struggle. This was also an important issue in Dande where so many people had died. The possessed medium of Bangomwe put it this way:

> (...) we go to [the] leader Mugabe. When he became the leader, he said: 'We want to practice our traditions'. There are children who died in the bush. There are Mhondoro whose things were destroyed during the war, and there are some mediums who died during the war like Mutota, Matare, Nehanda. Now Mugabe has not come to the spirit mediums to inform them that he took the country from the whites. He should bring beads and cloth for ritual ceremonies, to inform them that we took the country we were fighting for; as you are the elders you know about our traditions, I am very young. Wherever it is not good, you should point it out to me. What has troubled you, you should send your people to inform me. If I cannot come myself, I will send my juniors to see what the trouble is and how you want it to be solved. Now nothing has been done. Now the war has ended the Mhondoro are not happy with how people are living these days. If people come with a problem of rain, the spirits say they understand the problem and then there are Mhondoro which make rain. But none of the Mhondoro in the bush is happy. That is what happened, so we are just looking to what is being done and listening to what they are doing.

I noticed changes in the war stories, compared to the stories that were told when I first did research in Dande in 1988. In the mid-1980s, a number of ex-combatants decided to return to Dande looking for land. They were welcomed as heroes and received ample assistance. One of them was elected Ward Councillor, but, as mentioned in Chapter Three, was later betrayed and reported to the police for poaching an elephant. The first time I was in Dande, I heard mainly glorious stories about the guerrillas. As time went by, the stories changed and more and more people started telling me about how they were caught between two fires. Someone who in his teens had acted as a messenger and carrier for the guerrillas - a mujiba - and had spent a year in Chikurubi prison after he got caught, had told me proud stories of his war-time exploits when I first met him - though he never wanted to talk about the terrible things that happened to him in prison. Later he revised his story:

> I had to choose sides. I was beaten up by the Rhodesians who suspected I was a mujiba. Then, when I went to my father's field I came across some guerrillas who beat me up because they suspected I was a sell-out. If you chose sides at least you were beaten up by only one party. That is why I became a mujiba.

An old lady who had lost a leg during the war told me:

> We were the real victims. We were stuck in the keeps. They still wanted us to help them with food. But we were hungry too. There was not enough food in the keeps, many people could not go to their fields. Then one day there was a fight between the boys [guerrillas] and the MaBhunu [Boers, whites]. We were in the middle. They did not care about the people in the keep. Many bullets and bombs landed in the keep. That is how I lost my leg. Many people were killed, but not all were sell-outs. It was a bad time, we were always in the middle. And now they want to put us in keeps again, as if the war is not yet over.

She was, by the way, not the only one to draw parallels between the reorganised villages of the Mid-Zambezi Project and the 'keeps'.

Even the Mhondoro mediums had different stories to tell. One of the most notable changes concerned the story of how the medium of Nehanda was taken to Mozambique. She was travelling with the guerrillas in the valley in the company of the mediums of Chiodzomamera, Chipfene and Chidyamauyu, introducing the guerrillas to the villagers. The medium of Nehanda was old and feeble, and the guerrillas, fearing she would be caught, decided to take her to Mozambique. Earlier stories always read that at first she refused because she did not want to abandon her people, but eventually agreed to go to Mozambique (see also Lan 1985: 5) Now the medium of Bangomwe told a slightly different story:

> They [the guerrillas] took Nehanda, Chipfene, Chidyamauyu and Chiodzomamera. Chiwawa was also taken, but he ran away. Nehanda told them that she could not cross the Zambezi, 'I do not have to see my brother Samarengu[57]'. They told Nehanda that she should go because of the war. And when they were crossing the Zambezi her gano [ritual axe] fell into the

---

[57] According to the medium of Bangomwe, the spirit province on the side of the border to which she was taken belonged to the Mhondoro Samarengu. According to local myths Nehanda and her brother, Samarengu, had to commit incest to gain access to Dande to conquer the area of Bangomwe. Since then the two were forbidden to meet again, and this included a ban on their mediums visiting each other's spirit province.

Zambezi. This was a very bad sign. Nehanda managed to cross the Zambezi and they fought the war until it was over, but her medium died there.

The medium of Chidyamauyu also recalled Nehanda's gano dropping into the river and how that was a bad sign.

Attempts to bribe the mediums

In the meantime, the Project Manager was growing ever more desperate. In an interview I had with him, he complained that nobody in Matsiwo A wanted to assume responsibility of allowing his team to go ahead. After the meetings he had organised himself, he felt confident that the people were actually supporting the project and that he could set the demarcation team to work early in 1994. The Agritex land-use proposal that was issued in October 1993 mentioned that the implementation in Matsiwo A had been delayed '(...) due to the ancestral spirits of the area not accepting any developmental activities'. According to the same report (Agritex Provincial Planning Branch 1983: 4): 'However, ceremonies of appeasement have since been done in consultation with the chief of the area, Chief Matsiwo'. As we have seen, meetings with the medium of Chidyamauyu had taken place, but these were definitely not 'appeasement ceremonies', and the chief had changed his mind again and said that he did not dare to give his permission as long as -the medium of- Chidyamauyu refused. 'No one wants to take responsibility', the Project Manager told me.

> The village headmen refer the problem to the chief and the chief refers the problem to the medium of Chidyamauyu. Then the medium of Chidyamauyu says we have to wait for the medium of Nehanda. Nobody dares to say yes to the project. They are afraid that if they do so, and they will have problems [with rain] later, Nehanda will blame them for accepting the project and will order them to pay a fine for the violation of her sacred areas.

In June 1993, rumours started circulating about gifts that the government had presented to the medium of Chidyamauyu as well as to the new medium of Nehanda, as a reward for their support during the struggle for Independence. The Project Manager confirmed this. He told me that the gifts for Chidyamauyu had been handed over by senior government officials and a high ranking military officer, and that he himself had nothing to do with it. In fact, he was annoyed about the rewards. He said that these should not have been handed over until the medium had acquiesced in the project.

Nevertheless, many people made a connection between the gifts presented to the medium of Chidyamauyu and the approval of the project sought from him. It was a frequent topic of conversation at the many beer parties held to celebrate the abundant harvest of that year - the first after the severe drought of 1991/2. The medium himself was often absent during this period. I tried to interview him, but was unable to meet him until the end of August. Several village elders complained about his many trips away from Dande. Rumour had it that he frequently travelled to Harare (capital of Zimbabwe) to solve the witchcraft problems of rich businessmen. The elders complained that the medium had forgotten all about the problems of Dande. They suggested that he was more interested in money than in attending to his duties towards the people in his spirit province. Several people feared that the Mhondoro might leave the medium were he to continue to neglect the problems connected with the project. During this time, many people told me the stories of two mediums that had allegedly been killed by their Mhondoro for pursuing their own interests rather than those of their adherents. One village headman told me: 'The Mhondoro do not like their mediums to be so interested in money. Look what happened to the medium of Chiodzomamera, his Mhondoro killed him for that'. The medium of Chiodzomamera had opened a store after Independence. He frequently travelled to Harare, in civilian clothes, to buy goods for his store. A few years before I came to Dande, he was killed in a road accident on his way back from Harare.

The meetings organised by the Project Manager independently of the medium did definitely have certain effects. Some people actually believed that services and infrastructure in the Ward would only be improved if the Mid-Zambezi Project were accepted. Those who openly started to advocate the project were mainly young, reasonably well-educated men. The spokesman for this group was a young man who was a member of the Apostolic Church. He had recently returned to Dande from a job on the Plateau. In 1993 he stood as candidate for the post of Ward Councillor for Matsiwo A. The sitting Ward Councillor, though a member of the ZANU(PF), had been against the Mid-Zambezi Project. The new candidate had connections with the late Border Gezi, who at that time was the local MP. Contested elections were attended and observed by members from the Provincial Branch of the ZANU(PF) and officers of the Central Intelligence Office. To argue against secret balloting, they often used the high rate of illiteracy, and in the Matsiwo A elections, voters were asked to line up physically behind their preferred candidate. This procedure could have contributed to the victory of a candidate who was known to be supported by the local MP, even though the majority of residents were still opposing the Mid-Zambezi Project.

When I asked the new Ward Councillor why some people in the Ward had changed their mind about the project he said:

It was us, the youngsters, who wanted the project. We have travelled to other areas and we have seen the development there. There where the project was accepted we saw that (...) the roads are better, there are boreholes, schools, clinics. We want that development here. The older people refused. But we still have to see a lot, they are almost there, at the end, where they have to go. We want the development and we will have to teach the others to see the light of the project. (...) When we used to go to the [District] Council to ask for those things we were told that the Council does not give us development, only DERUDE and the project [do so]. That is how we came to understand it was good to accept the project and development.

The issue of the project and its supposedly developmental aspects may have exacerbated an already existing opposition between the elders and the younger generation. The advocates of the project not only stressed their youth; they also played on their religious affiliation. Village headmen and elders persevered in their opposition to the project. For most of the time, they obtained support from the medium of Chidyamauyu. They continued discussing the Mhondoro's dislike of the project and how that had been the major cause of the 1991/2 drought and the dry spells that had occurred since. They wanted the medium of Chidyamauyu to pronounce again that the project was wrong. The proponents of the project, on the other hand, emphasised their affiliation with Christian (mainly Independent) churches - the new Ward Councillor was a member of the Apostolic Church, a vapostori - rejecting 'the old people's backward traditions'. Resistance to the Mid-Zambezi Project was presented as resistance to development in general, as it was done by the authors of the Agritex Planning Branch report (1993: 4) who claimed that the ancestral spirits objected to '(...) any developmental activities'. Nevertheless, when I asked the new Ward Councillor whether he agreed with plans to demarcate arable plots at Tsokoto, the most sacred area of the spirit province - perhaps of the whole of Dande - he said:

> I would reject that. There are only few people living there, they guard the place. Why peg there? It is the place of our history. When people go there they will feel the history there. They cannot peg there.

In August 1993, I finally managed to see the medium of Chidyamauyu again. He confirmed that he had received gifts from the Ministry of Defence as a reward for his assistance during the war: seven head of cattle; an ox plough; black and white cloth; a spear; a dancing stick; and an axe plus some money. He mentioned Airforce Commander Perrence Shiri as one of the members of the delegation that visited him58. DERUDE officials had promised him that they would construct a house for him. He also said that the new medium of Nehanda, who was still residing in Karoi, had been rewarded handsomely by the Ministry of Defence for solving a problem at the building site of new army barracks near Harare. The medium of Chidyamauyu claimed that the reward constituted Z$ 20.000 (at that time about US$ 2500.-) and twelve head of cattle. Still, he maintained that despite this government reward, she opposed the resettlement project. Strangely enough, he also said that the official presenting him with the gifts had told Chief Matsiwo and the Project Manager (whom he said were

---

58 Perrence Shiri had built up a terrible reputation during the 'Gukurahundi', the government campaign in the 1980s to squash the so-called 'dissidents' in Matabeleland.

present when the gifts were presented, which was denied by the Project Manager) to listen to the medium of Chidyamauyu and stop the project:

> (...) [the Project Manager] was told to stop that pegging by Cde Shiri. Mbuya [grandmother] Nehanda said: If you want to peg the Dande, it is up to you, but if problems arise then do not come to me for help. Matsiwo then said to [the Project Manager]: You do not have to do anything in that area, as you have heard it yourself.

Later that month, the medium of Chidyamauyu publicly issued several statements against the project. From then on, I noticed that the rumours about his reputation and about Mhondoro killing or abandoning their greedy mediums ceased again.

Many elders expressed the hope that the new medium of Nehanda would finally come to her spirit province and give her verdict on the project. As time went by, I too became impatient and decided to try to visit the new medium of Nehanda at her home near Karoi. A friend of mine who was doing research on a Commercial Farm in Hurungwe had told me he knew where she lived. My friend, his research assistant and I went looking for her together in March 1993. We found the place where the medium was staying without any difficulties. The medium appeared to live in a brick house with a corrugated iron roof and windows, which stood in stark contrast with the huts of her neighbours. Around her house and yard, a new barbed wire fence with an iron gate had been constructed. At the gate, we were halted by two men, who, according to my friend's research assistant, were not from the area. They started to interrogate us about the motives for our visit and asked us to show them our IDs. We strongly suspected them to be CIO (Central Intelligence Office) officers[59] and spent an hour trying to convince them to let us speak to her local mutape, but to no avail. My friend's research assistant suggested to the two men that they take us to the local village headman, as the assistant knew the headmen well, but even this the two men would not allow. We were told that if we insisted on entering the village 'we would be in big trouble'. My friend and I did not want to put his assistant in danger, nor did we want to lose our research permits, so we gave up. All the time we were arguing with the two suspected CIO officers we did not see anybody coming out of the house. The only person we saw entering the gate was a herd boy, who brought in a large herd of cattle; I counted twenty-six. Some neighbours stood watching us from a distance, but did not interfere. We left without having spoken to anyone in the village, let alone to the medium herself. We all started to think that her heavy surveillance had something to do with the fact that she still had not come to Dande.

---

[59] At every police station in Zimbabwe's rural areas some CIO officers are stationed, patrolling the surrounding areas. After some time one learns to recognise them, as they usually have a certain way of addressing people.

What we had witnessed coincided with what the medium of Chidyamauyu told me later, in August. He said that the Air Force Commander had told him that CIO officers guarded the medium of Nehanda. The Project Manager also told me he had heard that this was the case. Furthermore, he told me he had heard that some white people had shown up at her place in Hurungwe trying 'to steal the medium'. I was not sure whether I should tell him that I had tried to visit her, and decided not to.

News about the handsome rewards for the medium of Nehanda and her surveillance spread through the Ward. After all this time of hoping she would come to Dande to deliver the final verdict on the Mid-Zambezi Project, the atmosphere changed. Many were disappointed and started to doubt the authenticity of her claims. As one person said:

> If she is the real medium, why does she not come down here and help her people? Have you heard of all the money they have given her? I think she just wants to sit down and enjoy her money. But what is she doing in Karoi [Hurungwe]? That is not her area. No, the real medium would look after her people.

Last attempts to introduce land reforms

After the installation of the new pro-project Ward Councillor, the chief was asked by both the project management and the new Councillor to approach the spirit medium once more. Despite his affiliation with an Independent Christian church that strongly condemns spirit mediums, the new Councillor tried to obtain the support from the medium of Chidyamauyu. He told the chief to tell the medium that most of his people had now come to accept the project. He also said he was convinced that the Mhondoro would understand the problems his people faced and that he would not want them to miss out on 'development'.

The chief returned from his meeting with the spirit medium highly upset. He claimed that he had suddenly felt sick during the meeting and had fallen unconscious. He was revived by the spirit medium that warned the chief never again to bring up the issue of the Mid-Zambezi Project. He related his story to me during an interview and said that he would refuse ever to see the spirit medium again, as he feared for his life.

The Ward Councillor was greatly disappointed. He and his fellow proponents denounced the Mhondoro cult as fake and claimed that Christianity was the only true religion. He tried to persuade the management of the Mid-Zambezi Project several times to continue with the implementation of the project, despite the directives of the spirit medium. The Project Manager promised the Ward Councillor that the re-distribution of land would finally take place, but nothing happened.

Why the Project Manager decided against introducing the project without the Mhondoro medium's permission while project staff had enforced the project in many other areas of Dande, remains somewhat obscure. Maybe he felt he could not abandon the strategy once embarked upon of consulting 'traditional' leadership without losing face and credibility. Also, fear on the part of the project staff members may have played a role. Quite a number of them were afraid that if they continued with their work the Mhondoro would punish them with illnesses, accidents and bad luck. During the final stages of the Mid-Zambezi Project, I came across one of the Resettlement Officers, who, without any encouragement on my part, started to tell me a story he had heard:

> You know what, did you hear that story about the Agritex team working on the dam in Chitsungo? The spirit medium of that area told them to stop. But they went ahead anyway. Then one day they went to the pool to take some measurements. On their way to the pool they were followed by bataleur eagles [believed to be messengers from the spirits]. One of the Agritex people got so scared, he got out of the car and went into the bush. They have never seen him again. When the others returned to their camp they found that all the figures had disappeared from their notebooks. And last week there was a car from DERUDE that had an accident, one person died. Did you hear that? You know, the people here are strong.

When I asked the Project Manager what he thought of the medium of Chidyamauyu he said:

> I don't understand why he keeps refusing the project. Now that he is living in a house built by us, he should know better. But it's the people, they are afraid of the new medium of Nehanda. These people here, they lived here very isolated [lives]. They are traditional and stubborn. They do not want to change, even if things will get better. Their traditions are very strong, and they have these (…) powers, well, (…) you know what I mean, you have been here long enough.

Having indeed become acquainted with the hidden ways in which people refer to certain issues, I assumed he was referring to witchcraft[60].

As already mentioned in Chapter Two, project staff was withdrawn from Dande in 1995 and DERUDE ended its activities. The remaining tasks were transferred to the District Development Fund. What would happen to the now officially illegal settlers was not clear. The project staff had referred the problem to the Rural District Council, but neither the government officials nor the Ward Councillors serving on the RDC had so far dared to deal with this problem. The Chief Executive Officer of the RDC reported in September 1995 that the Project Manager had been asked to retire.

---

[60] The Project Manager's remark reminded me of an article by Van Dijk (2001) on Born Again Christians in Ghana. They think of their Christianity as part of their modernity. Their pastors require them to break with the 'backward traditions' of the old people. Yet, they do not deny the powers of the spirits honoured by their relatives, or the powers of their witchcraft, but they have redefined both spirits and witches as evil forces emanating from the Devil.

I finished my second period of fieldwork by the end of August 1994. In the summer of 1995, after the withdrawal of DERUDE and the project staff, I briefly returned to Dande. It was then that I discovered that the medium of Chidyamauyu was suffering from a severe loss of popularity. The District Development Fund (DDF) had taken over the duties of DERUDE employees, and attempts to have the land-use reforms introduced were renewed by DDF and Agritex. Many people told me that the medium had refused to become involved and had not publicly denounced the project for a long time. Many people I spoke to connected his apparent withdrawal from the conflict with the fact that the house that DERUDE had promised him had finally been constructed, and that the medium was actually living in it.

The people in Matsiwo A were divided in their opinions concerning the land-use reforms. In villages where plots had been demarcated (but still not allocated), resistance was more general, among both elders and younger people, as people could see that the new land distribution would cause tremendous problems. In Mburuma, where I had lived for two years, I could not find anybody who supported the Mid-Zambezi Project. In areas where no land was demarcated yet, people disagreed among themselves. Most elders still opposed the land reforms, while younger people continued to place their bets on the development, which they were sure would follow the land-use reforms.

Opponents of the project said they feared that this time the Mhondoro Chidyamauyu had really left the medium. As one elder stated:

> Yes, he deserved a reward for his work during the war. He could have accepted the house for his wife and children. But how can he live in that house himself? Mediums are not supposed to live in these modern buildings. Mhondoro do not like corrugated roofs. You have spoken to many Mhondoro mediums. Have you ever seen one living in such a house? Mediums have to live in pole and daga [huts], not surrounded by bricks. I am sure Chidyamauyu has left the medium. He is displeased that his medium lives in a house, which is as good as accepting the project.

Proponents of the land-use reforms - or rather the development projects that were believed would follow in the wake of these reforms - were more divided in their opinions concerning the medium. Some agreed that the spirit of Chidyamauyu had left the medium. Others used the medium's 'betrayal' as proof that Mhondoro mediums in general are impostors and that Christianity is the only true religion.

When I visited the medium, I found him living in a three-roomed brick house with glass windows and a corrugated roof. I arrived after dark and the medium complained that there was still no electricity in the valley. He was content with his house and felt that he had earned it during the war. He said that the Mhondoro had no problems with the house. He also said that his Mhondoro still objected to the project but that his people were divided. When I asked him why the previous rainy season had been bad again, he said:

The drought is caused by people who no longer respect the Mhondoro. They cut down trees they are not allowed to cut down, they bathe in sacred pools. Maybe it will rain this year if they show remorse. But they have been misbehaving for a long time.

This time he did not blame the drought on the proposed land-use reforms.

Concluding remarks

In this chapter I have described the involvement of the Mhondoro mediums in the struggle against the Mid-Zambezi Project. They told, and enacted, a counter-narrative to the 'land degradation narrative' that was underlying the project. According to this counter-narrative, the real owners of the land are the Mhondoro, not the State. The royal ancestors control the rain and the fertility of the land, and hence have a greater power over it. The chiefs and headmen have managed the land on behalf of the Mhondoro in a fair and appropriate way, taking into account the needs and capacities of their subjects. The post-Independence government, which came to power with the help of the Mhondoro, is violating the rights of the population of Dande and neglecting their needs. The 1991/2 drought and all subsequent dry spells, which have harmed agricultural production, were taken to be signs that the Mhondoro disagreed with the government's land-use policy, and a show of power meant to demonstrate the Mhondoros' control over the land.

The counter-narrative did seem to have some effect on project staff members. Though many remained convinced that the project was needed - as I have described in the previous chapter - they did not dare to go ahead with it as long as the mediums had not given them permission. It is possible, however, judging from the statements made by some staff members, that they interpreted the counter-narrative in a different way to the way the opponents of the project did. Instead of attributing the problems they experienced to the Mhondoro, they have attributed them to witchcraft exercised by those wishing to stop the project.

The government's reaction to the involvement of the Mhondoro mediums was a little different. On the one hand, it seemed as if the counter-narrative was not taken seriously at all. Though project staff was withdrawn from Dande, this did not mean that the attempts to introduce the land reforms were completely aborted. DDF and Agritex continued to plan the implementation of the land-use plan developed by the Agritex Planning Branch, though when I returned in 2000 for a brief visit they still had not managed to do so. On the other hand, government did seem to take those who put forward the counter-narrative, the mediums, very seriously. The medium of Chidyamauyu was rewarded handsomely, allegedly for his contribution to the struggle for Independence, and the aspirant medium of Nehanda was kept under close surveillance.

The counter-narrative contained references to the struggle for Independence. According to the narrative this struggle was fought with the aim of 'returning to the old ways', which in this context was interpreted as returning local control over land. Perhaps surprisingly, it did not contain any references to a 'return of the stolen land', which featured in official government rhetoric concerning the causes and aims of the second chimurenga, and is now put forward in defence of the current land invasions.

The Mhondoro mediums were powerful actors or interpreters in the staging of the counter-narrative. In the first place because of the strong religious connection made between the Mhondoro, specific territories in Dande and the management of natural resources. Though the access of the mediums to the supernatural world may have been interpreted a little differently by those trying to impose land-use reforms, a connection with the supernatural world is made by virtually all local actors in the Mid-Zambezi Project drama, including project staff. The second reason for the importance of the mediums was probably the role attributed to the Mhondoro mediums during the struggle for Independence. Many people in Dande believed that this should throw in some weight against the government, and this seems to be confirmed by the way in which the government responded to the medium of Chidyamauyu and the woman claiming to be possessed by Nehanda. These responses can be interpreted as attempts to control the Mhondoro mediums. However, it is not only the Mhondoro who are able to transfer authority from one party to another, as Lan (1985: 211) argues. As I have shown in this chapter, adherents can also transfer authority from one medium to another, rendering any attempt by the government to control the mediums useless, since it renders them powerless.

This brings me to the final point I would like to make in this chapter, that of the influence of the adherents of the Mhondoro cult. The cases described illustrate an aspect of the cult that has been ignored in most literature on the role of the Mhondoro mediums in the struggle for Independence: the way pronouncements by possessed Mhondoro mediums appear to be shaped by the opinion of the adherents. The work of Bourdillon is an exception to this oversight; he has described how a Mhondoro medium had his calls to attend the installation ceremonies completely ignored when he supported the nomination by the Rhodesian government of a certain chief against the will of the majority of inhabitants of the chiefdom (Bourdillon 1979). In his later work, Garbett (1986; 1992), another authority on the Mhondoro cult, also attributes some influence to the adherents when he argues that the hierarchy of Mhondoro mediums is not determined solely by the perceived genealogical relations between the different Mhondoro at a given time, but also by a ranking of their mediums by adherents of the cult.

Mhondoro mediums are supposed to work for the benefit of the adherents. The Mhondoro spirits are believed to be ultimately benevolent and do what is best for their adherents. Since participation in the Mhondoro cult is largely related to a person's place of residence (and cultivation), the group of - potential

- adherents constitutes a fairly heterogeneous group: village headmen and elders, younger people, successful cash croppers, subsistence farmers with or without jobs in the city, cattle owners, teachers and shop-owners, and so forth. People with different interests who also occupy different positions in the local power equation will have different ideas about what the Mhondoro will consider best for them and about what will offend the Mhondoro. Therefore, one will often find at least some people complaining about Mhondoro mediums.

If a spirit medium is presented with many different views, he or she may find it hard to issue a clear social commentary. Despite this, some groups may have a stronger position in relation to the cult. Village headmen especially are in a powerful position, as many of them also serve as ritual assistants of the mediums. We have seen that the medium of Chidyamauyu attached great importance to their opinions. Cogently, this does not mean that village headmen will always have their interests represented by Mhondoro mediums. If a large enough group of adherents opposes the village headmen on a certain issue, it may be expected that the medium's utterances will reflect this.

I have described how over time, a group of potential adherents came to support the project and did·not find its opinions reflected in the pronouncements of the Mhondoro medium. For this group, the option of challenging the reputation of certain mediums was foreclosed as the village headmen and elders who were opposing the project had obtained the support of these mediums. As a result, those supporting the resettlement project challenged the cult itself. They emphasised Christian values and associated these with development as opposed to the 'backward traditions' of the Mhondoro cult. Yet, they did not dare to denounce the cult completely, as is shown in their objection to the demarcation of fields in the most sacred area of the spirit province, Tsokoto.

To those who have difficulties with certain pronouncements made by Mhondoro mediums, two courses of actions are open. One is to send a delegation to the possessed medium, pleading with the Mhondoro to change his or her mind. Many mediums as well as adherents related to me how initially most mediums in Dande pronounced that the Mhondoro were against the introduction of cotton. Since it was one of the few profitable cash crops that could be grown in the area, many villages then sent delegations to plead with the Mhondoro to change their minds. Almost all Mhondoro mediums pronounced that the Mhondoro responded positively to the pleas, and had decided reluctantly to allow the cultivation of cotton in their provinces. The new Ward Councillor also sent a delegation to convince the medium of Chidyamauyu, but he did not succeed in obtaining support for the Mid-Zambezi Project.

A second option is to express doubts that the medium is (still) genuinely possessed by the Mhondoro, as was shown in the case of the medium of Chidyamauyu and the aspiring medium of Nehanda. Mhondoro mediums need to make strong cases to establish and uphold their positions. The transformation of the sufferer into the healer, the 'wounded healer complex' (Eliade 1959; Janzen 1992), seems to play a major in this. In his book 'Ngoma', John Janzen

(1992) considers this transformation to be one of the core features of Ngoma institutions. Yet, in my view, many of the core features Janzen describes, especially the transformation of the sufferer into the healer, serve more as a legitimisation for those who 'do ngoma' than as the core of the cult itself (see also Reis 2000).

In most accounts of how people have become Mhondoro mediums (see also Lan 1985), much stress is put on the medium's initial resistance to the possession by the Mhondoro. People do not become a medium voluntarily; on the contrary, it is described as a very painful process. Both adherents and mediums say that mediums do not choose a career as a medium, but that the Mhondoro choose their medium. It might very well be that the tales of illness are strategically used to show that initially the medium was not receptive to signs from the Mhondoro and that only through the force of illness is the Mhondoro able to draw attention to its wish to possess someone. By stressing that the medium does not choose to become a medium, does not consider it a career option, the mediumship may become more genuine and credible.

Nevertheless, even if one accepts that the concept of the wounded healer has ideological overtones, this does not exclude the possibility that some mediums actually did experience illness or adversity prior to their establishment as mediums. Burck (1989) found that many male n'anga received their calling while facing problems with their working careers, and a considerable number of female n'anga were either divorcees or widows. Burck suggests that embarking upon a career as a n'anga is a socially acceptable possibility to escape financial misery without losing face. The life histories of some Mhondoro mediums in Dande suggest similar problems prior to possession. As I have already described above, quite a number of them told me that they experienced the first signs of possession while they were working outside of Dande, where they were beset by problems arising from the jealousy of colleagues.

Most mediums I have spoken to emphasise that they consider the mediumship a personal burden. The mediumship disrupts their lives and prevents them from working hard in their fields or building up an enterprise. Mhondoro mediums are supposed to work for the good of the communities in their spirit province. Unlike n'anga, Mhondoro mediums are not expected to use their position to acquire personal wealth (see also Garbett 1977; Lan 1985). Yet, as mentioned earlier, popular mediums are often believed to be powerful healers as well. As such, they may attract large numbers of patients. While part of the fees paid by their clients is spent on the upkeep of the shrines and providing hospitality to these clients, they may still earn substantial sums of money. The large number of clients may enhance their reputation, but when things happen that reduce the faith followers have in the medium, the wealth that resulted from this large number of clients may then serve to show that the medium has been working for his or her own interest only.

As I have described above, most mediums and adherents emphasise that mediums are total strangers, unrelated to the Mhondoro who possess them, and hence unrelated to the chiefs. This emphasis may serve to enhance the image of impartiality; the medium has no personal interests to defend. Pertinently, as mentioned earlier, I found that nearly all mediums I interviewed were born or grew up in Dande and that almost half of them actually did belong to the same clan as the Mhondoro possessing them.

In the pronouncements cited in this chapter references are made to 'the past'. The past not only plays a role in the sense of referring to an era when local authorities did have control over land; in my opinion it also plays an important role in authenticating mediums. Most séances start with a recitation of the heroic acts of the Mhondoro in past wars and the history of the area. The problems of the present are compared with the problems of the past. Possessed Mhondoro mediums often deal with modern developments, issue social commentaries that have to do with 'modern' conditions and certainly do not oppose all forms of 'modern development'. Yet they often claim they have no knowledge of the present. Before entering the medium's hut, shoes and watches have to be removed 'as the spirits do not know these things'. To give an example, the first time I consulted the possessed medium of Karembera, I asked him if I could tape the séance. The spirit then asked me to explain what a tape-recorder was. I did so, and he agreed that I could use it. Towards the end of the session, he asked me how I was going to get the words out of 'that little black box' again. I replayed part of the tape for him and he roared with laughter. He sang one of his favourite songs 'to put in the little black box'. After the session, the mutape took me to the hut of the medium, where he asked me to wait as the medium himself (and not the spirit) wanted to ask me something. Entering the hut, I discovered a huge ghetto blaster displayed on an elaborately decorated shelf[61].

This brings me to another issue. Both adherents and mediums stress that the medium and the spirit possessing him or her are completely separate. The medium is no more than an empty vessel that can be filled by the spirit. The separation between medium and spirit is usually made more clearly by younger mediums that have not been practising for a long time. After a séance, they often ask their vatape what the spirit has said. Older, more established mediums

---

[61] This incident also strengthened my opinion, which I share with Bourdillon (1987b: 271), that the refusal of many mediums to get into contact with modern, western items was not so much a sign of resistance towards pre-Independence white domination, but 'proof' that they really are possessed by a spirit that lived long ago.

were more likely to answer questions about their spirits' opinions while they were not possessed once they got to know me better.

The issues of the counter-narrative as well as of the role and position of the mediums come to the fore in the next chapter, which will describe the involvement of Mhondoro mediums in the resistance to yet another project that 'hit' Dande during the period I was doing my research there.

A new medium for Chitsungo:
Resistance against two
irrigation projects

Introduction

The inhabitants of Chitsungo Ward were especially 'hard-hit' by projects that were supposed to improve their living conditions. Here, the Mid-Zambezi Project had been implemented; the twelve acre-plots had been demarcated and allocated. Those who had managed to obtain a plot had moved to their new fields, others were still illegally cultivating their old plots or had moved to the grazing areas. While they were still trying to come to grips with the Mid-Zambezi Project, they were confronted with two new projects in their Ward. In Chitsungo two separate irrigation schemes were planned, independent of one another.

The first project, the Dande Irrigation Project, was initiated by the government Agricultural Rural Development Authority (ARDA). This was the more ambitious of the two, and would affect a large part of Chitsungo. Implementation of this project would entail an extension of the cotton estate in Mushumbi/-Chitsungo operated by ARDA, and a redistribution of land already redistributed under the Mid-Zambezi Project. The acreage available to local farmers would be reduced and the remaining twelve-acre (roughly five hectare) plots allocated under the Mid-Zambezi Project subdivided into two-hectare units. Farmers who had already been relocated under the Mid-Zambezi Project would have to relocate again.

The second project was initiated by Agritex and involved a smaller area, but still located within the Dande Irrigation Project area. At the time I was conducting my research, Agritex had already obtained funding for its project, and was trying to implement it. The population in Chitsungo generally was not aware of the existence of two separate projects, and associated all activities related to irrigation with Agritex.

The inhabitants of Chitsungo not exactly welcomed the prospect of relocating for the second time. This chapter will describe another case of the mobilisation of *Mhondoro* mediums in the struggle for local control over land. Again resistance to state appropriation of control over land took the form of the staging of a counter-narrative presenting the royal ancestors as the real owners of the land. The case also strengthens my argument about the influence of adherents on the *Mhondoro* mediums' pronouncements. In this case a new medium appeared on the scene when opponents of the irrigation scheme(s) feared that the established mediums would give permission to Agritex to start its activities.

Two competing irrigation projects

The Dande Irrigation Scheme was initiated by ARDA[62]. ARDA is the post-Independence successor to the Rhodesian Tribal Development Corporation (TILCOR), and is responsible for the operation of all state-owned farms and plantations. In Dande, ARDA was running two farming estates, one in Mzarabani and one in Mushumbi Pools (in Chitsungo Ward).

Consultants working on the feasibility study started working in the area in 1992, and a first version of the inception and feasibility report appeared in 1993. ARDA envisaged the building of a dam on the Dande River, on the Escarpment, in Kachuta Ward[63]. The estimated yield of the dam would be 46,600 million litres per year. With this yield about 5800 ha could be irrigated with so-called overhead irrigation, or 3700 ha with gravity irrigation. The main beneficiary of the project was to be the ARDA itself, or rather, the cotton-farming estate it exploits in Mushumbi/Chitsungo. According to the project feasibility study (Government of Zimbabwe 1993: viii), this estate comprises 1500 ha, of which 400 ha had been cleared and developed at the time I conducted my research. In order to convince donors to support the scheme, a 'community component' was introduced. This component involved the creation of 1500 to 2500 irrigated small-scale farm units. The authors of the feasibility study proposed that the size of the units be restricted to two hectare. On the basis of the 1992 Census it was assumed that 1788 families were living in the project area.

---

[62] During the course of my research the association changed its name several times. The name alternated between Agricultural Development Association (ADA) and Agricultural Rural Development Association (ARDA).

[63] The building of this dam will result in the displacement of five villages, harbouring about 1000 inhabitants, who will need to be resettled (Government of Zimbabwe 1993: viii).

The authors of the feasibility report were aware of the fact that the people in the project area had already been relocated under the Mid-Zambezi Project. This, they assumed would create some problems for the Irrigation Scheme, but it was not considered a real threat to its implementation: 'By far the majority of the people are willing to join the project. The major problem will be to get support for a reduction of size of the allocated plots. Presently these are about five hectare [the twelve acres allocated under the Mid-Zambezi Project]. The new (irrigated) plot size would be much less (ibid.: 44)'. The reduction in plot size was to be compensated by the possibility of double cropping on the irrigated plots. Cotton was recommended as the main summer crop, while beans could be grown in winter. Other crops suggested were maize, oil seeds and tree crops (e.g. cashew) (ibid.: ix). In private conversations with some of the consultants working on the project it emerged that the proposed cropping pattern would be the only one which would generate enough income for farmers to be able to pay their contribution to the scheme. However, they were dubious about whether it would be possible to produce oil seeds and cashew nuts in Dande. The same consultants expressed serious doubts about the social feasibility study conducted, which supported the conclusion that people in Chitsungo were willing to join the scheme. As will be shown below, these doubts were justified.

Under the Mid-Zambezi Project 4000 ha was allocated to 808 households. According to the authors of the irrigation feasibility report - who apparently did not fully understand the nature of the Mid-Zambezi Project - these households consisted of 'new settlers', migrants (ibid.: ix). Another 200 'indigenous households' were said to be farming 600 ha (ibid.: ix, 26); these were probably households that had not been able to acquire a plot through the Mid-Zambezi Project, but had refused to leave Chitsungo. It is not clear what happened to the remaining 780 households that were residing in the (irrigation) project area according to the 1992 Census. The conclusion that the scheme would be able to absorb more people than currently present in the area (ibid.: 44) therefore seems rather problematic.

The feasibility study for the Dande Irrigation Project has been funded by the African Development Bank, which would also finance the implementation of the project if it were found feasible. This is the same institution that funded the Mid-Zambezi Project, which means that the Bank would be responsible for relocating the inhabitants of Chitsungo twice within a short period, as well as allowing a second project to destroy the results of the first.

Private conversations with some of the consultants revealed that ARDA exerted considerable pressure on them to report positively on the project. The serious reservations they harboured were ignored. The feasibility report had to be rewritten several times before it was accepted by ARDA. Technical preparations for the Dande Irrigation Project also took considerable time. In order to transport the water from the dam to Chitsungo, a tunnel would have to be drilled through a range of granite mountains on the edge of the Escarpment, which significantly increased the costs of the project, and hence the fees which would have to be paid by the 'beneficiaries' of the project. Several alternative solutions were designed, which took a considerable amount of time. In 2001, however, the African Development Bank gave the green light, and in 2002 construction activities on the dam were started.

At about the same time the consultants for the Dande Irrigation Project were active in Chitsungo, Agritex officers were working on their own irrigation plans in the same area. The consultants of the Dande Irrigation Project were aware of the Agritex project, and mentioned it in their report (Government of Zimbabwe 1993: 44) but without any comments on how the two initiatives should interact. Agritex, on the other hand, only became aware of the existence of plans for the Dande Irrigation Project quite late.

The District Agritex Extension Officer of Guruve District (Agritex DEO) claimed that water for the irrigation scheme in Chitsungo had to come from the Mazvikadei dam, near Darwendale (close to the capital Harare). Plans to use water from that dam for the Communal Areas dated from the early days of Independence, he said, but only in the early 1990s did money become available. The Agritex DEO claimed that the government had provided most of the money, but donors had also assisted. He did not know which donors, but he thought the EU's predecessor, the EEC, was involved. The money was made available through the Province. The Agritex DEO said that the plans for the Chitsungo irrigation scheme dated from 1993.

Water for the Agritex irrigation scheme had to come down to Chitsungo solely by gravity. At Chitsungo the water would be collected in Mushongaende Pool and from there distributed farther for irrigation. The Agritex DEO claimed that once electricity would reach Chitsungo this could be used for the distribution of the water. To increase the storage capacity of the pool, the construction of a dam was envisaged. During one of our first meetings, the Agritex DEO talked about irrigating 100 hectares. However, on 18 May, 1994, an Agritex official reported to the Guruve Rural District Council that a total of 1000 hectares would be irrigated, using the 15 million cubic metres of water available from Mazvikadei.

This change in figures may be related to the donor requests. Initially, Guruve Council applied for funds for seven small earth dams. The EEC was willing to provide financial assistance, provided that the Council redesigned the dams, as the EEC preferred larger dams that would accommodate irrigation projects. The Council suggested Agritex should be given the task of redesigning the dams.

The Agritex DEO claimed that each household in the scheme would receive a two, to two and a half hectare plot. Consequently, the Agritex irrigation scheme would also entail subdivision of Mid-Zambezi Project plots - which at the time had been demarcated by Agritex staff - as well as the relocation of farmers. The Agritex DEO admitted that no thought had been given to how the irrigated plots would be allocated, though he referred to a set of standard regulations designed specifically for access to irrigation schemes.

The crops, which Agritex advised should be grown on the irrigated plots, were probably better suited to the area than those proposed by ARDA. Basically, they consisted of the crops that farmers were already growing: green mealies, cotton, groundnuts and beans.

Guruve Council was not aware of the existence of plans for two separate irrigation schemes in the same area. At one of the Council meetings, a high official from ARDA announced that Agritex was redesigning dams to conform to the wishes of the EEC. He never mentioned, however, that ARDA also had plans for an irrigation scheme. Agritex and the Councillors only learnt about the ARDA plans when the consultants working on the feasibility study ran into Agritex staff and the local Ward Councillor.

As mentioned earlier, most people in Chitsungo were not aware of the existence of two different project proposals either. They tended to associate all project activities in their Ward with only one irrigation project: the one proposed by Agritex. The different activities caused considerable confusion. As the team conducting the feasibility study for the ARDA project discussed the plans with local farmers, an Agritex team was already beginning to prepare the construction of a dam at Mushongaende Pool.

My attention was drawn to the irrigation projects by several things. One of the consultants working on the ARDA project approached me because he had heard that my research involved the mediums of the *Mhondoro* spirits. He wanted my opinion on the problems the consultants were experiencing at the proposed dam site in Upper Guruve. *Mhondoro* mediums living near the site objected to its construction stating that the area to be flooded was an important burial site where the remains of the important ancestor, Chigowo, are buried. In Chitsungo itself *Mhondoro* mediums were also reacting negatively to the plans. Several *vatape* and *Mhondoro* mediums I interviewed about the Mid-Zambezi Project told me of a sacred pool near Chitsungo and the mysterious things happening there since Agritex employees and consultants for the Dande irrigation scheme started meddling with it.

As my 'base' was in Mburuma village, about 80 kilometres away from Chitsungo ward, I could not always follow the developments concerning the irrigation schemes as closely as I could follow the developments in relation to the Mid-Zambezi Project in Matsiwo A Ward. However, I did travel to Chitsungo several times, staying for short periods. The following account is based on interviews I conducted in Chitsungo ward during these periods.

A new medium for Mhondoro Chitsungo

The pool that both ARDA and Agritex were planning to use for water storage is called 'Mushongaende' and is considered sacred. According to myths recounted in Dande this is the pool into which Chitsungo's head rolled when Biri beheaded him. *Mhondoro* Chitsungo belongs to the Mutota (invader) lineage, and the mythology says that he was engaged in a fight with Biri, who belongs to the Bangomwe ('autochthonous') lineage, about who could control the rains.

Speaking of the pool, the medium of Mashapiko, Dazimata Mushoshoma, said:

> In this [Mushongaende] pool there are a lot of things which belong to different Mhondoro. You can also see funny things there: fish of which you can only see the bones, wild animals emerging from the pool and going into the bush. There are njuzu and tsunguni [water spirits]. In the pool there are drums. At certain times you can hear them being beaten and you hear people singing traditional songs. Sometimes you can also see the water boiling while the fish are still swimming, even though, if you put your finger in, it will burn. People from the family of Chitsungo are not allowed to go to the pool as his head fell into the pool.

Early 1994, a team from Agritex started to work near the pool. Almost at the same time another team arrived in the area conducting surveys for the feasibility study of the ARDA project. The people in Chitsungo Ward had not been informed about the irrigation plans and wondered what was going on in their area. .People started questioning members of both teams and discovered that plans had been made to irrigate large tracts of land and then redistribute the land. The plans were received with great suspicion as many foresaw renewed chaos would come along with the redistribution of already redistributed land, and some feared a further loss of land.

Shortly after the arrival of the teams, several accidents occurred. Two car accidents took place in which at least one person was killed. Rumours circulated that some documents containing surveying data had disappeared. While the consultants working on the ARDA project experienced most of their *Mhondoro*-related problems in Upper Guruve, and became involved with spirit mediums there, in Chitsungo all attention was focused on the Agritex team. Within the villages close to the pool the story started circulating that the Agritex team was followed by *zvipungu*, bataleur eagles, whenever work had to be done near the sacred pool. The medium of Mashapiko said that the Agritex people had been warned:

> When the people from the irrigation came (...), they were told by the people here that the pool is sacred, that they would have to see the Mhondoro. The people from the irrigation project refused, they said that they were not here to consult Mhondoro but to do their job as they were trained to do. Then they came across problems when they started working. Then they went to a man called Boxing [a sabhuku], who took them to the chief. Then the chief came to consult the Mhondoro.

> When these people first went to work, when they were surveying, they wrote their measurements in their book. The following morning they wanted to check the figures in the book, but there was nothing in the book. Then the people accused Mr. Boxing, the sabhuku, of causing these problems. Then the sabhuku went to clap hands to the Mhondoro and the figures reappeared in the book. When the surveying was finished they went to an area upstream. The car was followed by birds, [called]

nengure. Then they stopped to cut down trees. They saw a person. The foreman said: it is just a person, like you and I, continue your work. When they were surveying one of the workers disappeared in the bush and returned after four days, struck dumb. One day they also saw wild animals emerging from the pool. Then a chipungu [bataleur eagle] appeared, flying towards the foreman. This chipungu managed to scare the people working there. Then they went to the headman of that area, who took them to the chief.

The Agritex team was very upset by the accidents. Some members feared for their lives and asked local people for explanations. The headman of the village closest to the pool told them that the accidents were signs from the *Mhondoro* of the area. The *Mhondoro* was said to be upset because the team had not informed the local authorities of their plans. The headman offered to take the team to the chief of the area, Chief Chitsungo. The leader of the team contacted the Agritex District Extension Officer who invited the chief to his office in Guruve.

The chief informed the Agritex delegation that he was upset that he had not been informed of the activities in his area. The chief ordered the Agritex delegation to arrange a meeting to be attended by him, the headmen, the Ward Councillor - who was also the Chairman of the Council -and villagers living within the project area. He stated that he could not give his permission for the irrigation project unless he knew the opinions of his headmen and subjects. When I interviewed chief Chitsungo about his contacts with Agritex he replied:

> I was invited once to attend a meeting in Upper Guruve; that was the first time I heard about the irrigation project. There had been meetings in Bindura [Provincial Agritex Offices], but I was not informed about those. I was told that my people want the project. But I wanted a meeting to be organised with the people. Then they organised this meeting. At the meeting the people said they did not agree to the irrigation project. Then I told them to consult the Mhondoro mediums.

Here again we see a chief directing a community problem to the *Mhondoro* mediums. Yet, as we will see later, when it looked as if the mediums were giving in to Agritex, Chief Chitsungo did show his discontent by staying away from a ritual to be conducted at Mushongaende pool.

At the meeting with the chief and the people of Chitsungo, the Agritex District Officer explained the plans for the irrigation scheme and the need to use Mushongaende Pool for storing the water. He emphasised the importance of the project to 'the development' of the area. When I spoke with some villagers who had attended the meeting, they told me that the people at the meeting had argued that of course, they were in favour of 'development' and would gladly acquiesce in the project, if it were not for their fear that the *Mhondoro* of the area did not agree with it. Pertinently, they also expressed their concern about the redistribution of the newly allocated twelve-acre plots. The chief expressed similar concerns:

I do not know what to think of the irrigation project, I have never seen one. But I know that the twelve-acre plots will be divided into smaller plots. Some people fear they will not qualify for an irrigated plot. They do not know where to go if they cannot have a plot. I think that what they want to do is wrong. First they give us twelve-acre plots and then they take them again. At the meeting people asked the Agritex DEO what would happen if they do not qualify for an irrigated plot. They were told they would get a twelve-acre plot in one of the grazing areas. The people from the project told the people that there will be more families living in the area, because there will be more plots. I asked where these families will live, because the residential stands have already been demarcated. The people from the irrigation scheme said that they would peg more stands, that the village will become like a 'location' [township]. It is not clear whether the irrigated plots can be inherited. I am afraid that the elders will not be able to cultivate a two-hectare irrigated plot. Where can they go? Maybe they will be moved to Chief Chapoto's or Chief Chisunga's area.

In discussions I had with people about the irrigation scheme, many people expressed fears about chaos and conflicts as the twelve-acre plots that had been distributed and allocated with so much difficulty under the Mid-Zambezi Project would have to be redistributed again. Yet, some people obviously found it difficult to be outspoken about the irrigation plan. They were not against irrigation per se, but were reluctant to accept it given the developments that already had taken place in the Ward. As one person said:

> When they were planning the Mid-Zambezi Project they should have reserved an area for irrigation. Then, people who are in favour of irrigation could have joined the irrigation scheme without disturbing anybody.

Elders especially were concerned that they would either not be fit enough or would not have enough labour available for the intensive farming required on an irrigated plot. They feared losing their fields if the Agritex extension workers were to deem their production insufficient. Many elders said they would have preferred to continue the practice of riverine cultivation as a strategy to cope with drought: 'That is our traditional irrigation, is it not?'

However, there were also proponents of the Agritex irrigation scheme. These were mainly found among younger people. Those who were not yet married at the time the twelve-acre plots were distributed under the Mid-Zambezi Project had not received any land. They were left with almost no prospect of obtaining a field for themselves. The Mid-Zambezi Project made them even more dependent on the elders. They could only hope for a share of the twelve-acre plot of their parents or an illegally allocated plot in the grazing areas. The irrigation scheme might increase their chances of a plot for themselves. As one recently married young men told me:

> When the twelve-acre plots were pegged, I was not yet married. Now I have a child and no field. Mr. M. [Agritex DEO] told us that there will be more plots because

they are going to make four plots out of every twelve-acre plot. Then we, the youngsters, can also have a field of our own.

Chief Chitsungo advised the Agritex DEO to visit two spirit mediums in the area and ask the *Mhondoro* for approval of the project. The *Mhondoro* of the area, Chitsungo, at that time did not have a medium, so the DEO was referred to other mediums living close to Chitsungo, whose spirits are believed to be related to Chitsungo: the medium of Mashapiko; the medium of Nyahuma; and the medium of Karembera. The medium of Mashapiko explained to me why the chief had sent the Agritex DEO to him:

> Nyahuma is [Mashapiko's] father, Karembera his brother, Katuu his grandchild, Kajowa and Chitsungo as well. Negomo and Tombwe are his children. Mashapiko belongs to Mutota's line. The area belongs to Mashapiko, but later he gave a portion to his grandchild, Chitsungo. The pool is in Chitsungo's area. The boundary is the Nyagugutu Stream. Mashapiko said he would take responsibility for all rituals for the pool and tell his grandchild who does not possess anyone.

The medium of Katuu, Mandreck Chajiwa, agreed with the medium of Mashapiko: 'Mushongaende Pool is for Mupariwa, Mupariwa is Chitsungo, together with Mashapiko and Nyajore'.

A session was organised with the mediums of Mashapiko and Nyahuma, attended by a delegation from Agritex and the Ward Councillor. The medium of Mashapiko remembered:

> When these people [of the irrigation project] came to ask advice from the Mhondoro, they came with the chief. The first time they did not agree on anything. Then the second time they came with the chief, the Mhondoro said that they should pay Z$ 400.- to be thrown into the pool and a piece of cloth 400 or 500 metres long without a joint [seam].

> The third time they came they only had Z$20.-, they said Z$400.- was too much to be thrown into the pool. The pieces of cloth were not long enough. That is why the ritual was not successful. Maybe the Mhondoro asked for a 400-metre length of cloth without seam because it is impossible to find it. Maybe it is a sign of refusal.

According to the Ward Councillor, however, the mediums had not said that the gifts were not suitable. He maintained that the mediums had declared that the ritual offering of the gifts could not be conducted because of the absence of the moon.

The new moon having arrived, the delegation returned to the *Mhondoro* mediums. The Ward Councillor said that the mediums agreed to take the delegation to the pool. However, when they tried to go to the pool, the Agritex car got stuck in the sand. After several hours of trying to free the car, the delegation gave up and returned home. This was interpreted by many people as another sign of the *Mhondoro*'s disapproval of the irrigation scheme.

The next time the delegation visited the *Mhondoro* mediums, the mediums said that the gifts had to be thrown into the pool by the *vatape* of the Chitsungo *Mhondoro* and Chief Chitsungo. The Ward Councillor then sent a Council vehicle to fetch the chief and the headmen/*vatape*, but neither the chief nor the headmen wanted to attend the ritual. There are several stories as to why they refused to attend. The Ward Councillor claimed they refused to leave the beer party they were attending[64]. But another Ward Councillor, of a neighbouring Ward, said that the chief had said that he and the headmen were the people who should deal with the spirit mediums and the traditional rituals. They were angry that a ritual was to be conducted without them having been informed beforehand. The medium of Nyahuma, Samson Mujungirira, had yet another story:

> I was asked to go with the medium of Mashapiko to Mushongaende to give the money and the cloth to the vatape and local people to throw into the pool. But when we arrived at the pool we found nobody there. When we asked why the people had not come to the pool, we were told that the people do not want the irrigation project. They are afraid they will lose their twelve-acre plots. They are also afraid that if they are not fit enough to cultivate an irrigated plot, they will lose the plot and it will be given to someone else.   .

The medium of Karembera, Record Mverere, interpreted the absence of the chief and headmen in a slightly different way:

> We went there and Nyahuma said he wanted the chief and other people to be there, but nobody turned up, so we gave back the things which had been brought by the people who wanted to do the irrigation. (...) All the Mhondoro's properties are in that pool, Mushongaende. So to construct a dam there is an absolute impossibility. But you[65], you say lets just construct the dam. That is how you are destroying the country. If the Mhondoro say that it is not good [to construct the dam], you say: 'We are going to arrest your mediums and put them in prison'. That is too bad.

> *M.S.*: Are the people in Chitsungo in favour of the irrigation?

> *Medium*: That is why we had called for a meeting to ask the people if they are the ones who asked for the irrigation or not, but they did not turn up.

---

[64] The beer parties feature prominently in the critiques of Christians on the 'traditional life-style'.

[65] As already described in the preceding chapter, I was sometimes suspected of being closely associated with the projects implemented in Dande. People are aware that many 'development' projects are sponsored by Western organisations and the connection was easily made. In Matsiwo A ward, most people understood eventually that I had nothing to do with the Mid-Zambezi Project, but in Chistungo Ward, were people saw less of me, my explanation of what I was doing was not always taken seriously.

When I asked the chief why he had not shown up for the ritual he said that he should have been informed beforehand. The chief complained to me that Agritex was not following the proper procedures. He said that at the time the meetings were organised, other people were already working at the pool without either his consent or that of the mediums. Possibly, the people surveying at the pool were working for the ARDA Dande Irrigation Scheme and were not aware of the negotiations going on between Agritex, the chief and the *Mhondoro* mediums.

The Ward Councillor was a staunch supporter of the irrigation scheme. He was the chairman of the Rural District Council, and the first Ward Councillor from Lower Guruve to be elected in that position. The Ward Councillors of Lower Guruve were regarded with some suspicion by the government officials sitting on the Council, especially after their abortive attempt to form the Lower Guruve Ward Council Development Committee, which was condemned by local CIO officers as a nothing less than a separatist movement. Whether this played a role in his support for the irrigation scheme or not, is not clear.

The Ward Councillor of Chistungo featured prominently in the stories about the attempted rituals. Chief Chitsungo and the medium of Mashapiko told me that the Ward Councillor had organised the collection of the money and the gifts. The medium of Mashapiko:

> C. [Ward Councillor] organised the money and the gifts. Later, he came to say that if the ritual was not successful the people who bought the cloth and gave the money wanted it back. The Mhondoro said that they could take it back.

The Ward Councillor later confirmed to me that he had indeed organised the money and gifts. When I asked him why he supported the irrigation schemes, he said that as a Ward Councillor and chairman of the Council he was there to promote development. He said that the people in his Ward did not want to be left behind and wanted the irrigation project. When I asked him about the problems with the *Mhondoro* mediums, he said:

> Well, yes, they are stalling the process. We gave them money, we gave them cloth, they should perform the chiumba [ritual to ask permission from the Mhondoro] soon. Some people, especially the elders, are afraid of these mediums, that is why they do not dare to support the irrigation project. But they too want the project.

However, this is not how the (possessed) medium of Nyahuma presented the relationship between the *Mhondoro* mediums and their adherents during a seance I attended:

> (...) there are difficulties with the construction [of the storage dam] because people dislike the dam - and it is not we, the Mhondoro, who do not want the dam, but it is the people. The people are saying if they accept the irrigation project they are going to lose their twelve-acre plots, that is why they are rejecting the project and we the Mhondoro we also dislike that.

M.S.: If the people reject something, do the Mhondoro support them?

N: The Mhondoro is just as good as a chief, because if a chief instructs his people to do something and they refuse that means you are not a chief, and it is the same with us, the Mhondoro. The people always want to see the Mhondoro doing good things for the people in order that they support the Mhondoro. And usually if a Mhondoro does something that the people dislike, they do not respect that Mhondoro. They will [then] refuse if you ask them to do something for you.

After the failed attempt to conduct the ritual at the pool, some people in the project area feared that the mediums of Mashapiko and Nyahuma had renounced their resistance to the irrigation project, or as one young man in the village close to the pool said: 'We are afraid they have been forced to accept'.

Then something unexpected happened. A new medium of the *Mhondoro* Chitsungo announced himself. After the death of the last medium of Chitsungo, the *Mhondoro* had been without a medium for a very long time. What was surprising was that the new aspirant medium was in fact an alleged descendant of the *Mhondoro*. As described in the preceding chapter, mediums are supposed to belong to a different clan than that of the spirit possessing him or her. This medium not only belonged to the same clan, but also was closely related to the chief and the headman of the village closest to the pool, who are both believed to descend from the *Mhondoro*. The man, who for years had had problems attributed to spirits, started claiming he might actually be possessed by Chitsungo. The headman supported his claim and informed the other *vatape*, who supported the claim as well.

The aspiring medium was in a hurry to take over responsibility for the irrigation project. However, in his haste to have his authority over the area recognised, he insulted the other mediums. The medium of Nyahuma told me:

I heard about the new medium who claims to be possessed by Chitsungo. But that medium has not undergone his test yet. Yesterday I was visited by someone who had a message from the new medium. The new medium asked me to come to his place. I refused. Someone who is not an established medium cannot ask an established medium to come simply by sending a message; he should come to see the medium himself.

Yet, in a way, the appearance of a new spirit medium of Chitsungo also seemed to suit the established mediums in that it would free them from dealing with the difficult issue of the irrigation scheme. The medium of Mashapiko informed the Ward Councillor that the latter would have to hand the case to the new medium. The medium of Nyahuma agreed, but stated that the aspiring medium should first pass his test. The Ward Councillor and the Agritex DEO were very upset by the appearance of someone claiming to be possessed by Chitsungo and tried to persuade the other mediums to 'stick to the deal they had struck'.

By the end of May 1994 I had interviewed the new medium, Biswork Saranyanga or Mupariwa Mupariwa as he is also called. Mupariwa is one of the praise names of the *Mhondoro* Chitsungo. The royal Chitsungo family is also referred to as the Mupariwa family. The interview took place in the village closest to Mushongaende Pool. The village headman was present at the interview and served as the *mutape*. The village headman used to be the Chief Chitsungo, but he retired because of health problems[66]. His son was appointed acting chief. The new medium was a full cousin to the present chief - that is, the son of the brother of the village headman (the former chief). Father's brother's sons are referred to as brother, and so the new medium referred to the present chief as his brother. Other people present during the interview were the village committee chairman, the VIDCO chairman, and some young and old relatives of the medium who lived in the village.

The aspirant medium had just returned to Chitsungo Ward. He had lodged with the medium of Nyachawa (in Hurungwe) for about six months. During the interview he said he could not say who was the spirit who possessed him, as he had not yet undergone his test, but he and the others present made strong suggestions that it might be Chitsungo. When the medium became possessed he left little doubt that we were speaking with Chitsungo. The seance started with severe critique of the medium of Mashapiko:

> This area does not belong to Mashapiko, he is not responsible for the Mushongaende Pool. Mashapiko did not even ask the people responsible, the Mupariwa [Chitsungo] family, if they like the irrigation. The project will not be successful if they do not consult the right people. Mashapiko came here one evening with six other Mhondoro mediums and asked village headman, Chitsungo, to tell people to gather for beating the drums. Mashapiko had black cloth and money he wanted to throw into the pool, which he had been given by the council. If they just go ahead constructing the dam without consulting the right people, they are going to see some miracles and people are going to die during the construction. I am very disappointed with these irrigation people who cut down some trees around the pool without my permission. But they found the trees with new leaves the following day and some were lost in the forest and some were beaten/hit by eagles.

When I asked the spirit/medium what the people thought about the project he began to cry. I felt a little embarrassed, but my assistant became excited. He whispered to me that this was a sign that the medium was really possessed by a *Mhondoro*[67].

> People truly want the project, that is, if the government is setting up the irrigation to help the people, not to exploit them. We know that the government is helping people with drought relief food and is wasting a lot of money in order that the people survive. We really know that the government has no money to keep on buying food for the people. The people like the project, that is, if there is no trick behind the irrigation project which will force the people of this area to shift. If there is a trick,

---

[66] During the war he was once beaten up severely by guerrillas who suspected him of being a sell-out.

[67] Lan (1985: 51) also mentions weeping as a sign taken to indicate true possession.

we will fight underground. If they just follow the right traditional process, they are going to construct the dam without any problems, but if they do not listen to the Mhondoro, well, they are not going to be successful. My medium was born here, and has been a resident for thirty-four years. He has been working at Mhangura mine as a mill operator, but his home was here. Chief Chitsungo is his brother. The only way the project should be done is by consulting the right people and the right Mhondoro responsible for this area and the pool. Then they have to follow the instructions they will be given by those people and the Mhondoro who are responsible.

When I asked about the 'trick', the VIDCO chairman explained that because of the Mid-Zambezi Project many people in the village had had to abandon their old fields, and had been allocated twelve-acre plots which were located right in the middle of an area that the elephants used to go to the river. Others had failed to obtain a new plot, and were now residing in the village illegally. People were afraid that with the implementation of irrigation scheme the land would be redistributed again and even more people would lose their land. The Agritex scheme would indeed entail the subdivision and redistribution of part of the twelve-acre plots. The ARDA scheme would have even bigger consequences for local access to land, since the area to be subdivided would be larger, and part of the land thus 'freed' would be taken over by the ARDA cotton estate.

In August 1994 I returned to The Netherlands. When I came back to Dande a year later, I discovered that Agritex had not made much progress with the project. A Ward Councillor informed me that the Agritex DEO had reported to the Council that the 'cultural problems' had been solved and that the construction of the storage dam should have commenced in May 1995. However, nothing had happened. The same Ward Councillor told me that the Ward Councillor of Chitsungo and the chairman of the Council Roads, Works and Planning Committee had visited the new medium of Chitsungo. They had spent the night at his homestead and had talked with the spirit. They were told that as long as the irrigation scheme would benefit the people, *Mhondoro* Chitsungo saw nothing wrong with it. He did not want any gifts from the Council as the scheme belonged to the people.

In the meantime Guruve had a new MP who also represented Lower Guruve (formerly represented by the MP for Centenary). The new MP publicly supported the irrigation scheme -though it was not certain whether he was referring to the Agritex or the ARDA scheme - and told the audience attending his rally that the scheme would benefit those left without land by the Mid-Zambezi Project. The twelve-acre/five hectare-plots would be subdivided in two hectare-plots, thus creating almost twice as many plots.

When I interviewed the Agritex DEO in September 1995, he informed me that the Ward Councillor of Chitsungo Ward was pressing him to go ahead with the irrigation scheme. He had also received complaints from Agritex officials at Provincial level that the project budget had not been spent and little progress had been made.

The Agritex DEO still maintained that the people in Chitsungo were in favour of the scheme. He claimed that the only problems Agritex was experiencing were 'of a cultural nature'. The irrigation specialists had started working near the pool before they were aware of the fact that the pool was considered sacred. Later during the interview, the Agritex DEO admitted that perhaps some people had had reservations, but that he thought the 1993/94 and 1994/'95 droughts in the valley were 'a blessing in disguise' as these convinced people of the need for irrigation. At the same time, however, he acknowledged that Chitsungo had not suffered as badly from the drought as other Wards. The Agritex DEO said he has spoken to the medium of Chitsungo and had received his permission to construct the storage dam at Mushongaende.

Interestingly, the Council's Senior Executive Officer interpreted the situation differently, taking a line that had more in common with what I heard in Chitsungo. According to the SEO, the problems experienced with the irrigation scheme and those with the Mid-Zambezi Project had similar origins: nobody ever asked the people in Dande whether they needed these projects. A further complication arose from the fact that the irrigation project was planned in an area where the Mid-Zambezi Project had previously been implemented:

> First people were allocated twelve-acre plots, now these plots will be divided in 2.5 acre plots. They should have implemented the irrigation scheme in another part of the valley and then invite people, also from outside the valley, to participate, people who really want to work on irrigated fields. And now the Agritex staff has approached the spirit mediums without consulting the chief and sabhuku first. One has to follow the proper procedures.

The medium of Chitsungo, who had passed his test during my absence and was now recognised by most other *Mhondoro* mediums in Dande, confirmed he told the councillor and the Agritex DEO to go ahead with the scheme:

> When you went [to the Netherlands], C. [the Ward Councillor] and his company came here. He talked with the spirit. The spirit said: ' am not stopping you from constructing the dam'. They argued, but still the spirit did not refuse. The spirit went on saying that those spirit mediums who accepted the piece of cloth, beads and money are the ones who know about Mushongaende. 'Go and return with those who accepted the gifts'. Then Mr. C. went to fetch the mediums who had accepted the gifts but they refused to come. Mr. C. returned with the gifts and he wanted to hand the gifts over to the medium of Chitsungo, but the Mhondoro refused the gifts. The medium told Mr. C.: 'Go and construct the dam, I will tell you what I want when you have completed your work'. Since that last meeting Mr. C. never returned again.

> (...) It was not possible for the Chitsungo Mhondoro to accept the gifts because he did not know how this issue started. The Mhondoro is not rejecting the project, but he referred the Councillor to the other mediums as they had once told the councillor that they could solve the problems of the dam. But if C. and his company had consulted me first, I could have told them what to do in order to obtain permission

for the dam, because the Mushongaende Pool does not belong to one Mhondoro. There are three Mhondoro responsible for the pool. These Mhondoro are: Chitsungo, Nyajore and Chingoo[68]. So I cannot give them permission when Chingoo and Nyajore are not present. The first Mhondoro to consult is Chitsungo Mupariwa because he is the owner of the pool. Then you go to Chingoo and then to Nyajore. We should not talk about the mountains, because they belong to Chiwawa. So Mashapiko and Nyahuma are responsible for this issue, because they are the mediums who charged all the gifts for the Mushongaende Pool. So now we are not able to refuse. It was better if this issue had started from Chingoo or Nyajore, we could have informed each other officially and we could have agreed on something about the dam because it is being constructed for our children. (…) These other mediums wanted to take advantage of the fact that they were possessed first. So I accept, but not wholeheartedly. They did it on their own excluding me because they wanted money, together with [the Ward Councillor]. If the Councillor had told the chief about the issue then the chief could have talked to the sabhuku. The sabhuku were going to inform their spirits and the spirits were going to tell them what to do. (…)

They [the other mediums] colonised us. We just simply acquiesced because they had already given permission. But we would like to see if they are going to be successful because the land, the pool and the heaven is ours. The Mhondoro said: 'You continue with what you were doing and, if you succeed, then you will come to us and tell us that you succeeded. If you do not succeed, then do not come because I am the owner of this land'. (...) If [the Ward Councillor] is saying that the Dande Mhondoro accepted the dam he is lying, we repudiate it because we were not informed. (...)

Now the Mushongaende pool has dried up. The reason is that there is a conflict between Mashapiko, Nyahuma, C. [the Ward Councillor] and me. So I want to see if these mediums really have the power to consult the Mhondoro of this pool, Chitsungo Mupariwa. I realised they were interested in the pool because it always has water in it. So we closed the pool and we will see if there is ever going to be water in it again (…). They wanted to destroy my home, but what are they going to destroy now as I have already destroyed my huts myself? I have moved the hippos, crocodiles and I covered the clay pots with sand. So now we wait to see what they are going to do with the pool.

The people you see here are the local people. They may accept the project because they use force. They are colonising us. The government wants to help us and we accept that, but we are against the things that were done because these colonised us. You [here, he suddenly identified me as someone involved in the project] were saying that you are going to arrest us if we refuse. So we just accepted because we were afraid of being put in prison. (...) Now, see if you can supply the people with water from Mushongaende. The heaven and land is ours. You are just in charge of

---

[68] Chingoo's territory includes the area in Upper Guruve where the dam for the Dande Irrigation Scheme is planned.

the topsoil, you, the government and the Christians. Two inches off the ground, and two inches below the ground that is where we start. We know where the rains come from and where the sacred things are. (...)

I told [the Ward Councillor] to remove the pegs [from the Mid-Zambezi Project], but C. did not do anything about it. The people here did not receive drought relief. I think C. tries to starve the people so that they would move.

When I visited the pool in September 1995, I was most surprised to see it had indeed completely dried up. This had not even happened during the 1991/1992 drought, which affected the whole of the Southern African region. However, as I already mentioned in the preceding chapter, this drought led to the construction of more dams on Commercial Farms in Upper Guruve. The 1993/1994 rainy season had not been a very good one either, and many Commercial Farmers may have decided to stock more water in their dams.

The Agritex DEO told me that the chief and village headmen had demanded to be taken on a 'look and learn tour'. They wanted to see other irrigation projects before they could accept the Agritex irrigation scheme. The Agritex DEO said he had no 'mileage' left, that is, the budget for running the Agritex vehicles had been spent. The Irrigation Officer of the Province was experiencing the same problem according to the DEO. The Agritex DEO claimed that because no 'look and learn tour' can be organised, the project had ground to halt. 'The cultural problems have been solved, the spirits needed to be appeased, but the project no longer has top priority'.

To this day the Agritex irrigation scheme never materialised. As I am writing this book, however, the Dande Irrigation Scheme feasibility study has finally been completed and accepted by ARDA. Despite the recent upheavals in Zimbabwe, the African Development Bank has approved a loan for the project, and the construction of the dam in Upper Guruve has started.

Concluding remarks

As in the case of the Mid-Zambezi Project, responsibility for expressing local opinions on the irrigation scheme was delegated to the *Mhondoro* mediums of the area by Chief Chitsungo. Once again, the *Mhondoro* were pitted against the state as the true owners of the land and the only ones who could give permission for the scheme. As the *Mhondoro* in whose territory the sacred pool was situated had no medium at the time Agritex started working in the area, the problem was referred to 'neighbouring' mediums. In the preceding chapter I have already shown how the medium of Chidyamauyu consulted the village headmen before he issued a verdict on the Mid-Zambezi Project. In this case, it was the medium of Nyahuma who stated quite openly that the adherents influenced mediums' pronouncements.

When people feared that the neighbouring mediums had accepted the irrigation scheme because they had been witnessed organising an acceptance ritual at the pool, the chief 're-assumed' his duty again by boycotting the ritual, an action in which he was joined by his village headmen. Apart from questioning the reputation of mediums, the boycotting of rituals is another strategy open to adherents when they seek to influence the mediums' pronouncements. Bourdillon (1979) has also described this strategy. He depicts village headmen who boycotted the installation rituals organised by *Mhondoro* mediums for a chief selected by the Rhodesian government, who lacked local support. There, the argument provided by the boycotting headmen was also that the proper procedures for organising the rituals had not been followed. Schoffeleers equally considers insistence on the 'proper' conduct of rituals to be an important influencing mechanism. He argues that the politically less powerful often become ritual conservatives, stalling decisions by insisting on the following of 'proper' procedures and rituals when the definition of what these 'proper' procedures are is often impossible (Schoffeleers 1992: 82).

In Chitsungo the adherents were boycotting rituals, rather than discrediting the involved mediums' reputations. Then an unexpected development took place: a new medium appeared who claimed to be possessed by the *Mhondoro*, who was believed to be the owner of the pool that was at the centre of the conflict with Agritex. I am convinced that the sudden appearance of this new medium was a reaction to the fear that the other mediums would go along with Agritex. The new medium was a rather unlikely candidate for the *Mhondoro* mediumship. Not only did he belong to the same clan as the *Mhondoro* possessing him - although that is apparently not so very strange, as I found more mediums belonging to the same clan as the *Mhondoro* possessing them - but he was even considered a direct descendant of Chitsungo. The new medium settled in the spirit's territory without the assistance of one of the local *Mhondoro* mediums, which was also highly uncommon. He then claimed responsibility for the pool before he passed his test.

Yet, despite his haste to take on the responsibility, the new medium did not denounce the irrigation scheme unambiguously. I was not able to ascertain whether he had given permission to Agritex when the pool had already dried up, thinking that the dry pool would prevent Agritex from implementing the scheme. The drying up of the pool indeed was a powerful image emphasising the *Mhondoro*'s power over the territory.

The possessed medium's earlier pronouncements, in which he stated that the project was good if there were no 'tricks' behind it, might be taken as a reflection of the uneasy feelings unsettling many people in Chitsungo. They were not against irrigation *per se*, and certainly did not want to be accused of being anti-development. The main problem the opponents of the scheme had was that it was introduced after they had already been resettled under the Mid-Zambezi Project. Those who were in favour of the irrigation scheme were the ones who had been left landless by the Mid-Zambezi Project. They hoped the scheme could solve their problems by providing them with land. However, even the supporters of the scheme realised that the irrigation scheme could create renewed conflicts over land. I do not have sufficient data to check the proponents' religious affiliation, but apart from the Ward Councillor, I never heard them commenting in such a negative way on the *Mhondoro* cult as the advocates of the Mid-Zambezi Project did.

The *Mhondoro* cult serves as an appropriate platform to discuss issues concerning the utilisation of natural resources. Yet, in my opinion, involving the *Mhondoro* mediums is not always an indication that people reject certain developments. They may be 'buying time'. The people of Chitsungo were not involved in the planning of the irrigation scheme. They were simply subjected to yet another project that was going to change their lives tremendously. They needed time to discuss what they thought of the project among themselves.

The people of Chitsungo and those working on the irrigation schemes tell different stories about what constitutes development and who owns the land. The problem lies in the fact that the project planners do not always seem to understand the people's stories. The planners in Guruve interpreted the problem as a cultural problem, which required nothing more than the following of 'the proper procedures' and 'appeasing the spirits'. Similar remarks could be found in the Agritex Planning Branch document on the Mid-Zambezi Project in Matsiwo A (Agritex Planning Branch 1993: 4). The consultants who wrote the report did not see - or perhaps did not wish to admit - that the problem was actually the proposed project itself, but maintained that the problems they were experiencing were of a 'cultural nature'. They also attributed too much power to the cult's mediums in terms of influencing people's ideas about their projects; whereas I believe the mediums' pronouncements reflected and were influenced by the attitudes of a considerable part of their adherents.

Planners and implementers always seem to underestimate the problems involved in obtaining support for interventions. All documents and interviews state that 'yes the people are in favour'. People indeed did say so, but they always added a 'but'. They seemed to understand the planners' narrative better, and did not want to be considered as opposing development, but they did have serious objections to certain aspects of the projects presented as 'development'. Project staff often ignored the 'buts'.

The Agritex employees who were working 'on the ground' partly spoke a similar language to that of the local population. They too believed in spirits. Yet, as mentioned in the previous chapter, they may not have agreed with the adherents of the *Mhondoro* cult that they were dealing with benevolent spirits, but may have attributed what was happening to witchcraft. Though I have no proof, I strongly felt that the lack of a budget for 'look and learn tours' was used as an excuse to abandon the project, being substituted for the main obstacle to the implementation of the scheme. It would be interesting to investigate if the implementers of ARDA's Dande Irrigation Project will come across the same problems as Agritex staff did when they move ahead with their even larger irrigation scheme.

8

Internal conflicts: Migrants, Mhondoro and witchcraft

Introduction

The preceding chapters have mainly dealt with resistance and resentment towards the proposed land reforms. Though I have described conflicts between opponents and supporters of the reforms and how some of the opponents came to change their minds, perhaps the stories presented in these chapters suggest a certain sense of unity and determination within the communities confronted with the reforms. Most of the time, however, this was not the prevailing sentiment. While some concerted acts of resistance were organised, as became clear especially in Chapter Six, attempts to implement the land reforms were accompanied by spates of serious clashes between villagers. These are the subject of the present chapter.

In many of the conflicts references were made to migration, from the Plateau of Zimbabwe into Dande, but also temporary out-migration as well as internal migration within Dande. This seems in agreement with the view of many policy makers and planners who often consider migration and mobility to be a problem. For a long time anthropologists also saw it as a phenomenon out of the ordinary that deserved study and explanation (Amselle 1976; Hecht 1985). However, more recently, a growing number of social scientists argue that the boot is on the other foot and it is in fact sedentarism that needs to be problematised (De Bruijn, Van Dijk & Foecken 2001). They argue that the way mobility is interpreted is often biased in the sense of what Scott (1998) refers to as 'seeing like a state': our lives are organised in bounded geographical spaces of the state, the city, the village, the house, the field and so on, forever determining identities in a static and localised mode. When mobility emerges it becomes a problem

In Chapter Two and Three I already argued that in Dande, migration has been a constant factor of life. Oral history abounds with stories of conquerors and migrants, people 'coming from elsewhere'. These different groups of people that settled in the area have left their traces in the religious domain, where each is represented by a royal ancestral spirit, a *Mhondoro* spirit. The *Mhondoro* cult with its 'spirit provinces', areas with relatively well-known boundaries controlled by a *Mhondoro* spirit, may seem to suggest close links between the ancestors and specific territories, between their descendants and these territories. Yet, on the basis of my fieldwork I will argue that it is precisely this focus on territoriality that contains many possibilities for the acceptance of migrants.

The government of Zimbabwe has tried to limit migration to Dande as well as to control local settlement patterns through the instrument of the Mid-Zambezi Project. These attempts have not been entirely successful, but ideas about migration and movement have changed as a result. This has also had repercussions in the religious domain: although the *Mhondoro* mediums did play an important role in local resistance to the project, their role in accepting migrants and transforming them into kinsmen has been considerably reduced. The project has put notions of 'autochthony' and 'stranger' at the forefront again, and has created conflicts in which official, bureaucratic identities and self-ascribed identities often clashed. Witchcraft played an important role in these conflicts.

Witchcraft is still an important issue in everyday life in Africa. It has not disappeared in the post-colonial Africa, on the contrary, it has proved highly flexible, alive to the rhythms of the world, as Geschiere has argued (1995; 1997). There are even authors who claim that witchcraft (accusations) have increased in post-colonial times (Colson 2000; Comaroff & Comaroff 1999; Rowlands & Warnier 1988). Many scholars argue that there is no intrinsic opposition between witchcraft and modernity; that modernity has not led to disenchantment (Comaroff & Comaroff 1993; Geschiere 1995; Thoden van Velzen 2001). The complex of images of the occult is forever changing and being recreated, and often expresses efforts to make sense of socio-political and economic changes, or even to control these (Thoden van Velzen & Van Wetering 1988; Geschiere 1995: 9).

The adaptive capacity of witchcraft images stems from their ambiguity. Geschiere (ibid.) argues that this ambiguity has to do with both political power and economic performance. This is in contrast with earlier theoretical work on witchcraft, which often considered witchcraft accusations as either consistently attacking power and wealth, or consistently supporting it. In English social anthropology in the 1950s and 1960s, emphasis was put on the 'levelling' tendencies of witchcraft (see e.g. Marwick 1965; Middleton and Winter 1963). Later publications stressed that witchcraft could have accumulative tendencies as well, and proposed to distinguish societies according to their tendencies of generating either 'levelling' or 'accumulating' witchcraft accusations. These tendencies were considered to be related to specific forms of kinship organisations (see e.g. Bourdillon 1990: 199-202). Since then studies on witchcraft have tended to focus almost entirely on the link between witchcraft and accumulation (see e.g. Rowlands and Warnier 1988; Austen 1993). Geschiere argues that in the modern context witchcraft simultaneously displays both levelling and accumulative tendencies. These tendencies are inextricably linked and it is the precarious equilibrium between the two that should be investigated if we want to study the modernity of witchcraft and the diverse interpretations witchcraft provides for new inequalities (Geschiere 1995: 25).

In this chapter I want to describe how migration as a continuing factor in Dande is reflected in the *Mhondoro* cult. With the introduction of the Mid-Zambezi Project the involvement of *Mhondoro* mediums in the integration of migrants in Dande was interrupted. The mediums hardly played a role in conflicts within the community over land. The conflicts were taken into another, but related, part of the religious domain: witchcraft. I will present some cases that seem to confirm Geschiere's remark about the ambiguity of witchcraft towards economic differentiation. Cogently, these cases show that people in Dande struggle with the relationship between modernity and witchcraft, and present conflicting stories on this issue.

The guardian spirits of the land: Territoriality and mobility

The concept of spirit provinces seems to emphasise territoriality, a link between ancestors and the land, and between their descendants and the land. Indeed, in the struggle to get the land back that was stolen by the white settlers, references were frequently made to ancestral spirits to strengthen claims to certain territories. Paradoxically, the use of the very same concept of territoriality within the *Mhondoro* cult allows for mobility, for flexibility in membership of the cult and the incorporation of migrants.

As I have already described in Chapter Six, membership of the *Mhondoro* cult is partly based on lineality; members of the chiefly clans that claim descent from one of the *Mhondoro* spirits can consult the mediums of their ancestor regardless of where they are living. For all others, membership is based on territoriality; that is, all persons living, and more importantly, cultivating land within a spirit province are supposed to honour the *Mhondoro* of this province and recognise the spirit's ownership of the land, regardless of whether that person is a descendant of the *Mhondoro* or not. In other words, strangers living and cultivating in *Mhondoro* territory are more or less automatically included in the cult.

Mobility is also reflected in the founding myths in which the *Mhondoro* play a role. In Dande it is possible to discern two main lines or lineages of *Mhondoro*:

the lineage which is headed by Bangomwe representing the 'autochthonous' ancestors and a lineage representing fifteenth century invaders of Dande headed by Mutota. But even the 'autochthonous' *Mhondoro* are believed to have come 'from elsewhere', as the mediums of Bangomwe, Nyahuma and Negomo told me.

The symbolic politics of inclusiveness

When newcomers arrive in the area they not only have to ask permission of the chief and village headman, but must also apply to the *Mhondoro* for permission to live and plough in the *Mhondoro's* territory[69]. A gift must be presented to the *Mhondoro* - either directly to the medium or indirectly through the village headman who often doubles as the medium's ritual assistant - and the newcomer will also have to take part in the rituals of the agricultural cycle. By doing so, strangers are accepted as and transformed into the grandchildren of the *Mhondoro*. In this way, the threat they may pose to the authority of the chiefly, royal lineage, is dispelled. The 'strangers who became kinsmen' are defined not . in terms of lineage, but in terms of territory (Lan 1985) and are included in the *Mhondoro* cult. All adherents have the right to consult *Mhondoro* mediums.

There can be several reasons for people to go and live in another chieftaincy; they could either be looking for better land to cultivate or trying to escape conflicts with their former chief or village headman. New economic opportunities could also be a pull factor: a cascade of myths as well as older people's life-histories mention the possibilities of elephant hunting and salt gathering as reasons for moving to Dande.

The practice of bride service in Dande too has contributed to the large number of 'strangers' living in the Dande chieftaincies. Because of the fact that Dande was infested with tsetse fly it was impossible to keep cattle there. Therefore, those who were not able to acquire prestige goods through participation in trade with the Portuguese, or in later times earn enough money in wage labour, could not pay bride prices. Instead, as described in Chapter Three, the groom had to perform agricultural tasks for his in-laws. The period of bride service could last for more than ten years. After the completion of their bond, many men decided to stay in the village of their in-laws where they had lived for so long, and would then be allocated their own fields. These men would be 'strangers', as marriage is as a rule clan exogamous.

One concept that shows the symbolic importance and inclusion of migration and the presence of 'strangers' in Dande is the concept of *sahwira* relationships. When a person dies, the deceased's body can neither be washed nor buried by

---

[69] As I have described in Chapter Three, most migrants I interviewed told me that they did not visit a *Mhondoro* medium personally to ask permission to stay, but that the village headmen did this on their behalf.

someone of the deceased's family, nor even by someone from the same clan. 'Strangers' are needed to bury the dead and each family has a special reciprocal relationship with one or more families that belong to a different clan to take care of each other's deceased. The members of these families refer to one another as *sahwira* (Bourdillon 1987: 61). *Sahwira* relations can be formed between people who belong to different ethnic groups; nor is difference in nationality a barrier. As I described in Chapter Three, I came across many examples of families who, during the periods they were working at commercial farms on the Plateau of Zimbabwe, initiated *sahwira* relations with families from Zambia and Malawi, who belonged to non-Shona speaking groups. In theory the *sahwira* relationships extend to following generations; they are patrilineally inherited. It is impossible to refuse hospitality to a *sahwira*.

The relationship between clan and territory is a complicated one (Bourdillon 1987). Bourdillon (ibid.: 24) claims that the word 'clan' may be a misnomer since '(...) it refers to an amorphous and scattered group of people whose only identity as a group is a common clan name'. This clan name (*mutupo*) is inherited through the father. The names of clans refer to totem animals or body parts that the members of the clans are forbidden to eat. Clans are subdivided in sub-clans, distinguishable by a praise name added to the clan name (e.g. *Nzou Samanyanga* means 'elephant', the name of the clan, and 'keeper of the tusk', which is the praise name). People often associate the sub-clan names with certain geographical areas, suggesting, Bourdillon claims, that they were originally local pockets of a particular clan (ibid.: 24).

Pertinently, there is a certain association between chiefly clan names and territories, but these territories can be extended or be lost to conquerors. Nevertheless, many people maintain that the name of a sub-clan - that is, the name of a clan in combination with a specific praise name - does indicate a certain place of origin. Clan membership also facilitates mobility: people who are not related to one another, and come from different parts of Zimbabwe (or even from Mozambique, provided they belong to a Shona-speaking group) but share the same totem animal, are supposed to offer one another hospitality, and such hospitality features in some of the migrants' life histories. In theory, clan membership cannot be changed. Yet, adopting a new clan name to facilitate settlement in a new area or even 'stealing' a clan's name to underpin one's claims to a conquered territory plays a prominent role in the founder myths in Dande. One myth, for instance, recounts how one of Mutota's children stole the elephant tusks that Bangomwe used as headrests. From then on Mutota's descendants claimed to belong to the same clan as Bangomwe: *Nzou Samanyanga*, Elephant, keeper of the tusks.

Mhondoro mediums and migrants

The Mid-Zambezi Project produced conflicts over land at two different levels. One was between the state and the opponents of the project. In the preceding chapters I have described how the mediums of the *Mhondoro* cult played an important role in the conflicts at this level, expressing grievances, contesting the state's authority over land by claiming that the ultimate owners of the land are the royal *Mhondoro* spirits, and threatening with supernatural punishments if these claims were not recognised.

The *Mhondoro* mediums were less influential in the other type of conflicts over land, the conflicts among the local population over who would have the rights to the twelve acre-plots, should the Mid-Zambezi Project not be stopped. In these conflicts questions of identity played an important role (see Chapter Four). Conflicts arose over the definition of `migrants' and `long-term residents'.

When I first arrived in Dande in 1988, the term 'migrants' was used primarily to indicate the group of newcomers who had arrived since Independence, and sometimes applied to those who had arrived in the late 1960s. This group was a very heterogeneous one, including Shona-speaking people from the southeast of Zimbabwe (speaking Karanga and Zezuru dialects), and former Commercial Farm labourers of Malawian, Mozambican and Zambian origin, with or without Zimbabwean citizenship. Some of the more recent settlers were Mozambicans from areas just across the border (sometimes originating from the same spirit province, since many of these provinces overlap the borders between the two countries), who were also referred to as Korekore. Initially they were not considered to be migrants, but as tension increased they were. While conflicts over land mounted, the definition of 'migrants' was broadened, and people started looking deeper and deeper into the past to find ancestors who did not originate from Dande.

As I described in Chapter Four, the conflicts among the inhabitants of Dande were related to earlier settlement patterns and the way these conflicted with project regulations. Just to remind the reader: most of the early inhabitants of the villages, those who considered themselves 'autochthons', had their fields on the banks of the many small rivers running through the area. As migration continued, it became increasingly difficult for migrants to gain access to riverine fields other than by borrowing or renting them. The fields allocated to the more recent newcomers by chiefs and headmen were generally situated farther away from the riverbanks. When existing villages were reorganised, migrants stood a better chance of obtaining fields, since they were often already farming in the upland areas demarcated by Agritex. This stood in contrast to long-term residents who had most of their fields near the rivers, and hardly ever had demarcation pegs in their fields.

Once Agritex had demarcated twelve-acre plots in a certain area, this was often followed by a scramble for land within the new boundaries. If a plot had been demarcated within an existing field, the farmer who cultivated the most acres within the plot could have that plot officially allocated to him[70], provided he had Zimbabwean citizenship and was officially registered at the Rural District Council (this was locally referred to as 'having district citizenship'). The last criterion had been adopted by project staff under pressure from the Council and was meant to protect the rights of the long-term residents. It did not always have the desired effect since many of the recent migrants had Zimbabwean citizenship and had registered themselves with the Council. Complications arose because some of the long-term residents had obtained their identity cards outside of the District, when they were working on Commercial Farms and in the cities, and had never verified the district number on their cards. In order to defend their rights to land, long-term residents suddenly claimed large parts of the newly demarcated fields, stating that a long time ago the chiefs had allocated that land to them for future use. They transferred all their labour to the new plots, clearing as many acres as possible in order to stand a better chance of having them allocated.

When the project was first introduced, many migrants welcomed it, thinking it would provide them with more secure rights to land than they felt chiefs and village headmen could guarantee them. After a while, as the project turned out to seriously disturb their relations with their hosts, most of them changed their minds and supported local resistance to the project. Despite this support, many of them saw their rights to land in Dande denied.

Violent clashes between migrants and long-term residents were rare; the killing of one migrant in a fight over a twelve-acre plot in Karai VIDCO was a sad exception. But tensions grew and the old mechanisms of inclusion were strained. Though in theory *sahwira* relationships cannot be broken, at the height of the conflicts over land I witnessed in Mburuma the breaking up of several *sahwira* relationships between migrant families and autochthonous families.

Many of the migrants who had arrived after 1985 had not been taken through 'the proper' procedures to ask permission from the *Mhondoro* for their settlement in the villages. The majority did report having paid a small sum to village headmen destined for the *Mhondoro* medium of the area they wanted to settle in, but of those who arrived after 1985 very few had had a *chiumba* performed. This meant that they had not become 'sons and daughters' of the *Mhondoro* and continued to be strangers.

Mhondoro mediums complained that they had not been informed about the continued migration, and therefore had not been able to check the migrants on any proneness to engage in witchcraft. The possessed *Mhondoro* mediums I interviewed were not unanimous in their attitudes towards the migrants. About

---

[70] The 'him' here is not a sign of gender bias on the part of the author but on the part of the project management that had not catered at all to women's rights to land.

half of them said they did not have any problems with the presence of the (most recently arrived) migrants in Dande. The other half did complain about the migrants, saying that they failed to respect the *Mhondoro*'s rules. Taking an opposite tack, the possessed medium of Katuu remarked that if migrants were not respecting the *Mhondoro*'s rules, this was the fault of the autochthons who were misinforming them or breaking the rules themselves. Looking at the question from a religious point of view, the possessed medium of Kadembo suggested that only migrants from the Mozambican part of the Zambezi Valley be accepted, since they knew the *Mhondoro* of the area. Cogently, during all the time I spent in Dande none of the mediums ever blamed droughts on the presence of migrants *per se*. Those who complained about the migrants all blamed their alleged disrespect of local rules on the introduction of the Mid-Zambezi Project. Some even attributed the arrival of so many people from outside the valley to the Mid-Zambezi Project. The possessed medium of Bangomwe, for instance, accused Mugabe of sending both the pegs and the migrants. Kadembo was another one who was convinced that the Mid-Zambezi Project had resulted in increased in-migration.

Consequently, the mediums continued to focus their critique on the Mid-Zambezi Project itself. They were less involved in the internal conflicts resulting from the introduction of the project.

Witchcraft and conflicts about land

Over time, conflicts within the communities over land amplified, more often than not involving accusations of witchcraft. With Marwick's ideas about witchcraft as a social strain gauge (Marwick 1982) in mind, I had expected this to happen. In the research proposal I developed in 1991/1992, before Geschiere's 1995 book came out, I stated that I wanted to study these accusations and analyse whether they were of a 'levelling' or of an 'accumulative' nature. David Lan's book 'Guns and Rain', which was my source of inspiration at the time, led me to expect that most of the accusations would be made by the better-off towards the less-well-off. Lan argued that 'envy is the motive most commonly ascribed [to witches], either envy of the rich by the poor or of the fertile by the barren' (Lan 1985: 36).

Moreover, Lan stated that witches are rarely strangers; they are first and foremost members of a person's own *dzinza* or *rudzi*, which means either lineage or people of a similar 'kind', belonging to the same clan. Nowadays in Dande the term 'rudzi' is also used to refer to ethnicity. Lan (ibid.) claims it was said that only members of the same clan could bewitch one another: 'An Elephant will help a Monkey to kill an Elephant (ibid.: 37)'. The second, less frequently encountered, category of potential witches, according to Lan, is that of close affines.

Lan describes the terrible acts committed by witches in Dande: 'The typical act of witchcraft is cannibalism or, more accurately, necrophagy. Witches kill people, including their own children, or rob graves to find human flesh to eat. They commit incest and adultery (ibid.: 35-6)'. Witches often use three animals as familiars (cf. Hammond-Took 1974): hyena, crocodiles, or snakes. The witches can either use these animals, or transform themselves into one of them. People can become witches involuntarily, when they are possessed by a *shave*, a non-human spirit, of one of the mentioned animals. They can also 'inherit' witchcraft from a parent, who has put medicine in the child's food to turn it into a witch. People may also become witches out of their own free will by apprenticing themselves to a practising witch and taking certain medicines. Lastly, it is possible to obtain medicines or witchcraft familiars from corrupt *n'angas* (healers) to use in specific cases, without becoming a 'full-time' witch engaging in necrophagy or nocturnal rides on the back of a hyena (Lan 1985: 35-7, see also Bourdillon 1987: 179).

Below I will describe two cases of a conflict over land involving witchcraft. These cases demonstrate that the pattern of accusations and threats was less consistent than Lan had led me to believe, and more in line with Geschiere's (1995) observations. The cases also illustrate that in Dande witchcraft did involve 'strangers'; non-kin accused of having imported new kinds of witch familiars. Identity became a key issue in claiming land through the Mid-Zambezi Project; yet, local labels and official bureaucratic identities did not necessarily coincide.

Case 1: The conflict between Sylvia and Lucia

The first case involves two women, Sylvia and Lucia. Lucia was born in Dande somewhere in the mid-1940s. Her parents had also been born in Dande. Her *mutupo* (clan) was Nzou Samanyanga, which is considered a 'local' clan, the same as that of the *Mhondoro*. When Lucia was about ten or eleven her parents died. She then moved to the Plateau of Zimbabwe with her sister and her brother-in-law where they worked on a white-owned commercial farm. When she was about seventeen she married a Mozambican farm labourer. When Lucia had had a divorce in 1983, she returned to Dande, accompanied by her sister's daughter and two of her own grandsons, all of primary school age. She did not return to the village where she was born, but instead moved to Chawasarira, where her uncle was living. She approached the village headman of Chawasarira to ask for a plot of land and was allocated about four acres. Since the village where she was born is located in a different spirit province to that of Chawasarira, she herself had insisted on a visit to the *Mhondoro* medium in the company of the village headman and had received his permission to cultivate the land. With the help of the three children, she cultivated maize and cotton.

Every now and then her children, who were still working at commercial farms, would send her a little bit of money. Her neighbour in Chawasarira was Sylvia.

Sylvia arrived in Dande in 1982, when she was in her late thirties. She was born on a white-owned commercial farm, as was her husband. In 1982 the owner of the farm sold his land and started a road construction firm. Sylvia's husband then started working as a driver for this firm and lived in town. When the farm was sold, both Sylvia and her husband decided it was time for her to secure a home for the family in a rural area. Since she was still capable of hard work, she wanted to make the farm as profitable as possible and planned to grow cotton. It was difficult to return to her birthplace as she and her husband originally came from one of the Communal Lands close to Masvingo - where the chi-Shona dialect referred to as Karanga is spoken - where land was very scarce. Her sister, who was married to someone from Dande, told her there was still plenty of land available in Dande. Sylvia and her husband approached the local Party Secretary and the village headman of Chawasarira and were allocated a plot of six acres. The village headman did not take the husband to see the *Mhondoro* medium, but instead clapped hands to the *Mhondoro* and asked him to protect this 'son of Zimbabwe'. He asked Sylvia's husband to pay him an acceptance fee that he said he would hand over to the *Mhondoro* medium. Sylvia cultivated the six acres - where she was growing maize, cotton, and groundnuts - with the help of her four youngest children and her mother. Occasionally, she hired labourers using the money her husband sent.

Both women said that prior to the demarcation of the fields they had good relations with each other. They exchanged groundnuts and vegetables and occasionally helped each other in the fields. Sylvia had established a branch of the ZANU(PF) Women's League in Chawasarira and Lucia became a member of this League.

In 1988 all inhabitants of Dande had to register with the Senior Resettlement Officer for resettlement under the Mid-Zambezi Project. Each household head had to show his or her identity card, to prove that they had Zimbabwean citizenship. Migrants also had to show official District Administration transferral letters, showing the date of migration. Sylvia and her husband were able to hand over all the required papers and were allocated a plot. This plot included the land Sylvia was already cultivating. Matters were not so smooth for Lucia who could not prove she was a Zimbabwean citizen. When she married, her Mozambican husband had arranged her papers and had registered her as a Mozambican citizen. At the time, Lucia did not think there would be any problem, and the village headman assured her that as a Korekore she had the right to a piece of land in Dande, and that he would make sure that she could keep the plot she was allocated by him.

Lucia soon discovered that the four acres the village headman had allocated to her fell within the boundaries of the twelve-acre plot officially allocated to Sylvia and her husband. She asked the Resettlement Officer where her plot would be, upon which she was told that as a Mozambican she would not be allocated a plot at all. Lucia then went to the village headman to complain. Together they approached the Senior Resettlement Officer at Mahuwe. The village headman complained that the land he had allocated to a Korekore woman had been given to a Karanga migrant. The Officer said that there was nothing he could do, since he had to follow the official procedures. The village headman then accused the Officer (who, like the other Resettlement Officers, was not a local man) of tribalism, arguing that some of the migrants who came from other Communal Areas without proper District transferral letters were still allocated a field. The Officer denied these allegations and repeated that there was nothing he could do for Lucia[71].

In Chawasarira many people who considered themselves 'autochthons' complained bitterly that they had either not received any land at all, or had been allocated land in a different village. They accused the Officer of favouring the migrants.

Lucia went to see Sylvia and demanded that she let her stay on her twelve-acre plot. She argued that she had more rights to the land, because she was Korekore, than Sylvia who was Karanga. Sylvia refused on the grounds that 'the government' had allocated her the plot, claiming that the government had the ultimate authority to decide how the land should be used. The village headman also put pressure on Sylvia to allow Lucia to stay. He argued that as a Korekore village headman it was he who had the ultimate right to allocate the land and that he had allocated the twelve-acre plot to Lucia.

Lucia then went to see the *Mhondoro* medium together with the village headman to ask for support. When I visited the *Mhondoro* medium, and asked him about the migrants and the Mid-Zambezi Project in general he made the following comment:

> Long back when these people were coming, they were first seeing the sabhuku [village headman]. If the sabhuku had land to allocate, he would take the person to the mutape [the medium's ritual assistant] and tell him to call sekuru [the Mhondoro] to inform him about the visitor and the sekuru would discuss with the visitor because this person might have murdered people where he was coming from or his ancestors might have bad spirits. (...) The wife of the mutape would be asked to grind sorghum meal and the meal would be given to the dunzwi [the medium's messenger]. The dunzwi would perform chiumba with the meal [that is, mix it with water, form a sort of ball with it and place that in the proposed field]. The following morning they would look at the chiumba to see whether it had spread [lost its ball-shape form] or not, and if it had spread, they would go back to the spirit to ask the spirit what to do with the person and the spirit would say what was to be done. If the chiumba had not spread, the person would be told in which areas he would be allowed to live (...). But these days these migrants, we just see them in this area and we do not know where these visitors are coming from. If the Mhondoro asks the

---

[71] Interviews with migrants, however, showed that the allegations of the village headman were not completely without foundation.

chiefs and the sabhuku [village headmen] about these migrants, he is told that this is done by his muzukuru [grandson] Mugabe [president of Zimbabwe]. The Mhondoro always says that although it is Mugabe who is allowing these people here, why can the [chiefs and sabhuku] not inform me about these migrants? (...) The [Rural District] councillors and the chiefs are the people who are responsible for allocating land to these migrants. The Mhondoro accepts these people, but he says we will see what will happen in the future.

The medium accused the government of denying local authorities' control over land and allowing strangers to settle by means of procedures that it considered legitimate, but were locally not accepted. He said he would back up Lucia's claim, but that the Resettlement Officer had to come and see him, not the other way around. The Officer refused to do so, denying the *Mhondoro's* authority over land.

A week after Lucia's visit to the medium, Sylvia's mother fell ill, suffering from headaches, stomach aches and fever. Sylvia suspected Lucia of bewitching her mother. When Sylvia's mother did not recover, despite the anti-malaria medication she had received at the local clinic, Sylvia went over to Lucia. Outside Lucia's hut, so that anyone passing might hear it, she accused Lucia of bewitching her mother. Lucia did not deny the accusations; on the contrary, she told Sylvia that if she would not let her cultivate her four acres, 'she would see what would happen'. Sylvia's mother died about a week later.

Two days later, the chairman of the Village Development Committee (VIDCO), the village headman and the local Party Secretary held a meeting. The village headman supported Lucia; the local Party Secretary ranged himself on Sylvia's side. The VIDCO chairman, being a migrant himself who had settled in Dande in 1966, was very hesitant about taking sides. After long hours of talking the following compromise was reached. Sylvia was urged to let Lucia cultivate the four acres till the next harvesting season. The village headman and the VIDCO chairman would accompany Lucia to the District Council in Upper Guruve to support her request for a change of citizenship. Lucia would then be able to register for resettlement in another village in Dande. Sylvia agreed to the solution.

Unfortunately, Lucia was unable to raise the money to pay for the fees to obtain citizenship, which had just been raised considerably. She was then allocated a field by the village headman in the area that had been designated as a common grazing area by the staff of the Mid-Zambezi Project. There she continued to farm with a number of other villagers who had not received a plot.

This first case seems to fit Lan's description of witchcraft motivated by envy. Lucia did not obtain a plot under the Mid-Zambezi Project and risked becoming officially classified as a squatter. She was accused of bewitching the mother of Sylvia, who did get a plot, which included the land that Lucia had been farming, and did not deny this.

One aspect of this case, though, neither confirms David Lan's nor Geschiere's analysis about the most common relationship between witch and victim. The victim and the accused were neither relatives nor even affines, and did not belong to the same '*rudzi*' - Lucia's clan was Elephant, Sylvia's clan was *Tsoko*, Monkey. Though the information I gathered does not preclude that a Monkey helped the Elephant to bewitch the Monkey, nobody seemed interested to find out whether this was the case. Lan states that when bewitching is suspected, the first reaction is to look for the culprit within one's own family. Here, neither the victims nor the villagers commenting on the case speculated about a possible helper within Sylvia's family. Apart from her children and mother, Sylvia's only relative in Dande was her sister, who was living with her in-laws in Chikafa, about a 100 kilometres away from Chawasarira.

Case 2: The village headman of Gonono

In Mburuma, the village where I lived, one of the villagers was a man who had been selected to be the successor to the late village headman of Gonono, a neighbouring village. This man had moved to Mburuma after Independence, before he became village headman, because he wanted to live closer to the road, so that it would be easier for him to transport his crops to the Grain and Cotton Marketing Board Depots in Mzarabani. He had been allocated both riverine fields and a large upland plot, where he cultivated cotton. Under normal circumstances he would have moved back to Gonono to take up his position, though that would not necessarily have meant he would have had to abandon his fields. However, because of the implementation of the Mid-Zambezi Project the man found himself in a difficult position. He had registered for a twelve acre-plot in Mburuma. His cotton fields were within the demarcation pegs of plot no. 1, and since he was the person cultivating most acres within the plot, he stood a very good chance of obtaining it. He refused to return to Gonono, because he feared he would not be able to obtain a twelve-acre plot there.

After a spell of drought in the middle of the rainy season, the medium of the ancestral spirit of the area, *Mhondoro* Chivhere, was consulted. He attributed the drought to someone who had committed incest, but he did not name the culprit. The village headman of Mburuma was not satisfied with this explanation and consulted the medium of Chidyamauyu, who offered a much more political explanation for the dry spell: the ancestors did not agree with the introduction of the Mid-Zambezi Project and the pegging of the plots.

One day I when I was walking through the village, I came across the village headman of Gonono. Almost without introduction he launched into the incest matter:

People think I was the person Chivhere accused of having committed incest. People think it was me because I usually have a very good harvest. They say I use magic.

Many people here do not like me, because I always have enough food. My son gave me money so that every month I can buy three bags [50 kg each] of mealie meal. So many people come to me to beg for food, but I have already given a bucket to each of my neighbours. And now they are trying to bewitch me to make sure I will not get plot number one. They want me to go back to Gonono.

About a month later I was sitting in the shade of a tree talking with some of my neighbours, when the headman of Gonono came running towards us. He started accusing my neighbours of inciting their herd-boys to take their cattle into his maize field. One of my neighbours said that he had been to the fields in the morning to check the damage, but that to him it looked as if people had cut the maize cobs, rather than that cattle had eaten them. Headman Gonono refused to accept this explanation and said he thought that cattle had been deliberately driven into his fields to scare him away. He threatened to report the case to headman Mburuma and demand compensation. In the meantime, the herd-boys appeared and started making fun of headman Gonono behind his back. When my neighbours started laughing, headman Gonono turned around and threatened to beat the boys. Then he told us that he had found a goatskin in his field that was smeared with hyena dung. 'I know what you are trying to do, you do not want me to have plot number 1, but you cannot scare me away'. He walked away, muttering under his breath.

The directions that the accusations took in this case, whether they served to attack prosperity or to support the accumulator's position, are much more ambiguous than in the first case presented. Here we have someone who was simultaneously accused of practising witchcraft, and a victim of witchcraft threats himself. He was accused of using magic to obtain good harvests and plenty of food. At the same time, some villagers were threatening to bewitch him - the soiled goatskin was interpreted as a witchcraft threat - apparently because they felt that the headman of a neighbouring village did not deserve to obtain plot no. 1 in Mburuma.

Migrants, modernity and witchcraft

Many of the conflicts over land took place between those who considered themselves 'autochthons' and those who were considered migrants; in other words, many of the witchcraft incidents involved both groups. Whenever someone fell ill within a family involved in conflict over land, the first reaction was to accuse the opposing party of using witchcraft, whether this party included members with the same clan affiliation or not. Bourdillon, though still maintaining that most witchcraft conflicts involve relatives, states that 'complete strangers are not above suspicions of witchcraft. A stranger is not normally allowed to come into contact with the food supply or with drying crops in case he should poison them (…) (Bourdillon 1987: 186)'.

In Dande, there were in fact two specific forms of witchcraft that were strongly associated with migrants. These involved the use of defined witch familiars, namely *zvishiri* and *chikwambo*. *Zvishiri* means birds, and in this case referred to birds that were kept in clay pots, and fed with blood, sugar and white mealie meal. They could be sent by their owners to obtain money or consumer goods from the victims. They were believed to tell the victim whom they were sent by, and would threaten the victims with illness or death if they did not hand over the desired money or goods. *Chikwambo* involved the use of a hare or a baboon for the same purpose. I was told that *zvishiri* and *chikwambo* were mainly used by poor people to attack those who were better off. The example I was given was that of a woman in the village where I lived. She was living in a run-down hut on the edge of the village. In the evenings, she could frequently be seen begging at the door of the hut of her son, who had recently returned from town with his wife and young children. A couple of times I saw how she was sent home by her son, empty-handed. When the woman's grandson died, her son accused her of having sent *zvishiri*.

The association of *zvishiri* and *chikwambo* with migrants struck me as strange, since in general, migrants were considered to be better off than autochthons. Migrants were considered to be better, 'more modern' farmers, more skilled at cultivating cash crops than autochthons (see Chapter Five). When I asked why these 'poor people's' witchcraft methods were so closely associated with migrants, I was told that:

> We did not have these methods before. You can buy zvishiri and chikwambo in Chipinge [in the east of the country], or from someone here who has bought them there. They cost a lot of money. But you can also inherit them from a relative. You can use them to become very rich. And you can also use them to collect money from people who have borrowed money from you but refuse to pay back. Everybody is always trying to borrow money from the Karanga because they are richer.

So witchcraft familiars, reputedly used out of spite against those who had accumulated, could also make the envious person an accumulator. Conversely, they could be used by accumulators to protect their wealth from levelling relatives and neighbours.

The migrants' alleged higher production was partly attributed to their 'modern' farming methods. As described in Chapter Three, migrant households were usually smaller than autochthonous households, and consequently had less family labour available, but they generally owned more cattle and compensated by having more draught power available. They also tended to have more income from sources other than agriculture alone, which they invested in agriculture. Occasionally, they could not escape the accusation of employing occult forces to increase their production. Apart from the *zvishiri* and *chikwambo*, they also risked being denounced for using a method that resembled the 'zombies' described by Fisiy and Geschiere (1991). One day I had a conversation with the local nurse and an 'autochthonous' farmer, which ran like this:

> Farmer: Did you see the cotton in F's field? Everybody has problems with the weeds [after a major drought, the present rainy season was very wet and many people complained about excessive growth of weeds], but his fields are clean. Some people say he uses magic.
>
> M.S.: What kind of magic?
>
> Farmer: There are people who can make you get up when you are asleep, without anyone knowing, and then they make you work in their fields all night.
>
> Nurse: That is nonsense, if I had started weeding in time my cotton fields would have been like his.
>
> Farmer: But he has so many acres, and not a big family.
>
> Nurse: But he has a son who sends him money so he can hire people.
>
> Farmer: So you don't believe in witching?
>
> Nurse: …
>
> Farmer: In Upper Guruve there was a boy who was killed by lightning. First the lightning struck his home, but he was not there. Then the lightning struck the house of a friend where he was staying, and that is when he got killed. All the others were alive, only the boy was killed. Such things mean that we can be sure of witching. You cannot explain this, can you?

Sanders (2001) describes how in Ihanzu, in Tanzania, migrants were also accused of using witchcraft at the expense of the autochthonous population. These migrants lost their grazing areas because of government intervention, and came looking for land in Ihanzu. They were likewise believed to be more successful, and were accused of using magic buses that 'ate' members of the autochthonous population. Sanders argues that the Ihanzu understood the politico-economic factors driving people to look for different places to live very well. Yet, the witchcraft stories made sense of why the Sukuma had been able to 'overrun' the territory of the Ihanzu, why they had been successful at it. 'Such imaginings shape the ways the Ihanzu cope with Sukuma inroads into their lands - whether they resist such movements, accept them as inevitable, or do both simultaneously in different contexts (ibid.: 44)'. Sanders believes that the Ihanzu distinguished between 'modernity' and 'tradition', but used both concepts when making sense of the migration movement.

Perhaps the people in Dande did the same, though their ideas about 'modernity' and 'tradition' in relation to witchcraft seemed to be somewhat messier, not so neatly separated. It was possible to increase production by employing both 'modern' farming methods and occult forces. The most powerful witchcraft familiars and medicines were believed to come from marginal areas in Zimbabwe like Chipinge - Dande also has quite a reputation for this in the rest of the country. The people in these areas were considered more 'traditional', speaking 'deep chi-Shona'. One could argue that people believed that traditional knowledge was necessary to develop strong witchcraft medicines, and that the more traditional people were considered to be, the stronger their witchcraft would be. This was countervailed by the fact that the more 'modern' people had more money available to travel to these marginal areas and pay for the familiars and the medicines, and hence were able to become not only more successful farmers, but also more successful witches. Both successes seemed to presuppose one another.

Concluding remarks

Migration has always been an important feature of life in Dande. This is reflected in the religious domain where the *Mhondoro* cult almost automatically includes migrants. Other mechanisms of inclusion, such as the *sahwira* relationship, also hint at the importance of 'strangers' in and for society. However, inclusion also means control: to be included in the cult means to accept the authority of the *Mhondoro* over land, and the social and moral rules prescribed by the cult.

Recently, with increased pressure on the land, the flexibility in attitude towards the latest migrants has lessened. The procedures for integrating them into the *Mhondoro* cult, thereby acknowledging their right to land, were no longer followed. The Mid-Zambezi Project, designed to control settlement patterns, and in particular spontaneous migration to the valley, created even stronger tensions between recent migrants and long-term residents. By replacing existing local land allocation procedures, the project made the application of earlier integration (and control) mechanisms almost impossible[72]. Inclusion and control were replaced by exclusion and conflict. The shortage of land created by the project resulted in conflicts, which placed identity as a means to claim land at the centre of attention. It was thought that the rights of 'local' people could be guaranteed by bureaucratic rules and regulations. However, in a country where most official papers are registered *ad hoc* and only for certain purposes, this can create serious problems. Just how complicated the issue of identity is in present-

---

[72] Here I would like to caution the reader: I am not arguing that no witchcraft problems could occur in communities where land allocation is done by local authorities. In Dande, however, prior to the implementation of the Mid-Zambezi Project access to land was not (yet) a problem, and communities *wanted* migrants to settle in Dande (see Chapter Three).

day Zimbabwe was shown in the first case described above, where official papers and (self-)ascribed identities seriously conflicted with one another.

Whereas the *Mhondoro* cult played an important role in the resistance to the Mid-Zambezi Project, its role in settling conflicts over land between the inhabitants of the spirit provinces was reduced. Witchcraft accusations, like those featuring in the case studies, were rife, but whether they actually increased as a result of the reduced role of the *Mhondoro* cult remains a supposition that is difficult to ascertain.

The results of my research on witchcraft reveal that local ideas about the directions witchcraft accusations and practices would generally take were not consistent. While migrants were considered to be more resourceful in every respect, including obtaining access to occult resources, in all of the witchcraft cases related to conflicts over land that I was able to study, the victims of witchcraft were migrants, and those threatening to use witchcraft were autochthons. The rumours and accusations flew both ways; both the 'haves' and the 'have-nots' were accused of witchcraft, confirming Geschiere's argument about the ambiguity of the relation between witchcraft, power and wealth (Geschiere 1995; 1997). Yet all the witchcraft threats I witnessed in the context of conflicts over land came from the 'have-nots', which also meant that 'autochthons' were adopting a more threatening stance more often than 'migrants' were. It must be said, however, that in other contexts I have witnessed 'the powerful' using witchcraft-threats to gain or maintain their position as well. A very corrupt District Councillor, for example, was re-elected after making veiled threats of witchcraft when the local Ward Committee proposed another candidate for the elections.

The interpretation of witchcraft accusations seems to depend upon which point of view is adopted, that of the accuser or the accused. For instance, Geschiere concludes that it is unclear whether villagers in his research area actually try to undermine government projects by witchcraft, or whether it is by the constant accusations of government officials that witchcraft is rendered a subversive force (1995: 11).

My study shows that in conflicts over land in Dande that involve witchcraft, kinship is not very important, and strangers accuse and threaten one another quite easily. Sanders (2001) confirms the occurrence of what he refers to as 'inter-ethnic imaginings' concerning witchcraft. Lately, this has also been an important theme in the work of Jean and John Comaroff (1999), who connect increasing xenophobia in South Africa with the development of ideas and fears about new forms of witchcraft attributed to migrants.

9

Conclusions

In the preceding chapters I have described the impacts of land reforms in Dande Communal Land. These reforms were supposed to increase agricultural production in Dande and at the same time help relieve the pressure on land in the Communal Areas on the Plateau of Zimbabwe. Instead, they created a large group of officially landless in an area where hitherto access to land had not been a problem. Before the introduction of the land reforms, Dande had been a refuge for people from the southeast of the country who felt they could not obtain enough land in their home areas, and for farm labourers who did not have a home area where they could claim land for 'retirement'. Spontaneous migration to Dande was one way of dealing with the shortage of land prevalent in most other Communal Areas of Zimbabwe. Government intervention, however, put a halt to this strategy. Furthermore, many people who considered themselves autochthonous to Dande officially lost access to their lands as well, and were labelled 'squatters'.

In Chapter Two I have described how in the mid-1980s the Zimbabwean government changed its stance towards the problem of unequal land distribution between the - mainly white-owned - Commercial Farmers and Communal Farmers. Policy focus shifted, from resettlement of Communal Farmers onto land in the Large Scale Commercial Farming Areas, to internal land reforms in the Communal Areas. The Mid-Zambezi Rural Development Project in Dande became a pilot project for these reforms, though it differed somewhat from other pilot projects. The original project plan foresaw in-migration from other Communal Areas, but in a limited and controlled way as opposed to the spontaneous in-migration that was already taking place. Controlling in-migration and rationalising local land-use practices were meant to boost agricultural production and the capacity to absorb Communal Farmers from elsewhere in

Zimbabwe and to prevent environmental degradation. In Chapter Four I have given evidence to demonstrate that the project has failed on all accounts.

The land reforms proposed for the Communal Areas closely resembled the reforms that the Rhodesian government tried to introduce through the Native Land Husbandry Act of 1951. Why did the post-Independence government revert to such a policy when its Ministers should have remembered that the NLHA had caused so much resentment, resentment that many commentators (see for example Ranger 1985; Drinkwater 1991) believe had fuelled the struggle for Independence? Today the government claims that the resettlement of Communal Farmers onto white-owned farms was sabotaged by the UK and other donor countries, and uses this argument to justify the invasions of commercial, white-owned farms by so-called war-veterans. Yet, given the - renewed - promises of financial support for the acquisition of land in the former European Areas made by those same donor countries at a donor conference in 1998 (scc Hammar & Raftapolous 2003), this hardly seems a valid explanation. Another explanation may be found if we look more closely at the ideas under-lying the internal land reforms.

Assumptions underpinning land reforms in Zimbabwe's Communal Areas

As described in the introduction to this book, Zimbabwe has not been the only African country to adopt land-use policies after Independence that show striking similarities to colonial policies. The Ujamaa experience in Tanzania, for instance, also shows remarkable parallels with programmes for agriculture and settlement initiated by the colonial regimes in East Africa, as Scott (1998) has noticed. Ujamaa was imposed upon rural Tanzania, despite the fact that one of the standard explanations for the success of Nyerere's TANU, prior to Tanzania's Independence, was nothing less than the widespread resentment of the colonial agricultural policy (see also Cliffe & Cunningham 1973). There are thus parallels both in time and place; parallels that suggest, according to Scott, '(...) that we have stumbled across something generic about the projects of the modern developmentalist state (Scott 1998: 224)'. Post-Independence govern-ments determined to develop and modernise their countries were confronted with the same difficulties as were their colonial predecessors: the illegibility of local settlement and of land-use practices. 'Simplification' of settlement patterns was apparently the only possibility for the new governments to deliver development services such as schools, clinics, and clean water efficiently (ibid., see also Sender & Johnston 2004). Pertinently, this process also facilitated bureaucratic - as well as political - control over rural dwellers. Thirdly, many post-Independence governments believed that 'simplification' of settlement and land-use patterns would improve the efficiency of agricultural production (Scott 1998.: 224-5).

The word 'believe' is appropriate here, as both Scott (ibid.) and Keeley & Scoones (2000: 7-8) argue, since the scientific data supporting policies of 'simplification' are more often than not quite meagre, and extrapolated from situations that differ markedly, heedless of context (see also Leach & Mearns 1996; Delius and Schirmer 2000). The policies were backed up by, or embedded in so-called 'development narratives' (cf. Roe 1991; 1995), stories developed by planners to help them deal with complex realities, often presented in a simplified cause and effect form.

In the introduction and in Chapter Five I have described how during the colonial era a specific development narrative evolved in Southern and East Africa that linked concern for agricultural production in those areas assigned to African farmers with environmental concerns (see Leach & Mearns 1996; Keeley & Scoones 1999; McKenzie 2000). In this narrative, African land-use practices were considered to be the cause of soil erosion, which in turn led to declining agricultural production in these areas. 'Modern' agricultural techniques, but even more importantly, 'proper', scientific land-use planning was believed to be the panacea. The development of this narrative coincided with an increasing congestion in the Reserves and Tribal Trust Lands as a result of continuing evictions of African farmers from formally classified 'European Areas'. Yet, this process was not accorded any significance in the 'land degradation narrative'. Science was what was going to prevent a collapse of African agriculture, not politics. Delius and Schirmer (2000: 721), however, argue that although the narrative emphasises the importance of science; in fact, the nature and extent of the environmental crisis in those areas set aside for African farmers was assumed rather than researched. In Rhodesia the 'land degradation narrative' culminated in the introduction of the Native Land Husbandry Act of 1951, the implementation of which caused huge resentment amongst African farmers.

Not long after Independence the political definition of the land issue, which allegedly had played such an important role during the struggle for Independence, was again reformulated as a technical problem requiring a technical solution, not a political one; a return to colonial discourse. The major donor countries and organisations supported this policy shift. No doubt political motives played a role in this support, perhaps not so much support for white farmers who originated from some of the donor countries, as a strong belief in the economic benefits of private land ownership and large-scale agricultural production[73]. Though there is an ongoing debate about the relative productiveness of large-scale versus small-scale farming (see Moyo 2000; Sender & Johnston 2004), large-scale commercial farming did bring in the bulk of foreign currency, geared as it was towards export. Donors bought into and helped the spreading and developing of the 'land degradation narrative'. Local land-use practices were often not understood and linked to Hardin's (1968) 'Tragedy of the Commons', which - as so many on natural resource management have pointed out - describes a free access or 'no management' situation rather than communal natural resource management (see for example Hulme & Murphree 2001). Donor organisations experienced similar problems in 'reading' local land-use practices as governments did. A quote from a feasibility study for another land-use planning project for Dande[74] shows how right Scott was in choosing the term 'illegibility' for the common technocratic bias towards local practices. The rationale for this new project was formulated as follows: '(…) the current intricate communal land system based on customary land rights does not permit anyone to know who precisely owns what land. This system hinders any effective control by the relevant authorities (in: Derman 1995: 57)[75]'.

The planners of the Mid-Zambezi Project had similar problems while interpreting the local land use situation when they were designing the programme of land reforms for Dande. As I have described in Chapter Four, the project had a number of goals that were difficult to reconcile. It was designed to prevent environmental damage by controlling spontaneous migration to Dande, and moving people away from 'non-arable' land. At the same time local land-use practices were to be 'improved', to make land-use more 'efficient' and thereby create space for 3000 new households from the overcrowded Communal Areas on the Plateau.

The basic assumptions underlying the project stemmed from the 'land degradation narrative' and were shared by both the government and the donor organisations that had played a role in initiating and funding the project. The

---

[73] Sender & Johnston (2004) describe how in recent years donors, influenced by the World Bank, have shown a change of heart and now consider small-scale farming more productive, and support market-led land redistribution.

[74] During the implementation phase of the Mid-Zambezi Project several new land-use plans were already being developed for different parts of the Zambezi Valley, including Dande. Most of these resembled the Mid-Zambezi Project closely, and were developed in a similar top-down manner, without consulting the local population. Donor organisations did not co-ordinate their activities and seemed neither aware of each other's plans, nor of projects already implemented.

[75] The plan from which the quote was taken was developed *after* the implementation of the Mid-Zambezi Project, but the situation in Dande is described as if that project had never happened.

first of these was that allocation of land was still done by 'traditional' authorities on the basis of 'customary' rights and was therefore inefficient. As the policy document on land reforms in the Communal Areas stated: 'The Communal Land Bill transfers legal authority over land allocation away from the traditional leaders to elected local councils (District Councils). (...) If successful the measures will leave the traditional, conservative leaders with little more than a spiritual function (...) and will allow substantive innovation provided that matters are not forced too quickly (Government of Zimbabwe 1985: 17)'. The document specifically refers to Hardin's article on the commons (ibid.: 44). The second assumption was that the allocation of clearly demarcated arable plots and residential stands would increase security of tenure for individual farmers (ibid.:79). This, combined with improved efficiency, would help prevent environmental damage - the third assumption (ibid.: 79).

The 'inefficiency' of local land-use practices was never verified by the project planners. How these practices worked was mainly sheer guesswork, and, as I have described in Chapter Four and Five, based on stereotypical ideas of what communal tenure was supposed to be - and there are some authors who claim that these ideas were to a 'large extent colonial inventions (see for example Cheater 1990). No thought was given to how these practices might have changed over time. Planners, for instance, assumed that women held no rights to land in their own right, and excluded them from the project. Yet, as I have shown in Chapter Three and Four, many widows and divorcees had obtained substantial plots in their own right, from various sources of authority - including 'traditional' village headmen. The Guruve (Rural) District Council did manage to obtain a concession from project management, which ensured that widows with minor dependants would be able to obtain a small plot, but women's rights to land deteriorated significantly with the implementation of the project.

If planners already considered 'communal tenure' based on 'customary land rights' complex and unclear, they would have been baffled even more had they taken the trouble to actually study local land-use practices in Dande. Land allocation prior to the implementation of the Mid-Zambezi Project involved various authorities. People looking for land, whether new settlers or children who had reached adulthood, approached different authorities, varying from the village headmen to VIDCO chairmen and ZANU(PF) party officials, depending on their own personal position, history and network. This 'shopping' for land can probably be linked to alternating movements from reinforcing the positions of 'traditional' leadership, to strengthening 'modern', bureaucratic local government institutions that I have described in Chapter Two. It was not until the early 1990s that the government of Zimbabwe began to realise that 'communal' tenure was a complicated matter, and established the Commission of Inquiry into Appropriate Agricultural Tenure Systems, under the Chairmanship of Professor Mandivamba Rukuni (Government of Zimbabwe 1994).

Many people in Dande were not convinced that the land reforms would result in more efficient land-use than did their own complex set of practices. In their eyes, 'efficiency' was both linked to production *and* access to land. When project management discovered that the number of people residing in the project area had been seriously underestimated, the migration component of the project was cancelled. No new settlers were allowed into Dande. Worse, according to the project plans, there was not even enough arable land for all those already present in Dande at the time the project was implemented. About a third of the households could not obtain a twelve acre-plot and became officially landless (see also Derman 1993). Many considered the allocation of standard sized plots, regardless of family size or availability of farming input, an inefficient way of distributing land. As Scott has remarked, simplifying land-use patterns in fact also means simplifying farming households (1998: 225). Before the introduction of the project, land was allocated on the basis of production capacity. Households were allocated land on the basis of what they could manage, and if their capacity increased, they could apply for additional land. Many considered the allocation of standard-sized twelve acre-plots one of the reasons why suddenly, since the implementation of the project, there was not enough land to accommodate all households residing in the project area[76].

Another reason, and an important bone of contention between project planners and local farmers, was the fact that large areas already under cultivation were suddenly labelled 'non-arable'. Especially the attempted enforcement of the ban on riverine cultivation was greatly resented. The riverine fields, *mudimba*, are crucial resources for food security in Dande (see also Lynam et al. 1996). Research elsewhere in Zimbabwe has shown that their cultivation does not automatically lead to siltation and erosion, which was the reason provided for the ban (see for example Dambo Research Unit 1987). However, under the Mid-Zambezi Project the *mudimba* were classified as 'non-arable' land and designated as grazing areas.

Instead of increasing security of tenure, the project in fact has created growing *in*security. As has just been pointed out, about a third of the population present in Dande at the time of implementation are now officially classified as landless and labelled squatters. In Chapter Four I have described that most of the 'squatters' still live and farm in Dande, either in the grazing areas, or 'outside the project', that is, in areas that have not been demarcated under the

---

[76] Here I would like to remind the reader that I am not arguing that over time, with continued in-migration, no problems would have arisen in Dande concerning access to and distribution of land. The argument here is that the project quite suddenly created a land shortage for people who hitherto *did* have access to land in Dande and that this caused great resentment.

Mid-Zambezi Project. So far, no attempts have made to evict them, but their security of tenure has definitely diminished. In Chapter Six I remarked that quite a number of migrants initially did think that the project would increase their security of tenure. Most of them managed to obtain a twelve acre-plot, yet, the many conflicts this caused in their host communities led to increased feelings of insecurity as many feared that if the situation escalated they could be chased away from the communities through violence or witchcraft attacks. As a result, most migrants changed their mind about the project. Given the present chaotic political situation in Zimbabwe and the renewed focus on resettlement of black farmers on white-owned farms, it is not likely that an eviction exercise targeting 'squatters' in Dande will be organised soon. However, when I was in Zimbabwe in June 2002, I heard that the 'squatter' label had been used on some occasions to justify the harassment and driving out of people suspected of being members of the opposition party MDC.

The third assumption underlying the project has been falsified as well. The Mid-Zambezi Project has not prevented environmental degradation. In fact, the opposite is true. The relocation of farmers, and sometimes of entire villages, has increased deforestation. Conflicts between people and wildlife have increased, resulting in more demands for Problem Animal Control. Though it has become more difficult for new settlers to obtain land in Dande, in-migration has not entirely stopped.

Project planners and Dande residents seemed to have conflicting ideas about the landscape of Dande. Local people saw it as a relatively empty area with plenty of land for cultivation. They told stories about successful cotton and maize farmers in Dande who, before the war for Independence started, had been able to buy tractors and cars. During the war, when people were placed in 'Protected Villages', or 'keeps', these assets were lost; large parts of the cultivated lands were reverted to bush again and wildlife gained significant territory. After Independence this bush had to be taken back, and migrants could assist in this. The message about all the land available in Dande seems to have been spread among fellow farm labourers and in town, and the influx of new settlers, disrupted during the war, regained momentum. Migrants attracted new migrants, and even former guerrillas who had fought the Rhodesian Forces in Dande returned to cultivate the former frontline. This development was not unique to Dande, it happened in other parts of the Zambezi Valley as well, nor was it something new (see for example Nyambara 2001). In-migration seems to have been a continuous feature in the history of Dande, which is reflected in the founding myths of villages and stories recited about the royal ancestors.

The picture that emerges from the project documents is rather different. According to these Dande could indeed serve as an 'overflow' for overpopulated Communal Areas on the Plateau. Yet, the supply of arable land was considered limited, and the environment fragile, requiring protection against the hordes of migrants expected to flock to the area following tsetse eradication. Once project staff discovered that many more people were residing in the area than had been foreseen, Dande was considered 'overpopulated' by project staff and government officials serving on local government institutions. Paradoxically, in some other government departments it was still considered an empty area, where the Mazoe squatters and entrenched Mutorashonga miners could be relocated.

All parties, including Dande residents, seemed to agree that the area needed to be developed. However, the kind of development needed was a disputed subject. Improvement in infrastructure and government services - mainly in the domain of education, healthcare and the marketing of agricultural products - was a wish that project planners, project staff and residents shared, and a component of the project greatly appreciated by Dande residents. Nevertheless, both project staff and local residents considered the land reforms to be the main component of the project, and these were greatly resented by the population.

Project staff, that is, the Project Manager, the Resettlement Officers as well as the Agritex and Veterinary Officers assisting them, were all outsiders, 'people from up there'. In Chapter Five I have described how they all seemed to adhere to the 'land degradation narrative' underpinning the project. Almost all of them thought that the land reforms would contribute to the development of Dande and help prevent environmental damage by moving people away from 'non-arable' land. Many staff members showed a considerable bias against 'autochthonous' residents, whom they considered to be bad farmers, applying 'backward' farming methods and producing far less than the 'progressive' migrants, whose settlement they were supposed to control. At the same time, however, they were the ones experiencing the cutting edge of the problems associated with a top-down planning exercise. Already at an early stage, some of them predicted that the project would not be completed in time. It was their discovery that the number of people already present in the project had been grossly underestimated. As a result, the proposed in-migration of 3000 new families was cancelled. The Project Manager and Resettlement Officers negotiated with the Councillors of the Rural District Council, and were forced to compromise on some of the allocation criteria, for example the allocation of small plots to widows with minor dependants and the preferential treatment of those with District citizenship. Yet, the basic principles of the land reform exercise were never the subject of negotiations. As it became clear that not enough plots were demarcated to cater for the entire population, Ward Councillors would continually ask for more plots to be pegged, but their pleas were doomed to be unheard. The Councillors from Dande did not receive much backing from the government officials serving on the Council, who grew to dislike the project, complained about the top-down manner in which it was implemented, but never questioned its necessity. The same applied to many of the project staff members. Over time some of them adjusted their attitudes towards local farmers and their agricultural practices somewhat. Most notably, Agritex officers started doubting whether riverine cultivation was really that harmful. The Project Manager and some of the Resettlement Officers took up twelve acre-plots in Dande and their production methods did not differ greatly from those of their neighbours. Some of them spent years in Dande, and were not blind to the social unrest the project created. Against all odds, most continued to defend the basic principles of the project right until the end.

Conflicts and the development of a counter-narrative

In the project documents no attention was paid to the practicalities of relocating large numbers of people: to the way people had to be convinced to move to new plots or even new villages. It was assumed that people were 'familiar with the concept of resettlement' and no problems were expected (ADF 1986: 37). Though the similarities with the Native Land Husbandry Act were not lost on the people in Dande, especially not on the migrants coming from the southeast of the country, it did not necessarily follow that they appreciated the project. Many compared the project with the relocation to the 'keeps' during the war. When the first metal pegs appeared to mark the new fields, a protest march was organised, which met with military intimidation. Since then, resistance to the project has continued, albeit in different forms.

In Chapter Four I have described that most of the people who did not obtain a twelve-acre plot, and were consequently labelled squatters, have not left Dande. They are still cultivating land they have obtained from various sources. Those who had riverine fields are still using them, despite the ban on riverine cultivation. Others have been allocated land by village headmen or VIDCO chairmen in the newly designated grazing areas - including the riverine areas. This has increased conflicts over cattle destroying crops. Some of the 'squatters' have been allocated land - again by village headmen and VIDCO chairmen - 'outside the project', that is, in areas that have not officially been demarcated for cultivation. Others are borrowing or renting land from people who have been allocated twelve acre-plots, but do not have enough labour or inputs available to cultivate all of their land themselves. Most of the people who are farming illegally in the villages are people who did not qualify for a twelve-acre plot. Others were allocated a plot, but refused to take it up because it was located in a village too far away from where their relatives were staying, or from services and roads. Especially in the northern zone of the project there are still plots that have not been taken up.

It was especially in the first villages subjected to the project, that this form of resistance was rife. Mahuwe, which was one of the villages where I conducted my research, is a case in point. When the fields there were demarcated and allocated, those who were lucky enough to obtain a plot quickly transferred their labour to the plot to occupy it. It was then that the full extent of 'the shortage of plots' became clear. Conflicts broke out within the communities between legal plot-holders and those who had not obtained plots. These conflicts were about who really belonged in Dande - and hence had the right to a plot - and who did not. As I have explained in Chapter Four, recent newcomers were farming mainly in those areas that project planners considered 'arable' and stood better chances of obtaining twelve-acre plots than those who considered themselves 'autochthons', who were mainly farming in areas considered 'non-arable' by the project planners. This created conflicts over land, which entailed disputes about identity. Before the implementation of the project migrants had been more than welcome in Dande. Now, sharp boundaries were drawn between 'autochthons' and 'migrants'. Definitions of autochthony became narrower and narrower, as even people from just across the Mozambican border - speaking the same chi-Shona dialect, who were believed to share the same ancestors - became 'strangers'.

These conflicts induced other villages, which had not yet had their land redistributed, to reject the project entirely. There was even a whole Ward that resisted relocation. It was in this Ward - Matsiwo A Ward - that I have spent most of my time. The mediums of the *Mhondoro* spirits backed the resistors by claiming that the ancestors did not approve of the project. The mediums provided the opponents of the project with an alternative story about land, a counter-narrative to the 'land degradation narrative'.

Project staff found they had little control over people who refused to move, or settled 'outside the project'. In the project documents it had always been assumed that people would move to their new plots of their own accord - and by their own means; no provision had been made for transport and no compensation for abandoned fixed assets had been provided. This turned out to be a highly problematic assumption. Project management then decided on a change of strategy. The 'traditional leaders', who had not been assigned a role in the project, were to be mobilised in order to convince their subjects to conform to project regulations. The Project Manager approached Chief Matsiwo, in whose chiefdom the rebel Ward was located. He, however, referred the Project Manager to the *Mhondoro* spirits of the area, whom he spoke of as the 'real owners' of the land, the only ones who could give permission.

Both the Project Manager's change of strategy and the referral by the chief provided the *Mhondoro* mediums with possibilities to make their counter-narrative heard. It can by no means be ruled out that the recounting of this narrative by the opponents of the project had inspired the Project Manager to mobilise 'traditional leadership' in the first place.

The counter-narrative is the instrument by which the authority of the state over land in Dande is challenged. The ultimate owners of the land were said to be the *Mhondoro*, the royal ancestral spirits, since they provided rain and fertility without which the land would be useless. The severe droughts that occurred during the implementation phase of the project were explained as a show of control by the *Mhondoro* over the land, and a sign that they did not agree with the project. The counter-narrative also maintained that the authority over land should revert to the chiefs - and through them to the village headmen - who are after all direct descendants of the *Mhondoro*. Apart from their powers to withhold the rains, the superiority of the *Mhondoro* over the state was emphasised in another way. The *Mhondoro* were put forward as those who had helped the present government to power by supporting the armed struggle for Independence. Many of the possessed mediums argued that they did so because they expected that the stolen lands would be taken back from the whites, and that the authority of 'traditional' leadership over this land would be restored, a 'return to the old ways'.

At first glance it may seem that the narrative put forward by the *Mhondoro* mediums does not really constitute a counter-narrative to the land degradation narrative. The counter-narrative does not comment upon the validity of the assumption that proper, scientific land use planning prevents soil degradation. Some people in Dande even believed part of the narrative, thinking that their production techniques were indeed 'backward'. Adams and Hulme (2001), however, argue that point-by-point rebuttals are not necessarily effective in challenging dominant narratives. A narrative that tells a better story is. The land degradation narrative served to de-politicise the land issue in Zimbabwe. One could argue that the counter-narrative re-politicised the land issue again since it stated that the struggle for Independence was fought to regain control over land. Both narratives are based on different interpretations of what the Mid-Zambezi Project was about; the vision of the planners and implementers was that it was about rationalising and increasing agricultural production and preventing environmental degradation. The proponents of the counter-narrative interpreted it as an attempt to take control over the land away from local communities. Yet, at the same time, both narratives have more in common than appears at first sight. Though the land degradation narrative stresses the importance of science, in fact it seems to be more about stereotypes of what communal farming practices are like. The counter-narrative tells the story of how efficient and fair these practices are. In this, it shares a characteristic with the land degradation narrative, namely that it simplifies complex land use practices. The counter-narrative ignores, for instance, the role that Ward Councillors and VIDCO chairpersons have played in the allocation of land in Dande.

The recounting of the counter-narrative produced mixed effects. Project staff were not insensitive to the supernatural threats issued by the possessed mediums. They did not dare to go ahead with the implementation without permission from the spirits, as was shown in Chapter Six and Seven. In that sense, the counter-narrative proved to be a powerful story. However, in other ways, project staff were not convinced by the counter-narrative, perhaps because it did not explicitly address the validity of the 'science' part of the land degradation narrative. Most staff members continued to think that the Mid-Zambezi Project was needed to improve agricultural production and prevent soil erosion. They could not give up the project altogether and continued to try to convince the chief, the village headmen and the villagers to accept it. They did so by threatening that all development would be withheld from those who did not agree to being relocated, that is, that no schools or clinics would be built, no roads upgraded. This strategy worked only partially. It divided the communities into those who were willing to accept land reforms if this would bring improvement of infrastructure and services, and those who persevered in resisting the project. The proponents were supported by the new Ward Councillor, who in turn was backed by ZANU(PF), but failed to obtain support from the spirit mediums. They began to argue that the mediums were remnants of a 'traditional, backward lifestyle', and emphasised their own membership of Independent Christian churches. Through the Ward Councillor they tried to convince project management to·go ahead with the implementation of the project despite continued disapproval of the *Mhondoro*. The implementation of the project, however, was never completed. In 1995 the Project Manager retired and all other project staff were withdrawn from Dande. This, however, did not mean an enduring victory for the opponents of the project, as I will explain in the last section of this chapter.

The role of Mhondoro mediums

The study of the role of the mediums in the conflicts over the land in Dande as described in Chapter Six and Seven gave me some insights into the functioning of the *Mhondoro* cult and its role in Dande.

The mediums expressed local resentment against the government's interference with land allocation and land-use. They invoked the 'real owners of the land', the royal ancestors, in their opposition to the state's claim to the land in Dande. Land, and the control over it, is a central issue in the *Mhondoro* cult. Its rituals are concerned with the fertility of the land. The *Mhondoro* themselves are believed to have struggled among themselves for the control over land. Most of the myths related to the cult are about the tricks and schemes that Mutota's descendants deployed to steal the rain-making powers - and thus the control over land - from the autochthonous Bangomwe and his children (see Garbett 1977; 1992; Lan 1985). Such re-enacted conflicts between 'invaders' and 'autochthons' are quite common in spirit medium cults all over Southern Africa (see for example Werbner 1977; Schoffeleers 1978; Ranger 1999). Therefore, the involvement of the *Mhondoro* mediums in the struggle against the land reforms may have seemed a logical option to both mediums and adherents of the cult.

Access to and control over land is central to political control in Zimbabwe, even in areas where land has lost most of its productive value, as Andersson (2001) maintains. Much of the literature on the *Mhondoro* mediums deals with their political authority derived from their ties to the land. They play an important role in the succession procedure when a chief dies (see Garbett 1966a). But most of all, they have been credited with mobilising resistance to the Rhodesian white settler regime - both in the first revolt against white dominance in 1896/1897 and during the armed struggle which led to Zimbabwe's Independence in 1980 (see for example Ranger 1967; 1985; Fry 1976; Lan 1985). Bourdillon (1987b) has questioned the mediums' mobilising power, and argues that perhaps the freedom fighters have done more for the reputation of the mediums than the other way around. Whatever the case, the association between spirit mediums and the war for Independence is readily made, by the mediums, by many of their adherents, and even by the state (see Weiss 1986; Ranger 1993b). At Independence festivities in the National Stadium banners depicting the late medium of Nehanda decorate the stadium, and the ancestral spirits are thanked for their support. The association of *Mhondoro* mediums with resistance to the (white settler) state may also explain why they became involved in the resistance against the land reforms in Dande. In their pronouncements the mediums frequently refer to their contribution to Zimbabwe's Independence to increase the legitimacy of their claims to the land vis-à-vis the state. This may also explain why the government tried to control the mediums rather than denounce them, as witnessed by the protection (resulting in isolation) of the new medium of Nehanda and attempts by a senior government official to buy the support of the medium of Chidyamauyu.

Some of Bourdillon's doubts concerning the mobilising capacity of mediums appear to be confirmed in this book. The cases described in Chapter Six and Seven suggest that perhaps the opponents of the projects mobilised the mediums for their struggle rather than the other way around. The medium of Chidyamauyu gained a wealth of support when he fiercely denounced the land reform project - which he did after he had consulted the village headmen. After he had received gifts and a house in reward for his contribution to the armed struggle for Independence, he kept rather quiet about the project. Immediately rumours started circulating that he had been bribed, that he was looking after his own interests more than after those of the adherents and even drastically suggesting that the spirit had left the medium. A renewed public denouncement of the project gained him some support again, but when he moved into his new house and refused to attribute the drought to the project, he lost respect and was seldom consulted any longer by the communities he was supposed to serve. The matter of the irrigation project seems another case in point. Here, the adherents of the *Mhondoro* cult transferred their support to the new medium of Chitsungo - even though this medium had not yet passed his test - when other mediums appeared to be willing to accommodate Agritex staff by conducting an acceptance ritual for the irrigation project.

Little has been written about the influence of adherents on spirit mediums and their pronouncements. Garbett (1969) has hinted at the support mediums need, but Bourdillon (1979) has been more explicit. He describes how villagers boycotted the ceremonies organised by spirit mediums for the installation of a new chief who did not have popular support. However, in most of the literature on the role of spirit mediums during the struggle for Independence the influence of adherents has been neglected, if not denied. Nor is it a current theme in literature on spirit possession in other countries in the region (see Van Dijk, Reis & Spierenburg 2000).

The explanation of droughts or other climatological mishaps offers possibilities for mediums to offer social commentaries. In the course of my fieldwork, gradually, the idea began to take shape that the *Mhondoro* cult serves as a major platform for discussions on new developments and socio-political issues. These discussions can be held openly during possession seances and rituals, but also more covertly outside the sites officially associated with the cult. Many individuals and groups, all with different economic interests and political affinities participate in these debates. Each interest group may be seeking support from the *Mhondoro* cult. Not only do spirit mediums exert themselves to have their messages accepted as real expressions of the *Mhondoro* spirits; the followers of the cult also wish to see their interests reflected in the mediums' pronouncements. The resulting process of alternately questioning and preserving the medium's reputation is a crucial element in the power equation.

The adherents of the *Mhondoro* cult believe that the *Mhondoro* have the best intentions towards the people in their spirit provinces - including their direct descendants, the chiefs and their families - and they expect the possessed mediums' pronouncements to reflect these intentions. Since participation is based on territoriality, that is, all those living and farming in an area belonging to the *Mhondoro* are supposed to participate in the cult's rituals, *Mhondoro* mediums are confronted with a very heterogeneous group of potentials followers. Hence, in some cases adherents may differ in opinion on what exactly is the best; in others there may be more cohesion among them. The more cohesion there is amongst adherents, the stronger expectations of the mediums' pronouncements become. When the pronouncements do not match the expectations, adherents may start doubting if a medium is still possessed by a royal ancestor. Mediums are believed to be completely separate from the spirits possessing them. The spirits are believed to choose their mediums and not the other way around. Allegedly, spirits can decide to abandon a medium if this medium is found to be acting in his or her own interests rather than in the interests of the adherents. In that case, earlier successes can act against the medium. The more popular a medium, the more he or she is consulted by individuals (or families) in cases of illness or bad luck. Though mediums are not supposed to earn money from their duties to the communities, they are allowed to accept handsome rewards for assisting individuals. The wealth accumulated in this way can be taken as a proof of greed if and when a medium's pronouncements do not confirm expectations.

The complete separation between mediums and the spirits possessing them allows for pronouncements that contain critiques of the more powerful in society. The spirit mediums denouncing the projects could not be held responsible for the critique expressed through their mouths. It also allowed the mediums to oppose the chief, who let himself be talked into assisting project management in attempts to convince villagers of the need to accept the land reforms. Chiefs do hold some leverage over mediums, since the mediums' assistants - who play an important role in deciding whether a medium is genuine or not (see Lan 1985: 54, 199) - are often village headmen who have been appointed by the chiefs. However, if a majority of adherents believe that a medium's pronouncements are genuine, even though they go against the interests of the chiefs or headmen, it will be difficult for the latter to challenge the reputation of the medium.

Since the spirits have the interests of all those living in their provinces at heart, adherents may try to negotiate with them when they feel that certain pronouncements militate against their interests. Many people - and some of the possessed mediums as well - told me stories of how the *Mhondoro* of Dande had issued a ban on the cultivation of cotton when this crop was first introduced into the area. Villages then sent delegations to the spirit mediums to convince the spirits that cotton was the only cash crop that could be cultivated in Dande, and that the ban should be lifted; and it was. Cogently, when opinions differ considerably, not everyone can be satisfied, and people may start doubting mediums altogether, looking for an alternative in the religious domain. Various churches are active in Dande and some are in fierce competition with the *Mhondoro* mediums, denouncing them as charlatans or mediums of evil spirits; others co-operate with the mediums and do not forbid participation in rituals to honour the spirits.

To emphasise the separation between spirits and mediums, many people - mediums and adherents alike - maintain that mediums are 'strangers' to their spirits, that they belong to different clans (see also Lan 1985: 51). My research, rather than confirming this, brought to light that nearly half of the mediums I interviewed in fact do share their *mutupo* with the spirit possessing them.

The *Mhondoro* cult certainly does not ban 'strangers'. In theory their mediums should be strangers, though in practice this is not often the case. Some of the *Mhondoro* themselves are said to be strangers who invaded Dande. In principle, every person living and farming in a spirit province can participate in the cult, whether they are 'strangers' or 'autochthons'. In Chapter Eight I have described the importance of 'strangerhood' in Dande. Perhaps for this very reason, the internal conflicts in the villages over who would be excluded from rights to land should the land reforms be continued, were hardly ever taken to the spirit mediums, but were fought out through witchcraft.

Though project staff members were not insensitive to the pronouncements of the *Mhondoro* mediums, many told me that they considered the *Mhondoro* cult a remnant of the past, a 'backward' tradition. In their pronouncements many of the mediums referred to the past; they even demanded 'a return to the old ways', that is, a return of the authority of the chiefs over the land. Nevertheless, their rejection of the land reforms and the irrigation project cannot simply be classified as a rejection of 'modern development'. 'Modern' though these projects may be, whether they contribute to development remains very doubtful. As I have tried to show in this book, the projects have had serious flaws attributable to the misreading of local land-use practices, and the denial of their dynamics. The rejection of 'traditional' religions as 'backward looking' (see Thoden van Velzen and Van Wetering 1988: 399; Werbner 1997) is a misinterpretation which fails to recognise that the images of the ancestors and the past are simultaneously products of economic and political forces, as well as promises and visions of a future. They contribute to people's attempts to make sense of the present or even change present conditions (Thoden van Velzen and Van Wetering 1988: 400-1; see also Comaroff & Comaroff 1993; Geschiere 1995: 23; Behrend & Luig 1999: xiii). The fact that the spirit mediums in Dande offer a critique on 'modern' land reforms by referring to the past does not mean that they reject 'modernity' in general; some of the spirit mediums themselves grow cotton and hybrid maize, and drive tractors. Planners and implementers would do better to question why certain of their schemes are rejected, rather than simply assuming that local communities are conservative by nature

10

Epilogue

Though the *Mhondoro* mediums' intervention managed to stall the implementation of the Mid-Zambezi Rural Development Project and the Agritex Irrigation project, this did not mean the government suddenly ended its attempts to implement land reforms in Dande. Project staff may have been sensitive to the pronouncements made by the *Mhondoro* mediums; the government was not. This is not to say that it did not take the mediums seriously. On the contrary: I have described how attempts were made to bribe the medium of Chidyamauyu, and how the new medium of Nehanda was tightly controlled and prevented from moving to the Zambezi Valley. The arguments put forward by the possessed mediums, however, were not taken seriously. After the Mid-Zambezi Project staff left, the District Development Fund Officers were charged with implementing land reforms in those areas which had resisted them, but so far they have not been pursuing relocation very actively. The Dande Irrigation Project described in Chapter Seven continued, though seriously delayed. Construction work on the dam started in 2002. A new programme was designed, the Mid-Zambezi Valley Land-Use Programme, which would include Dande. The aim of this programme was very similar to that of the Mid-Zambezi Project. No attempts have been made to learn from the failure of the Mid-Zambezi Project. All plans share the idea that without proper land-use planning people cannot be controlled and that local communities cannot themselves be empowered to engage in such planning (see also Derman 1995: 71). South-west of the area covered by the Mid-Zambezi Project lies Kanyurira Ward where communities have fairly successfully engaged in such planning under the banner of the CAMPFIRE programme, yet the lessons from this programme have not been taken into account either.

The current political and economic situation, though, has disrupted the new land-use planning exercises, with the exception of the Dande Irrigation Project. Most donor organisations have halted their activities, apart from drought relief, and government does not have the necessary funds to carry out further land-use planning in the Communal Areas. All attention has now shifted to the invasions of farms in the Large Scale Commercial Farming Areas, and the government organisations once responsible for the internal land reforms in the Communal Areas are now working on the implementation of the 'Fast Track Resettlement Programme' on invaded Commercial Farms. On the surface it may seem that the post-Independence government has finally returned to its promise of returning the stolen lands to the peasants. Whether this will be an enduring change of policy that indeed is aimed at improving the situation of land hungry Communal Farmers remains to be seen. The invaders have been told not to construct any permanent structures, and many have already been removed from invaded farms to make way for ZANU(PF) politicians or businessmen with strong ties to the party. Recently, newspaper articles have appeared about a number of white farmers who have been given back their farms after concluding deals with senior government officials (The Herald, 18 May 2004). The main victims of the land invasions, however, were not just the farm-owners; even worse off are the thousands of farm labourers who have lost their jobs and are not considered potential participants in the Fast Track Resettlement Programme. They are often considered foreigners and large numbers of them await their fate in refugee camps near the bigger towns and cities.

Looking at other developments in Zimbabwe, the invasions seem to be an instrument for political control deployed by the ruling party. Severe violence has been used against members of the opposition party. The free press has been attacked, literally with bombs - the critical newspaper Daily News has had its presses bombed - and with new legislation. Local government authorities have been attacked and taken over by 'war veterans' (see McGregor 2002). The 2002/3 harvest failed in the wake of the disruptions in the countryside, failure to provide inputs to the land invaders and a serious drought. Food aid has been hijacked by the ruling party, and there are numerous reports that drought relief is only given to those who can produce a ZANU(PF) membership card (see for example Amnesty International Press Release 14 May 2004).

Spirit mediums have not remained quiet, but this time the separation between medium and spirit was not so readily accepted: one medium by the name of Takatukwa Mamhova Mupawaenda was murdered just before the presidential elections by ZANU(PF) supporters who accused him of mobilising chiefs and headmen against Mugabe (The Daily News 19 February 2002). A group of mediums calling themselves Mhondoro Dzedzimbahwe protested against the murder. They issued the following statement to a journalist from The Daily News:

We, the spirit mediums of Zimbabwe, are outraged by this horrendous crime perpetrated against one of our own. We have also been outraged by all politically motivated murders that have taken place since 1980. (...) We implore you, the people of Zimbabwe, to stand steadfastly against such atrocities. Let it be remembered that we, spirit mediums, are the protectors of the country of Zimbabwe and everyone in it. The perpetrators of this evil act will themselves never know peace. Let it also be known that even if you kill us, we will not stop campaigning for justice, peace, tolerance and prosperity for our land, Zimbabwe. (In: The Daily News 7 March 2002)

The journalist continued: 'The spirit mediums said they took courage from great spirit mediums, Sekuru Kaguvi and Mbuya Nehanda, killed for resisting colonialism in the 1890s.They said Kaguvi and Nehanda were killed for standing up against the same brutal policies now being perpetrated by ZANU(PF)'.

What will happen to the Communal Areas of Zimbabwe is not easy to predict. It is tempting to say that, given the endurance of the land degradation narrative in the 1980s and 1990s, and the eviction of a number of land invaders to make way for the elite, in the future the government policy will attempt to consolidate the Commercial Farms again and return to a policy of internal land reforms in the Communal Areas. Yet, such a policy requires some stabilisation of the political situation, and stability is still far away. The present government seems determined to stay in power at all costs. These costs are tremendous. The economic situation of the country is disastrous and the vast majority of the population can no longer make ends meet. Unfortunately, unless the elite itself is affected by the economic crisis, the present political course will not easily be abandoned. The government of Zimbabwe has, as Alexander (2003) and Raftapolous (2003) argue, even resorted to attacking the structures of the state; it has undermined the judiciary system by removing independent and critical judges and has all but destroyed local government (see McGregor 2002). Alexander (2003) also maintains that the land invasions and political chaos have led to a sidelining of technocrats within the ministerial departments. She cites an article from the Independent (16 May 2000, in Alexander 2003: 113) in which some of them are lamenting that the plans produced by their '(…) serious scientific analysis of Zimbabwe's agricultural needs were now dead'. These developments make a return to the implementation of land reforms in the Communal Areas less likely. Nevertheless, this does not mean that the interests of farmers in these areas will be taken at heart. The chaotic situation in terms of the provision of farming implements, the loss of jobs, and the difficulties experienced in marketing of produce as a result of even stricter price controls have not improved the situation in the Communal Areas.

Many commentators have speculated about the lessons that can be learnt from the Zimbabwean situation for the case of South Africa. I would like to conclude by concurring with Alexander (2003), Raftapolous (2003) and Cousins (2003) that it is important to remember that the struggle for Independence of Zimbabwe was fought for a more equitable distribution of land but also, and perhaps even more important, for good governance and democracy. A lack of the latter two can lead to the abuse of the land issue for political reasons.

References

Abraham, D.P. (1959) The Monomotapa Dynasty. *NADA*, 36: 58-84.
Abraham, D.P. (1966) The Roles of "Chaminuka" and the *Mhondoro*-cults in Shona Political History. In: E. Stokes and R. Brown (Eds.) *The Zambezian Past*. Manchester: Manchester University Press, 28-46.
Adams, Willan & David Hulme (2001) Conservation & Community, Changing Narratives, Policies & Practices in African Conservation. In: David Hulme & Marshall Murphree (Eds.) *African Wildlife & Livelihoods. The Promise and Performance of Community Conservation*. Oxford/Portsmouth: James Currey Publishers/Heinemann, 9-23.
ADF, African Development Fund (1986) *Appraisal Report for the Mid Zambezi Valley Rural Development Project*. Agricultural and Rural Development Department.
Agritex Planning Branch (1993) Land Use Plan for Matsiwo A Ward, Dande Communal Area, Mashonaland Central. Harare: Agritex.
Alexander, Jocelyn (1995) Things Fall Apart, The Centre Can Hold: Processes of Post-War Political Change in Zimbabwe's Rural Areas. In: N. Bhebe and T. Ranger (Eds.) *Society in Zimbabwe's Liberation War: Volume Two*. Harare/ London/ Portsmouth: University of Zimbabwe Publications/James Currey/Heinemann, 175-91.
Alexander, Jocelyn (2003) Squatters, Veterans and the State in Zimbabwe. In : Amanda Hammar, Brian Raftapolous & Stig Jensen (Eds.) *Zimbabwe's Unfinished Business : Rethinking Land, State and Nation in the Context of Crisis*. Harare : Weaver Press, 83-118.
Alexander, Jocelyn, JoAnn McGregor & Terence Ranger (2000) *Violence & Memory, One Hundred Years in the 'Dark Forests' of Matabeleland*. Oxford/Portsmouth/Cape Town/Harare: James Currey/Heinemann/David Philip/Weaver Press.
Amselle, J.L. (1976) Aspects et Significations du Phenomene Migratoire en Afrique. In: J.L. Amselle (Ed.) *Les Migrations Africaines, Resaux et Processus Migratoires*. Paris: Maspero, 9-39.
Anderson, Benedict (1985) Imagined Communities, Reflections on the origin and spread of nationalism. London: Verso.
Andersson, Jens (2002) Going places, staying home. Rural-urban connections and the significance of land in Buhera district, Zimbabwe. PhD thesis, Wageningen University.
Austin, Ralph A. (1993) The moral economy of witchcraft: an essay in comparative history. In: J. Comaroff & J.Comaroff (Eds.) *Modernity and its malcontents; ritual and power in postcolonial Africa*. Chicago, London: University of Chicago Press, 89-110.
Bank, Leslie (2002) Beyond Red and School: Gender, Tradition and Identity in the Rural Eastern Cape. *Journal of Southern African Studies*, 28 (3), 631-649.

Barrett, John (1994) Economic Issues in Trypanosomiasis Control: Case Studies from Southern Africa. Unpubl. PhD Thesis, University of Reading.

Barrow, Edmund & Marshall Murphree (2001) Community Conservation. From Concept to Practice. In: David Hulme & Marshall Murphree (Eds.) *African Wildlife & Livelihoods. ThePromise & Performance of Community Conservation.* Oxford/Portsmouth: James Currey/ Heinemann, 24-37.

Batagglia, D. (1995) On Practical Nostalgia: Self-Prospecting among Urban Trobrianders. In: D. Battaglia (Ed.) *Rhetorics of Self-Making.* Berkeley, Los Angeles/London: University of Berkeley Press, 77-94.

Bate, S.P. (1997) Whatever Happened to Organizational Anthropology? A Review of the Field of Organizational Ethnography and Anthropological Studies. *Human Relations*, 50(9), 1147-1175.

Beach, D.N. (1980) *The Shona and Zimbabwe, 900-1850.* Gweru: Mambo Press.

Beach, D.N. (1984) Zimbabwe Before 1900. Gweru: Mambo Press.

Beach, D.N. (1986) War and Politics in Zimbabwe 1840-1900. Gweru: Mambo Press.

Beach, D.N. (1994) *The Shona and their Neigbours.* Oxford (U.K.)/Cambridge (U.S.A.): Blackwell.

Behrend, Heike & Ute Luig (1999) Introduction. In: Heike Behrend & Ute Luig (Eds.) *Spirit Possession, Modernity & Power in Africa.* Oxford/Kampala/Cape Town/Madison: James Currey/Fountain Publishers/David Philip/University of Wisconsin Press, xi-xxii.

Beinart, W. (1984) Soil erosion, conservationism and ideas about development, 1900-1960. *Journal of Southern African Studies*, 11 (1), 52-83.

Beinart, W. (1989) Introduction; the politics of colonial conservation. *Journal of Southern African Studies*, 15, 143-162.

Berry, Sara (1993) No Condition is Permanent: The social dynamics of agrarian change in Sub-Saharan Africa. Madison: University of Wisconsin Press.

Bhebe, Ngwabi and Terence Ranger (1995) Volume Introduction: Society in Zimbabwe's Liberation War: Volume Two. In: N. Bhebe and T. Ranger (Eds.) *Society in Zimbabwe's Liberation War: Volume Two.* Harare/London/Portsmouth: University of Zimbabwe Publications/James Currey/Heinemann, 6-34.

Blanckenburg, Peter Von (1994) Large Scale Commercial Farmers and Land Reform in Africa. The case of Zimbabwe. Aldershot: Avebury.

Bourdillon, M.F.C. (1970) Peoples of Darwin: an Ethnographic Survey of the Darwin District. *NADA*, 10, 103-114.

Bourdillon, M.F.C. (1979) Religion and Authority in a Korekore Community. *Africa*, 49, 172-181.

Bourdillon, M.F.C. (1981) Suggestions of Bureaucracy in Korekore Religion: Putting the Ethnography Straight. *Zambezia*, IX, 119-136.

Bourdillon, M.F.C. (1987) *The Shona Peoples. An Ethnography of the Contemporary Shona, with Special Reference to their Religion.* Revised edition. Gweru (Zimbabwe): Mambo Press.

Bourdillon, M.F.C. (1987b) Guns and Rain: Taking Structural Analysis too far? Review article. *Africa*, 20, 263-274.

Bratton, M. (1978) Beyond Community Development: The Political Economy of Rural Administration in Zimbabwe. Gwelo: Mambo Press.

Brickhill, Jeremy (1995) Daring to Storm the Heavens: The Military Strategy of ZAPU 1976 to 1979. In: N. Bhebe & T. Ranger (Eds.) *Soldiers in Zimbabwe's Liberation*

War. Volume one. Portsmouth/London/Harare: Heinemann, Currey/University of
   Zimbabwe, 48-72.
Bruce, John W. (1990) *Legal Issues in Land Use and Resettlement.* Zimbabwe
   Agricultural Sector Memorandum. Washington: World Bank Report.
Burcke, Deliane Jannette (1989) Kuoma Rupandi (The parts are dry). Ideas and
   Practices concerning Disability and Rehabilitation in a Shona Ward. Research Report
   no.36. Leiden: African Studies Centre.
CASS/WWF/Zimtrust Coordinating Committee (1989) Wildlife Utilization in
   Zimbabwe's Communal Lands Collaborative Programme Activities. Harare: Unpubl.
   Report.
Catholic Commission for Justice and Peace in Zimbabwe (1997) *Report on the 1980s
   Disturbances in Matabeleland and the Midlands.* Published on the World Wide Web,
   http://www.mg.co/mg/zim/zim/zimtitle.html.
Cavendish, William (1999) The complexity of the commons: environmental resource
   demands in rural Zimbabwe, WPS/99-8. Oxford: CSAE Publ. Working Paper Series.
Chambers, R. (1983) Rural development: putting the last first. Horlow: Longman.
Chambers, R. (1993) *Challenging the Professions: Frontiers for Rural Development.*
   London: Intermediate Technology Publications.
Cheater, A.P. (1990) The Ideology of 'Communal' Land Tenure in Zimbabwe:
   Mythogenesis Enacted? *Africa,* 60,188-207.
Chennells, Anthony (1995) Rhodesian Discourse, Rhodesian Novels and the Zimbabwe
   Liberation War. In: N. Bhebe and T. Ranger (Eds.) *Society in Zimbabwe's Liberation
   War: Volume Two.* Harare/London/Portsmouth: University of Zimbabwe
   Publications/ James Currey/ Heinemann, 102-129.
Chibudu, C., G. Chiota, E. Kandiros, B. Mavedzenge, B. Mombeshora, M. Mudhara, F.
   Murimbarimba, A. Nasasara and I. Scoones (2001)   Soils, Livelihoods and
   Agricultural Change: The Management of Soil-Fertility in the Communal Lands of
   Zimbabwe. In: Ian Scoones (Ed.) *Dynamics and Diversity: Soil Fertility and
   Farming Livelihoods in Africa,* London: Earthscan, 116-163.
Cliffe, Lionel & Griffiths L. Cunningham (1975) Ideology, Organization, and the
   Settlement Experience of Tanzania. In: Lionel Cliffe & John S. Saul (Eds.) *Policies,
   vol. 2 of Socialism in Tanzania: An Interdisciplinary Reader.* Nairobi: East African
   Publishing House, 131-140.
Cliffe, Lionel & John S. Saul (1975) (Eds.) *Socialism in Tanzania: An Interdisciplinary
   Reader.* Nairobi: East African Publishing House.
Clifford, J. & G. Marcus (1986) (Eds.) *Writing Culture: The Poetics and Politics of
   Ethnography.* Berkeley: University of Berkeley Press.
Cobbing, Julian (1977) The Absent Priesthood: Another Look at the Rhodesian Rising
   of 1896-1897. *Journal of African History,* 8, 61-84.
Comaroff, Jean & John Comaroff (1993) Introduction. In: Jean Comaroff & John
   Comaroff (Eds.) *Modernity and its Malcontents. Ritual and Power in Postcolonial
   Africa.* Chicago/London: University of Chicago Press.
Comaroff, Jean & John Comaroff (1999) Alien-nation: Zombies, immigrants and
   millennial capitalism. *CODESRIA Bulletin,* no.3/4, 17-28.
Cousins, Ben (2003) The Zimbabwean Crisis in its Wider Context: The Politics of
   Land, Democracy and Development in Southern Africa. In : Amanda Hammar, Brian
   Raftapolous & Stig Jensen (Eds.) *Zimbabwe's Unfinished Business : Rethinking
   Land, State and Nation in the Context of Crisis.* Harare : Weaver Press, 263-316.

Cutshall, C.R. (1989) Masoka/Kanyurira Ward- A Socio-Economic Baseline Survey of Community Households. Occasional Paper. Harare: Centre for Applied Social Sciences (University of Zimbabwe).

Cutshall, C.R. (1990) Kanyemba/Chapoto Ward- A Socio-Economic Baseline Survey of Community Households. Occasional Paper. Harare: Centre for Applied Social Sciences (University of Zimbabwe).

Cutshall, C.R. (1991) *Angwa/Chisunga Ward- A Socio-Economic Baseline Survey of Community Households.* Occasional Paper. Harare: Centre for Applied Social Sciences (University of Zimbabwe).

Dabengwa, Dumiso (1995) ZIPRA in the Zimbabwe War of National Liberation. In: N. Bhebe and T. Ranger (Eds.) *Soldiers in Zimbabwe's Liberation War Volume One.* Harare/London/Portsmouth: University of Zimbabwe Publications/ James Currey/ Heinemann, 24-35.

Dambo Research Unit Loughborough University, U.K. (1987) *Utilisation of Dambos in Rural Development, a discussion paper.* Unpubl. report, University of Zimbabwe.

Daneel, M.L. (1970) The God of the Matopo Hills. The Hague: Mouton.

Daneel, M.L. (1971) The Background and Rise of Southern Shona Independent Churches. The Hague: Mouton.

Daneel, M.L. (1977) The Growth and Significance of Shona Independent Churches. In: M.F.C. Bourdillon (Ed.) *Christianity South of the Zambezi, vol. 2.* Gwelo: Mambo Press, 77-129.

Daneel, M.L. (1987) *Quest for belonging: introduction to a study of African independent churches.* Gweru: Mambo Press.

Daneel, M.L. (1991) Healing the Earth: Traditional and Christian Initiatives in Southern Africa. Paper presented at the conference "*Wholeness, Healing and Resistance; on the role of religion in the management of personal, social and ecological crises in a changing South Africa*", 26-27 September 1991, University of Utrecht.

Daneel, M.L. (1998) Mwari the liberator: oracular intervention in Zimbabwe's quest for the 'lost lands'. In: James L. Cox (Ed.) *Rites of passage in contemporary Africa : interaction between Christian and African traditional religions.* Cardiff : Cardiff Academic Press, 94-125.

De Bruijn, Mirjam, Rijk Van Dijk & Dick Foecken (2001) Introduction In: Mirjam de Bruijn, Rijk van Dijk and Dick Foecken (Eds.) *Mobile Africa, Changing patterns of movement in Africa and beyond.* Leiden: Brill, 27-46.

Delius, Peter & Stefan Schirmer (2000) Soil Conservation in a Racially Ordered Society: South Africa 1930-1970. *Journal of Southern African Studies,* 26 (4), 719-743.

Derman, W. (1990) The unsettling of the Zambezi Valley. An Examination of the Mid-Zambezi Rural Development Project. Occasional Paper. Harare: Centre for Applied Social Sciences (University of Zimbabwe).

Derman, W. (1993) Recreating Common Property Management: Government Projects and Land Use Policy in the Mid-Zambezi Valley, Zimbabwe. Occasional Paper. Harare: Centre for Applied Social Sciences (University of Zimbabwe).

Derman, W. (1995) *Changing Land-Use in the Eastern Zambezi Valley: Socio-Economic Considerations.* Report submitted to World Wide Fund for Nature-Zimbabwe and the Centre for Applied Social Sciences, University of Zimbabwe.

Derman, W. & A. Ferguson (2000) The Value of Water: Political Ecology and Water Reform in Southern Africa. Paper presented at the *Panel on Political Ecology for the*

Annual Meetings of the American Anthropological Association, San Francisco, November 15-19, 2000.

Derman, W. and J. Murombedzi (1994) Democracy, Development, and Human Rights in Zimbabwe. A Contradictory Terrain. *African Rural and Urban Studies, 1, 119-143.*

De Wet, Chris (1989) Betterment Planning in a Rural Village in Keiskammahoek, Ciskei. *Journal of Southern African Studies*, 15 (2), 326-345.

Douglas, Mary (1986) Institutionalized Public Memory. In: J.F. Short (Ed.) *The Social Fabric*. London: Sage.

Douglas, Mary (1995) Forgotten Knowledge. In: M. Strathern (Ed.) *Shifting Contexts: Transformations in Anthropological Knowledge*. London/New York: Routledge.

Drinkwater, Michael (1991) *The State and Agrarian Change in Zimbabwe's Communal Areas,* Basingstoke/London: MacMillan.

Dzingirai, Vupenyu (1995) *Take back your CAMPFIRE*. NRM Occasional Papers Series, Harare: Centre for Applied Social Sciences (University of Zimbabwe).

Eliade, M. (1959) *The Sacred and the Profane. The Nature of Religion.* New York, London: Harcourt Brace Jovanovich.

Fabian, Johannes (1983) *Time and the Other: How Anthropology Makes its Object.* New York: Columbia University Press.

Fardon, Richard (1990) Introduction: Localizing Strategies; The Regionalization of Ethnographic Accounts. In: Richard Fardon (Ed.) *Localizing Strategies. Regional Traditions of Ethnographic Writing.* Edinburgh: Scottish Academic Press, i-x.

Ferguson, James (1990) *The Anti-Politics Machine*. Cambridge: Cambridge University Press.

Fisiy, C.F. & P. Geschiere (1991) Sorcery, Witchcraft and Accumulation. Regional Variations in South and West Cameroon. *Critique of Anthropology*, 11, 251-278.

Fortmann, Louise & Calvin Nihra (1992) *Local Management of Trees in Zimbabwe: A Tenurial Niche approach.* Harare: Occasional Papers Series, Centre for Applied Social Sciences (University of Zimbabwe).

Frederikse, Julie (1982) *None But Ourselves. Masses vs. Media in the Making of Zimbabwe.* Johannesburg: Ravan Press.

Frederikse, Julie (1984) *None But Ourselves. Masses vs Media in the Making of Zimbabwe.* London: Heinemann.

Fry, Peter (1976) Spirits of Protest: Spirit Mediums and the Articulation of Consensus among the Zezuru of Southern Rhodesia. Cambridge: Cambridge University Press.

Garbett, Kingsley (1966a) Religious Aspects of Political Succession among the Valley Korekore (N. Shona). In: E. Stokes & R. Brown (Eds.) *The Zambezian Past.* Manchester: Manchester University Press.

Garbett, Kingsley (1966b) The Rhodesian Chief's Dilemma: Government Officer or Tribal Leader. *Race*, 8, 307-426.

Garbett, Kingsley (1967) Prestige, Status and Power in a Modern Valley Korekore Chiefdom, Rhodesia. *Africa*, 37,307-325.

Garbett, Kingsley (1969) Spirit Mediums as Mediators in Valley Korekore Society. In: J. Beattie & J. Middleton (Eds.). *Spirit Mediumship and Society in Africa.* London: Routledge & Kegan Paul, 104-127.

Garbett, Kingsley (1977) Disparate Regional Cults and a Unitary Field in Zimbabwe. In: R. Werbner (Ed.) *Regional Cults.* London: Academic Press, 55-92.

Garbett, Kingsley (1986) From Conquerors to Autochthons: Structural Transformation in Korekore Regional Cults. Paper presented at the conference on *Culture and Consciousness in Southern Africa*, University of Manchester, September 1986.

Garbett, Kingsley (1992) From Conquerors to Autochthons: Cultural Logic, Structural Transformation, and Korekore Regional Cults. *Social Analysis, Journal of Cultural and Social Practice*, no.31, 12-43.

Geertz, Clifford (1973) *The interpretation of cultures.* New York: Basic Books.

Gelfand, M. (1956) *Medicine and Magic of the Mashona.* Cape Town: Juta.

Gelfand, M. (1962) Shona Religion with Special Reference to the MaKorekore. Cape Town: Juta.

Geschiere, Peter (1982) Village Communities and the State. Changing Relations among the Maka of South-east Cameroon since the Colonial Conquest. London: Kegan Paul.

Geschiere, Peter (1995) Sorcellerie et Politique en Afrique, La viande des autres. Paris: Karthala.

Geschiere, Peter (1997) *The Modernity of Witchcraft: Politics and the Occult in Postcolonial Africa.* Charlottesville: University Press of Virginia.

Government of Zimbabwe (1984) *Structure of Village Development Committees, Ward Development Committees and Extension Services.* Harare: Government Printer.

Government of Żimbabwe (1985) Ministry of Land, Resettlement and Rural Development. *Communal Lands Development Plan. A 15 Year Development Strategy.* First draft. Harare: Government Printer.

Government of Zimbabwe (1985b) Ministry of Land, Resettlement and Rural Development. *Resettlement and Rural Development. Intensive Resettlement Policies and Procedures. Revised Version.* Harare: Government Printer.

Government of Zimbabwe (1986) Ministry of Lands Agriculture and Rural Resettlement. *Conceptual Framework for the Communal Lands Development Plan.* Harare: Government Printer.

Government of Zimbabwe (1993) Euroconsult in Association with Burrow Binnie Ltd. Zimbabwe. *Dande Irrigation Feasibility Study.* Unpubl. Report.

Government of Zimbabwe (1994) Commission of Inquiry into Appropriate Agricultural Tenure Systems, under the Chairmanship of Professor Mandivamba Rukuni, *Volume One: Main Report.* Harare: Government Printer.

Government of Zimbabwe (1999) Ministry of Local Government and National Housing, *Discussion Paper on the Vision of Local Government in Zimbabwe*, draft January 1999.

Government of Zimbabwe (1999b) Ministry of Local Government and National Housing, Rural District Councils Capacity Building Programme, Fourth Six Monthly Programme Review Report 1st January to 30th September 1999, Draft November 1999.

Grindle M.& J. Thomas (1991) *Public Choices and Policy Change.* Baltimore: Johns Hopkins University Press.

Hammar, Amanda (1998) Speaking with Space: Displacements and Claims in the Politics of Land in Zimbabwe, paper presented at *CODESRIA General Assembly*, Dakar (Senegal) 14-18 December.

Hammar, Amanda & Brian Raftapolous (2003) Zimbabwe's Unfinished Business : Rethinking Land, State and Nation. In : Amanda Hammar, Brian Raftapolous & Stig

Jensen (Eds.) *Zimbabwe's Unfinished Business : Rethinking Land, State and Nation in the Context of Crisis.* Harare : Weaver Press, 1-48.

Hammond-Toke, WD (1974) The Cape Noun witch familiar as a mediatory construct. *Man*, IX, 128-136.

Hardin, G. (1968) The Tragedy of the Commons. *Science*, 162, 1234-1248.

Hasler, Richard (1996) Agriculture, Foraging and Wildlife Resource Use in Africa. Cultural and Political Dynamics in the Zambezi Valley. London/New York: Kegan Paul.

Hastrup, Kirsten (1993) Hunger and the hardness of facts. *Man*, 28(4), 727-739.

Harries, Patrick (1989) Exclusion, Classification and Internal Colonialism: the Emergence of Ethnicity among the Tsonga-speakers of South Africa. In: Leroy Vail (Ed.) *The Creation of Tribalism in Southern Africa.* Berkeley/Los Angeles: University of California Press, 82-117.

Hecht, Robert M. (1985) Immigration, Land Transfer and Tenure Changes in Divo, Ivory Coast, 1940-1980. *Africa*, 55,319-335.

Hendricks, Fred T. (1989) Loose Planning and Rapid Resettlement: The Politics of Conservation and Control in Transkei, South Africa, 1950-1970. *Journal of Southern African Studies*, 15 (2), 306-325.

Hill, K.A. (1994) Politicians, Farmers, and Ecologists. Commercial wildlife ranging and the politics of land in Zimbabwe. *Journal of African and Asian Studies,* xxix, 226-248.

Holleman, J.F. (1952)   *Shona Customary Law.* London: Oxford University Press.

Hulme, David & Marshall Murphree (2001) Community Conservation in Africa, an Introduction. In: David Hulme & Marshall Murphree (Eds.) *African Wildlife & Livelihoods, the Promise & Performance of Community Conservation.* Oxford: James Currey, 1-8.

Isaacman, A.F. (1976) The Tradition of Resistance in Mozambique: Anti-Colonial Activity in the Zambezi Valley 1850-1921. London: Heineman.

Isaacman, A. & B. Isaacman (1977) Resistance and Collaboration in Southern and Central Africa, c. 1850-1921. *International Journal of African Historical Studies*, 10, 31-62.

James, Deborah (1985) Family and Household in a Lebowa Village. *African Studies*, 19 (1), 93-109.

Janzen, John M. (1992) 1992   *Ngoma. Discourses of Healing in Central and Southern Africa.* Berkeley, Los Angeles, Oxford: University of California Press.

Kamsteeg, Frans & Harry Wels (Forthcoming) Anthropological perspectives on power, performance and organizational politics. *Intervention, Research Journal for Culture Organisation and Management.*

Keeley, James and Ian Scoones (1999) *Understanding environmental policy processes: a review*, IDS Working Paper, no. 89. Brighton: Institute of Development Studies.

Keeley, James and Ian Scoones (2000) Environmental policymaking in Zimbabwe: Discourses, science and politics. Brighton: Institute of Development Studies.

Kramer, Eira (1997) The early years: extension services in peasant agriculture in colonial Zimbabwe, 1925-1929. *Zambezia*, XXIV, 159-179.

Kramer, Eira (1998) A Clash of Economies: Early Centralisation Efforts in Colonial Zimbabwe, 1929-1935. *Zambezia*, 25(1), 83-98.

Kriger, Norma (1988) The Zimbabwean War of Liberation: Struggles within the Struggle. *Journal of Southern African Studies*, 14, 304-326.

Kriger, Norma (1991) *Zimbabwe's Guerrilla War. Peasant Voices.* Cambridge: Cambridge University Press.

Kriger, Norma (2001) Les veterans et le parti au pouvoir: Une cooperation conflictuelle dans la longue durée. *Politique Africaine,* 81 (March): 80-100.

Lan, David (1985) *Guns and Rain. Guerrillas & Spirit Mediums in Zimbabwe.* Harare: Zimbabwe Publishing House.

Lawry, Steven W. (1989) *Tenure Policy toward Common Property Natural Resources.* Madison (Wisconsin): Land Tenure Center.

Leach, Melissa & Robin Mearns (1996) Environmental Change & Policy: Challenging Received Wisdom in Africa. In: Melissa Leach & Robin Mearns (Eds.) *The Lie of the Land: Challenging received wisdom on the African environment.* Oxford/Portsmouth: James Currey/Heinemann, 1-33.

Lévi-Strauss, Claude (1966) *The Savage Mind.* Chicago: Chicago University Press, second edition.

Long, Norman (1968) *Social Change and the Individual: a Study of the Social and Religious Responses to Innovation in a Zambian Rural Community.* Manchester: Manchester University Press.

Lynam, T.J.P., J. Chitsike, M. Howard, P. Hodza, M.A. Khumalo, W. Standa Gunda (1996) Assessing the Contributions of Renewable Resources to the Livelihoods of Communal Area Households in the Zambezi Valley of Zimbabwe. Paper presented at the *'Pan African Symposium on Sustainable Use of Natural Resources and Community Participation',* 24-27 June 1996, Harare, Zimbabwe.

Mafu, Hezekiel (1995) The 1991-92 Zimbabwean Drought and Some Religious Reactions. *Journal of Religion in Africa,* XXV(3), 288-308.

Malkki, Liisa H. (1995) Purity and Exile. Violence, Memory and National Cosmology among Hutu Refugees in Tanzania. Chicago/ London: University of Chicago Press.

Mamdani, Mahmood (1996) Citizen and Subject. Contemporary Africa and the legacy of late colonialism, London: James Currey.

Marks, Shula (1989) Patriotism, Patriarchy and Purity. In: Vail, Leroy (Ed.) *The Creation of Tribalism in Southern Africa.* Berkeley/Los Angeles: University of California Press, 215-240.

Marongwe, Nelson (2003) Farm Occupations and Occupiers in the New Politics of Land in Zimbabwe. In : Amanda Hammar, Brian Raftapolous & Stig Jensen (Eds.) *Zimbabwe's Unfinished Business : Rethinking Land, State and Nation in the Context of Crisis.* Harare : Weaver Press, 155-190.

Martin, J. (1992) *Cultures in Organizations. Three perspectives.* New York: Oxford University Press.

Martin, R.B. (1986) *Communal Areas Management Programme for Indigenous Resources. Working Document no.1/86, revised version.* Harare: Branch of Terrestrial Ecology, Department of National Parks and Wildlife Management.

Martin, D. and Johnson, P. (1981) *The Struggle for Zimbabwe: The Chimurenga War.* London: Faber.

Marwick, Max (1965*) Sorcery in Its Social Setting. A Study of the Northern Rhodesia Cewa.* Manchester: University of Manchester Press.

Marwick, Max (1982) Witchcraft as a Social Strain-gauge. In: Marwick, Max (Ed.) *Witchcraft and Sorcery.* Harmondsworth: Penguin, 300-313.

Mawere, Abraham & Ken Wilson (1995) Socio-Religious Movements, the Sate and Community Change: Some Reflections on the Ambuya Juliana Cult of Southern Zimbabwe. *Journal of Religion in Africa*, XXV(3), 253-287.

Maxwell, David (1995) Christianity and the War in Eastern Zimbabwe: the Case of Elim Mission. In: N. Bhebe and T. Ranger (Eds.) *Society in Zimbabwe's Liberation War: Volume Two.* Harare/London/Portsmouth: University of Zimbabwe Publications, James Currey, Heinemann, 58-90.

McAllister, P.A. (1989) Resistance to 'Betterment'in the the Transkei : A Case Study from Willowvale District. *Journal of Southern African Studies*, 15 (2), 346-368.

McGregor, JoAn (1995) Introduction. *Environment and History*, 1, 253-256.

McGregor, JoAn (1995b) Conservation, Control and Ecological Change : The Politics and Ecology of Colonial Conservation in Shurugwi, Zimbabwe. *Environment and History*, 1, 257-279.

McGregor, JoAn (2002) The Politics of Disruption: War Veterans and the Local State in Zimbabwe. *African Affairs*, 101, 9-37.

McKenzie, Fiona A. (2000) Contested Ground: Colonial Narratives and the Kenyan Environment, 1920-1945. *Journal of Southern African Studies*, 26 (4), 697-718.

McLaughlin, Janice (1995) Avila Mission: a Turning Point in Church Relations with the State and with the Liberation Forces. In: N. Bhebe and T. Ranger (Eds.) *Society in Zimbabwe's Liberation War: Volume Two.* Harare/London/Portsmouth: University of Zimbabwe Publications/James Currey/Heinemann, 91-101.

Metcalfe, S. (1993) Rural Development and Biodiversity: Prospects for Wildlife Habitat on Communal Lands in Zimbabwe's Zambezi Valley. Paper produced for the Southern African Wildlife Management Association Symposium on *'Biodiversity in Practice'*, Port Elizabeth, 29 June-1 July 1993.

Metcalfe, S. (1994) The Zimbabwe Communal Areas Management Programme for Indigenous Resources (CAMPFIRE). In: David Western and R. Michael (Eds.) *Natural Connections: Perspectives in Community Based Conservation.* Washington D.C.: Island Press.

Middleton, J. and E.H. Winter (1963) (Eds.) *Witchcraft and Sorcery in East Africa.* London: Routledge and Kegan Paul.

Mitchell, Clyde J. (1983) Ethnography and Network Analysis. In: Schweizer, T. (Ed.). *Netzwerkanalyse. Ethnologische Perspektiven.* Berlin: Dietrich Reimer Verlag.

Moyo, Sam (1986) The Land Question. In: Mandaza (ed.) Zimbabwe: The Political Economy of Transition 1980-1986. Dakar: Codesria.

Moyo, Sam (1990) *Agricultural Employment Expansion: Smallholder Land and Labour Capacity Growth.* Monograph Series No.2. Harare: ZIDS.

Moyo, Sam (1994) *Economic Nationalism and Land Reform in Zimbabwe.* Occasional Paper Series No. 7. Harare: SAPES Books.

Moyo, Sam (1995) *The Land Question in Zimbabwe.* Harare: SAPES Books.

Moyo, Sam (2000) The Political Economy of Land Acquisition and Redistributionin Zimbabwe, 1990-1999. *Journal of Southern African Studies*, 26(10): 5-28.

Moyo, Sam; Peter Robinson, Yemi Katerere, Stuart Stevenson & Davison Gumbo (1991) *Zimbabwe's Environmental Dilemma, Balancing Resource Inequities.* Harare: ZERO.

Moyo, S.; B. Munslow, P. O'Keefe and D. Weiner (1985) Land Use and Agricultural Productivity in Zimbabwe. *The Journal of Modern African Studies*, 23, no.2.

Munro, W. (1995) Building the Post-colonial state: villagization and resource management in Zimbabwe. *Politics and Society,* 23,107-40.

Murirwa, Kudakwashe, Jurgen Hagmann & Edward Chuma (2001) Mainstreaming participatory approaches to SWC in Zimbabwe. In: Chris Reij & Ann Waters-Bayer (Eds.) *Farmer Innovation in Africa. A Source of Inspiration for Agricultural Development.* London/Sterling: Earthscan, 300-309.

Murombedzi, J. (1990) The Need for Appropriate Local Level Common Property Resource Management Institutions in Communal Tenure Regimes. Harare: Centre for Applied Social Sciences.

Murombedzi, J. (1991) Wetlands Conservation under Common Property Management Regimes in Zimbabwe. Harare: Centre for Applied Social Sciences (University of Zimbabwe) NRM Occasional Papers.

Murombedzi, J. (1992) *Decentralization or Recentralization? Implementing CAMPFIRE in the Omay Communal Lands of te Nyaminyami District.* Harare: Centre for Applied Social Sciences (University of Zimbabwe).

Murphree, M.W., J. Murombedzi & R. Hawks (1989) *Survey of In-migration to Portions of the Kariba, Guruve and Kanyati Districts.* Unpubl. report, Centre for Applied Social Sciences (University of Zimbabwe).

Murphree, M.W. (1995) *Traditional and State Authority/Power in Zimbabwe.* NRM Occasional Papers Series. Harare: Centre for Applied Social Sciences (University of Zimbabwe).

Nabane, Nontokozo (1994) *A Gender Sensitive Analysis of a Community Based Wildlife Utilization Initiative in Zimbabwe's Zambezi Valley.* NRM Occasional Papers Series. Harare: Centre for Applied Social Sciences (University of Zimbabwe).

Nabane, Nontokozo; Vupenyu Dzingirai, & Elias Madzudzo (1994) *Membership in Common Property Regimes. A Case Study of Guruve, Binga, Tsholotsho and Bulilimamangwe CAMPFIRE Programmes.* NRM Occasional Papers Series. Harare: Centre for Applied Social Sciences (University of Zimbabwe).

Nyambara, Pius S. (2001) Immigrants, 'Traditional' Leaders and the Rhodesian State: the Power of 'Communal' Land Tenure and the Politics of Land Acquisition in Gokwe, Zimbabwe, 1963-1979. *Journal of Southern African Studies,* 27, 771-791.

Olivier de Sardan, Jean-Pierre (1992) Occultism and the Ethnographic "I". The Exoticizing of Magic from Durkheim to "Postmodern" Anthropology. *Critique of Anthropology,* 12, 5-25.

Olthof, Wim (1995) Wildlife Resources and Local Development: Experiences from Zimbabwe's CAMPFIRE Programme. In: J.P.M. van den Breemer, C.A. Drijver & L.B. Venema (Eds.). *Local Resource Management in Africa.* New York: Wiley, 111-128.

Palmer, Robin (1977) The agricultural history of Rhodesia. In: Palmer, R. & Parsons, N. (Eds.) *The roots of rural poverty in Central and Southern Africa.* Los Angeles: University of California Press, 221-254.

Palmer, Robin (1990) Land Reform in Zimbabwe, 1980-1990. *African Affairs,* 89, 163-81.

Pels, Peter (1993) *Critical Matters. Interactions between Missionaries and Waluguru in Colonial Tanganyika, 1930-1961.* Amsterdam, Unpubl. PhD. Thesis, Amsterdam School of Social Research (PhD thesis).

Phimister, Ian (1977) Peasant production and underdevelopment in Southern Rhodesia, 1890-1914, with particular reference to the Victoria District. In R. Palmer & N.

Parsons, N. (Eds.) *The roots of rural poverty in Central and Southern Africa.* Los Angeles: University of California Press.

Potts, D. (2000) Worker Peasants and Farmer Housewives in Africa: the Debate about 'Committed'Farmers, Access to Land and Agricultural Production. *Journal of Southern African Studies*, 26 (4), 807-832.

Potts, D. & Mutambirwa, C. (1990) Rural-urban linkages in contemporary Harare: Why migrants need their land. *Journal of Southern African Studies*, 16 (4), 677-698.

Ranger, Terence O. (1967) *Revolt in Southern Rhodesia 1896-7.* London: Heinemann.

Ranger, Terence O. (1982) Survival, revival and disaster: Shona traditional elites under colonialism, Paper presented to the Round Table on *Elites and Colonisation*, Paris.

Ranger, Terence O. (1985) *Peasant Consciousness and Guerrilla War in Zimbabwe.* Harare: Zimbabwe Publishing House.

Ranger, Terence O. (1991) Religion and Witchcraft in Everyday Life in Contemporary Zimbabwe. In: Preben Kaarsholm (Ed.) *Cultural Struggle & Development in Southern Africa.* London: James Currey, 149-165.

Ranger, Terence O. (1993) The Communal Areas of Zimbabwe. In T.J. Basset & D.E. Crummey (Eds.) *Land in African Agrarian Systems,* Madison: University of Wisconsin Press.

Ranger, Terence O. (1993b) The Invention of Tradition Revisited. In: Terrence Ranger and Olufemi Vaughan (Eds.) *Legitimacy and the State in Twentieth-Century Africa. Essays in honour of A.H.M. Kirk-Greene.* London: Macmillan, 62-111.

Ranger, Terence O. (1995) Religious Pluralism in Zimbabwe. *Journal of Religion in Africa*, XXV(3), 226-251.

Ranger, Terence O. (1999) *Voices from the Rocks. Nature, Culture & History in the Matopos Hills of Zimbabwe.* Harare: Baobab; Bloomington (Indianapolis)/Oxford: Indiana University Press/James Currey.

Ranger, Terence and Mark Ncube (1995) Religion in the Guerrilla war: the Case of Southern Matabeleland. In: N. Bhebe and T. Ranger (Eds.) *Society in Zimbabwe's Liberation War: Volume Two.* Harare: University of Zimbabwe Publications, London: James Currey; Portsmouth: Heinemann, 35-57.

Reis, Ria (2000) The 'wounded healer' as ideology. The work of ngoma in Swaziland. In: R. Van Dijk., R. Reis & M. Spierenburg (Eds.) *The Quest for Fruition through Ngoma, Political Aspects of Healing in Southern Africa.* Cape Town/ Zomba/ Lusaka/ Gweru/ Oxford/Athens: David Philip/ Kachere/ Bookworld/ Mambo Press/ James Currey/ Ohio University Press, 61-75.

Reij & Waters-Bay (2001) Entering research and development in land husbandry through farmer innovation. In: Chris Reij & Ann Waters-Bayer (Eds.) *Farmer Innovation in Africa. A Source of Inspiration for Agricultural Development.* London/Sterling: Earthscan, 3-22.

Reynolds, Norman (1984) *Land Tenure and Agricultural Productivity in a Developing Country - Economic Aspects and Models.* Harare: Institute for Agricultural Extension Zimbabwe Symposium, Monograph 3.

Ribot, Jesse (1999) Decentralisation, participation and accountability in Sahelian Forestry: legal instruments of political-administrative control. *Africa*, 69, 23-65.

Richards, Paul (1985) *Indigenous agricultural revolution: ecology and food production in West Africa.* London: Hutchinson.

Roe, Emory (1991) Development narratives, or making the best of blueprint development. *World Development,* 19, 229-232.

Roe, Emory (1992) *Report on the amalgamation of district councils and rural councils.* NRM Occasional Papers Series. Harare: University of Zimbabwe, Centre for Applied Social Sciences.

Roe, Emory (1995) Except-Africa: postscript to a special to a special section on development narratives. *World Development*, 23 (6), 1065-69.

Rowlands, M. & J.P. Warnier (1988) Sorcery, Power and the Modern State in Cameroon. *Man*, 23,118-132.

Rutherford, Blair (2001) Working on the Margins. Black Workers, White Farmers in Postcolonial Zimbabwe. London/New York: Zed Books.

Sanders, Todd (2001) Territorial and magical migrations in Tanzania. In: Mirjam De Bruijn, Rijk Van Dijk and Dick Foecken (Eds.) *Mobile Africa, Changing patterns of movement in Africa and beyond.* Leiden: Brill, 27-46.

Schoffeleers, J.M. (1978) Introduction. In: J.M. Schoffeleers (Ed.) *Guardians of the Land.* Gwelo: Mambo Press, i-xii.

Schoffeleers, J.M. (1992) River of Blood: The Genesis of a Martyr Cult in Southern Malawi, c. a.d. 1600. Madison: University of Wisconsin Press.

Scoones, Ian (1996) Range Management Science & Policy. Politics, Polemics & Pasture in Southern Africa. In: Leach, Melissa & Mearns, Robin (Eds.) *The Lie of the Land, Challenging Received Wisdom on the African Environment.* Oxford/London: James Currey, Heinemann, 34-53.

Scoones, Ian (2001) Transforming Soils: The Dynamics of Soil-Fertility Management in Africa. In: Scoones, Ian (Ed.) *Dynamics and Diversity: Soil Fertility and Farming Livelihoods in Africa*, London: Earthscan, 1-44.

Scoones, I. and Cousins, B. (1991) *Contested Terrains: The Struggle For Control over Dambo Resources in Zimbabwe.* London: Drylands Programme, IIED.

Scoones, I. and Cousins, B. (1994) Struggle for control over wetland resources in Zimbabwe. *Society and Natural Resources*, 7, 579-94.

Scott, James (1985) Weapons of the Weak: Everyday Forms of Peasant Resistance. New Haven: Yale University Press.

Scott, James (1998) Seeing Like a State. How certain schemes to improve the human condition have failed. New Haven: Yale University Press

Sender, John & Deborah Johnston (2004) Searching for a Weapon of Mass Production in Rural Africa: Unconvincing Arguments for Land Reform. *Journal of Agrarian Change,* 4 (1/2), 142-165.

Shore, C. & Wright, S. (1997) Policy: a New Field in Anthropology. In: C. Shore & S. Wright (Eds.) *Anthropology of Policy: Critical Perspectives on Governance and Power.* London: Routledge.

Shotter, John (1990) The Social Construction of Remembering and Forgetting. In: D. Middleton and D. Edwards (Eds.) *Collective Remembering.* London: Sage.

Sibanda, B.M.C. (1986) Impacts of Agricultural Microprojects on Rural Development. Lessons from Two Projects in the Zambezi Valley. *Land Use Policy*, October 1986, 311-329.

Spierenburg, Marja (1994) The Role of the Mhondoro Cult in the Struggle for Control over Land in Dande (Northern Zimbabwe): Social Commentaries and the Influence of Adherents. NRM Occasional Papers Series. Harare: Centre for Applied Social Sciences (University of Zimbabwe).

Spierenburg, Marja (1998) Healing the Ills of Development: The Role of the Mhondoro Cult in the Struggle against an Irrigation Project in Dande. In: Heike Schmidt &

Albert Wirz (eds.) *Afrika und das Andere, Alteritaet und Innovation*. Hamburg: LIT Verlag.

Spierenburg, Marja (1999) Conflicting Environmental Conservation Strategies in Dande, Northern Zimbabwe. CAMPIRE versus the Mid-Zambezi Rural Development Project. In: Bernhard Venema & Hans van den Breemer (eds.) *Towards Negotiated Co-management of Natural Resources in Africa*. Hamburg: LIT-Verlag.

Spierenburg, Marja (2000) Social Commentaries and the Influence of Adherents: The Role of the *Mhondoro* Cult in the Struggle over Land in Dande (northern Zimbabwe). In: R. Van Dijk., R. Reis & M. Spierenburg (Eds.) *The Quest for Fruition through Ngoma, Political Aspects of Healing in Southern Africa*. Cape Town/ Zomba/ Lusaka/ Gweru/ Oxford/ Athens: David Philip/ Kachere/ Bookworld/ Mambo Press/ James Currey/ Ohio University Press, 76-98.

Spierenburg, Marja (2001) Moving into another Spirit Province, Immigrants and the Mhondoro Cult in northern Zimbabwe. In: M. De Bruijn, H. Van Dijk, D. Foecke (eds.) *Mobile Africa, changing patterns of movement in Africa and beyond*. Leiden, Brill, 47-62.

Strathern, Marilyn (1995) Nostalgia and the New Genetics. In: D. Battaglia (Ed.) *Rhethorics of Self-Making*. Berkeley: University of California Press.

Thoden van Velzen, H.U.E. (2001) Dangerous Creatures and the Enchantment of Modern Life. In: Paul Clough & Jon. P. Mitchell (Eds.) *Powers of Good and Evil*. New York/Oxford: Berghahn.

Thoden van Velzen, H.U.E. & W. Van Wetering (1988) The Great Father and the Danger. Religious Cults, Material Forces and Collective Fantasies in the World of the Surinamese Maroons. Dordrecht: Foris.

Thomas, Stephen J. (1992) *The Legacy of Dualism and Decision-making: The Prospects for Local Institutional Development in CAMPFIRE*. Harare: Centre for Applied Social Sciences / Branch of Terrestrial Ecology, Department of National Parks and Wildlife.

Tungamirai, Josiah (1995) Recruitment to ZANLA: Building up a War Machine. In: N. Bhebe and T. Ranger (Eds.) *Soldiers in Zimbabwe's Liberation War Volume One*. Harare/London/Portsmouth: University of Zimbabwe Publications/ James Currey/ Heineman, 36-47.

UNEP (1986) *Assessment of the present and future activities related to the Zambezi Action Plan*. Report by the UNEP Mission of Experts to the Zambezi Countries 2nd June – 3rd July 1986.

Vail, Leroy (1989) Ethnicity in Southern African History. In: Vail, Leroy (Ed.) *The Creation of Tribalism in Southern Africa*. Berkeley/Los Angeles: University of California Press, 1-19.

Van Binsbergen, W.M.J. (1999) Creating "a Place to Feel at Home", Christian church life and social control in Lusaka, Zambia (1970s). In: Piet Konings, Wim van Binsbergen & Gerti Hesseling (Eds.) *Trajectoires de liberation en Afrique contemporaine*. Paris/Leiden: Karthala/African Studies Centre, 223-50.

Van Binsbergen, W.M.J. (1995) Four-tablet Divination as Trans-regional Medical Technology in Southern Africa. *Journal of Religion in Africa*, 25 (2), 114-40.

Van Binsbergen, Wim & Matthew Schoffeleers (1985) Introduction: Theoretical explorations in African religion. In: Wim van Binsbergen & Matthew Schoffeleers (Eds.) *Theoretical Explorations in African Religion*. London: Kegan Paul, 1-43.

Van Binsbergen, W.M.J. & H.A. Meilink, H.A. (1978) Migration and the Transformation of Modern African Society. *African Perspectives*, 1978(1), 7-20.

Van Dijk, Rijk (2000) Ngoma & born-again fundamentalism. Contesting representations of time in urban Malawi. In: R. Van Dijk., R. Reis & M. Spierenburg (Eds.) *The Quest for Fruition through Ngoma, Political Aspects of Healing in Southern Africa*. Cape Town/ Zomba/ Lusaka/ Gweru/ Oxford/ Athens: David Philip/ Kachere/ Bookworld/ Mambo Press/ James Currey/ Ohio University Press, 133-154.

Van Hekken, P.M. & Thoden van Velzen, H.U.E. (1971) *Land Scarcity and Rural Inequality in Tanzania. Some Case Studies from Rungwe District*. The Hague: Mouton.

Van Velsen, J. (1967) The Extended-case Method and Situational Analysis. In: A.L. Epstein (Ed.). *The Craft of Social Anthropology*. London: Tavistock, 129-149.

Weiner, D., S. Moyo, B. Munslow & P. O'Keefe (1991) Land use and agricultural productivity in Zimbabwe, in: N.D. Mutizwa-Mangiza and A.H.J. Helmsing (Eds.) *Rural Development and Planning in Zimbabwe,* Aldershot: Avesbury.

Weiss, Ruth (1986) *The Women of Zimbabwe*. Harare: Nehanda Publ.

Wels, Harry (2003) *Reciprocity and Joint Ventures in Private Wildlife Conservation. The Savé Valley Conservancy and its Gift to the Neighbouring Communities in Zimbabwe*. Leiden: Brill.

Wels, Harry (2000) Fighting over Fences. Organisational co-operation and reciprocal exchange between the Savé Valley Conservancy and its neighbouring communities. Amsterdam: Vrije Universiteit, PhD thesis.

Werbner, Richard P. (1977) Introduction. In: R.P. Werbner (Ed.) *Regional Cults*. ASA Monographs. London/New York/San Fransisco: Academic Press, ix-xxxviii.

Werbner, Richard P. (1991) *Tears of the Dead. The Social biography of an African Family*. Harare: Baobab Books.

Werbner, Richard P. (1996) Introduction, Multiple Identities, Plural Areas. In: Richard Werbner & Terence Ranger (Eds.) *Postcolonial Identities in Africa*, London & New Jersey: Zed Books, 1-25.

Werbner, Richard P. (1997) The Reach of the Postcolonial State. Development, Empowerment /Disempowerment and Technocracy. Paper presented to the *Association of Social Anthropologists Conference Power, Empowerment and Disempowerment in Changing Structures,* 7-9 January, Harare, University of Zimbabwe.

Werbner, Richard P. (1998) Smoke from the Barrel of a Gun: Postwars of the Dead, memory and Reinscription in Zimbabwe. In: Werbner, Richard (Ed.) *Memory and the Postcolony. African Anthropology and the Critique of Power*. London/New York: Zed Books, 71-102.

Worby, Eric (1995) Tyranny, Parody, and Ethnic Polarity: Ritual Engagements with the State in Northwestern Zimbabwe. *Journal of Southern Africa,* 24, 561-579.

Wynne, B. (1992) Uncertainty and environmental learning: reconceiving science and policy in the preventive paradigm. *Global Environmental Change*, 2 (2), 111-27.

Newspaper Articles and Press Releases

Amnesty International, Press Release 14 May 2004, Index:AFR 46/014/2004, News Service No: 124. Website: (last consulted on 24 May 2004):
http://web.amnesty.org/library/Index/ENGAFR460142004?open&of=ENG-ZWE
The Daily News (Zimbabwe), 19 February 2002, *Spirit medium murdered.*
The Daily News (Zimbabwe), 7 March 2002, *Spirit mediums condemn terror.*
The Herald (Zimbabwe), 28 January 2002, Spirit mediums meet to prepare for ceremony.
The Herald (Zimbabwe), 18 May 2004, *Confusion hits farming sector.*
Zimbabwe Independent, 5 July 2002, *War veterans refuse to act.*

Index

1. A sculpture of President Mugabe (photo by Marja Spierenburg, 1994)

2. A meeting of the Village Development Committee (photo by Marja Spierenburg, 1994)

3. Distribution of food aid (photo by Marja Spierenburg, 1994)

4. The medium of Nyahuma and assistant (photo by Marja Spierenburg, 1994)

Printed in the United States
by Baker & Taylor Publisher Services